SOLDIERS
OF THE
DRAGON

SOLDIERS
OF THE
DRAGON

Chinese Armies 1500 BC–AD 1840

C J Peers

First published in Great Britain in 2006 by Osprey Publishing, Midland House, West Way, Botley, Oxford OX2 0PH, United Kingdom.
443 Park Avenue South, New York, NY 10016, USA.
Email: info@ospreypublishing.com

Previously published as Men-at-Arms 218: *Ancient Chinese Armies 1500–200 BC*; Men-at-Arms 284: *Imperial Chinese Armies (1) 200 BC–AD 589*; Men-at-Arms 295: *Imperial Chinese Armies (2) 590–1260 AD*; Men-at-Arms 251: *Medieval Chinese Armies 1260–1520*; and Men-at-Arms 307: *Late Imperial Chinese Armies 1520–1840*, all written by C J Peers.

A CIP catalogue record for this book is available from the British Library

ISBN 10: 1 84603 098 6
ISBN 13: 978 1 84603 098 7

Page layout by Ken Vail Graphic Design, Cambridge, UK
Index by Alison Worthington
Typeset in Baskerville MT, Helvetica, LegacySan, RotisSemiSerif and RotisSerif
Originated by United Graphics, Singapore
Printed and bound in China through Bookbuilders

06 07 08 09 10   10 9 8 7 6 5 4 3 2 1

For a catalogue of all books published by Osprey please contact:

NORTH AMERICA
Osprey Direct c/o Random House Distribution Center
400 Hahn Road, Westminster, MD 21157, USA
E-mail: info@ospreydirectusa.com

ALL OTHER REGIONS
Osprey Direct UK, P.O. Box 140, Wellingborough, Northants, NN8 2FA, UK
E-mail: info@ospreydirect.co.uk

www.ospreypublishing.com

Front cover: Chinggis Khan fighting the Chinese in the mountains. A miniature painting illustrating a scene from Ahmad Tabrizi's *Shahanshahnama*. (Permission British Library Or 2780 f49v)

Title page: Huang Ch'ao's peasant army attacks Ch'ang-an, the T'ang capital, in 874. (© Stephen Turnbull)

Contents

Introduction

China is the oldest of the world's surviving civilizations, and its history forms a continuous narrative stretching back 3,500 years. Though it has always been admired for its contributions to art and science, China's military achievements have until recently been underrated in the West. This book aims to redress this balance and show the enormous contribution that the Chinese fighting man has made to the theory and practice of war. It includes a brief outline of the major wars and campaigns, as well as a survey of the development of weaponry, organization and methods of command.

This book's general structure follows the traditional division of Chinese history into dynasties, each of which took its name from its ruling family or from a title adopted by the regime's founder. Not all of the rulers of these dynasties were native Chinese, as conquering tribes like the Mongols and the Manchus routinely adopted the customs and administrative methods of their subjects. The approach used here covers all those regimes that ruled over at least part of what is now China and adopted a native dynastic title. This is not always ideal, especially when discussing times when several such dynasties flourished simultaneously, but it does help to divide this enormous subject into more manageable periods. The most important of the 30 or so dynasties covered in this book are as follows:

SHANG, *c.* 1500 to *c.* 1027 BC
CHOU, *c.* 1027 to 256 BC
CH'IN, 221 to 207 BC
HAN, 202 BC to 220 AD
T'ANG, 618 to 907 AD
SUNG, 960 to 1279 AD
YÜAN (Mongol), 1260 to 1368 AD
MING, 1368 to 1644 AD
CH'ING (Manchu), 1644 to 1911 AD

Scholars – both Western and Chinese – have traditionally described China's history as a series of cycles. Successive dynasties rose and united the country

OPPOSITE The Simatai section of the Great Wall north of Peking. (© Stephen Turnbull)

7

under a single emperor, who ushered in a period of peace and prosperity, then gradually declined in virtue and the ability to govern. Eventually the 'mandate of heaven' would be withdrawn from the regime, leading to natural disasters, popular rebellions and the collapse of central authority. A period of fragmentation and chaos would follow – lasting perhaps only a few years, perhaps a century or more – until the next dynasty arose in its turn. To some extent this scheme does reflect reality, and it is worth looking briefly at some of the conflicting factors that combined to impose these cycles.

Most Chinese accepted in principle the ancient idea that the empire should have a single ruler – the 'One Man' of Chou tradition – but it was also understood that the people were entitled to depose and replace an emperor who failed to fulfil his obligations. An emperor's control over his empire was complicated by China's susceptibility to various natural disasters, such as floods and earthquakes. In a society where the emperor was regarded as an intermediary between earth and heaven, such phenomena could easily be blamed on his shortcomings. The process of centralization was hindered by the fact that China is geographically diverse and criss-crossed with rivers and mountains that present formidable barriers to campaigning armies. A recurring theme through the centuries is the split between northern China, centred on the Yellow River valley, and the lands south of the Yangtze. Northern China was influenced by the nomads of the steppes, and provided pasture land for horses, while southern China was largely a rice-growing region, inhospitable to cavalry, where most communication was by water. Areas beyond the Yellow and Yangtze rivers, centred on fertile plains encircled by mountain ranges, resisted most attempts at conquest from the outside. Predominant among these were ancient Ch'in, the 'land within the passes' in the north-west; and the modern province of Szechwan (ancient Shu) west of the Yangtze gorges.

As a result of these conditions, internal conflict in China, to say nothing of wars against foreign invaders, was almost continuous. The sources that describe these conflicts are extensive. Written history has a long pedigree in China, and numerous chronicles and memoirs survive, dating back as far as the Chou era. Although much traditional historical writing is of uncertain date or provenance, its overall reliability is impressive. For example, the list of Shang dynasty kings given by the Han historian Ssu-ma Chien, writing a millennium later, corresponds closely to the names on oracle bones excavated from Shang sites by modern archaeologists. The 'official histories', which were customarily produced for each dynasty by its successor, tend to be rather dry records of government business, but can contain useful details on military organization. There are also numerous surviving military manuals, ranging from the philosophical works of the Chou era to the illustrated encyclopaedias of the Ming. A small but growing proportion of this material is available in translation. A great deal of

Looking down from Jiaoshan mountain towards the flatlands of northern China. (© Stephen Turnbull)

archaeological work has also been done in recent years, much of which is now being published outside the country.

Pronunciation of names and technical terms can be a problem for Western readers. It is almost obligatory to provide a note on this subject, but it is difficult to give guidance that is both brief and useful. Chinese pronunciation has changed dramatically over the centuries, and in its modern form uses a system of tones our alphabet is unable to reproduce. I have retained the modified Wade-Giles system of transliteration, which is still the most commonly encountered in scholarly works, despite a strong challenge from the Pinyin system favoured by the current government of China. Words transliterated using the Wade-Giles system are also more accessible to the English-speaking reader, and if they are pronounced as if they were English, the results, although not entirely accurate, are at least recognizable. Thus we will at least avoid such increasingly prevalent absurdities as 'Kwin' for the Ch'in dynasty of Shih Huang-ti (written 'Qin' in Pinyin, but pronounced approximately like English 'chin'). Nevertheless there is not always consistency even within these systems, and readers should be aware that the names of people, places and dynasties may appear elsewhere in different forms. Thus the Eastern Chou state, which I have called Tsin, and the much later Kin dynasty founded by the Jurchen people, are both referred to in some English works as 'Chin'. Where such different versions appear in published works, I have selected the one least likely to give rise to confusion.

Chronology

c. **1500 BC**	Introduction of advanced bronze-casting. Rise of Shang state.
c. **1300 BC**	Introduction of chariot. Permanent Shang capital established at Yin.
c. **1027 BC**	Chou revolt. Battle of Mu. Chou conquest of central China.
c. **880 BC**	Hsung K'eu of Ch'u takes title of 'king'. Chou king forces him to give it up and reduces him to vassalage.
771 BC	Invasion by Jung barbarians. Fall of Chou capital, Hao. Eastern Chou dynasty established at Lo-yi; kingdom divided into two parts.
750 BC	Chou kingdom reunited by King Ping.
707 BC	King Huan defeated by rebel ministers at Hsu-ko. Chou realm fragments into hundreds of small states.
685–643 BC	Duke Huan of Ch'i, first hegemon.
632 BC	Tsin defeats Ch'u at Ch'eng-p'u.
595 BC	Ch'u defeats Tsin at Pi.
584 BC	Wu-ch'en of Ch'u organizes Wu army on Chinese lines.
576 BC	Ch'in expedition decisively defeated by Tsin at Ma-sui.
575 BC	Tsin defeats Ch'u at Yen-ling.
506 BC	Wu invades Ch'u. Fall of Ying.
479 BC	Death of Confucius.
473 BC	Yueh overruns and destroys Wu.
453 BC	Coalition of ex-allies defeats Tsin at Ching Yang. Tsin breaks up into three parts – Wei, Han and Chao.
350 BC	Lord Shang begins his political and military reforms in Ch'in.
333 BC	Ch'u conquers Yueh.
318 BC	Coalition led by Ch'u crushed by Ch'in.
316 BC	Ch'in conquers Shu and Pa.
307 BC	Wu Ling of Chao forms China's first cavalry units.
285 BC	Yen overruns Ch'i.
279 BC	Yen defeated at Chi Mo and expelled from Ch'i.
256 BC	Ch'in deposes the Chou king. Official end of Chou dynasty.
246 BC	Accession of King Cheng in Ch'in.
223 BC	Final defeat of Ch'u by Ch'in.
221 BC	Ch'in conquers Ch'i. China unified under King Cheng, the First Emperor.
210 BC	Death of the First Emperor.
207 BC	Ch'u rebels destroy Ch'in army at Hsin-an. Second Emperor commits suicide.
206 BC	Ch'in dynasty disintegrates. China divided between Hsiang Yu and Liu Pang.
202 BC	Liu Pang defeats Hsiang Yu and takes title of Han Kao-ti. China reunited under Han dynasty.
200 BC	Kao-ti defeated by Hsiung-nu at P'ing-ch'eng.
177–166 BC	Major incursions by Hsiung-nu.
154 BC	Revolt of the king of Wu.

141 BC	Accession of Wu-ti, the 'Martial Emperor'.
139–113 BC	Chang Ch'ien's explorations in the far west.
133 BC	Beginning of Han offensive against Hsiung-nu.
121–119 BC	Wei Ch'ing and Huo Ch'u-ping defeat Hsiung-nu.
111–108 BC	Conquest of Tien and K'un-ming in Yunnan.
108 BC	Conquest of Ch'ao-hsien in Korea.
104–101 BC	'War of the Heavenly Horses' against Ferghana.
51 BC	Peace agreed with Hsiung-nu.
AD 8–25	Hsin dynasty of Wang Mang.
18–27	Red Eyebrow rebellion.
23	Wang Mang defeated by Han forces at K'un-yang.
25	'Eastern' or 'Later' Han founded by Liu Hsiu.
40–43	Revolt of the Trung sisters in Yueh.
73–89	Renewed offensive against Hsiung-nu.
108–111	Great Ch'iang raids into Yellow River plain.
184	Outbreak of Yellow Turban revolt.
189	Palace coup by Tung Cho. Collapse of Han power.
220	Death of Ts'ao Ts'ao, whose son is proclaimed king of an independent Wei state. Formal end of Han dynasty.
263	Conquest of Shu Han by Wei.
280–316	Temporary reunification under Ts'in dynasty.
c. 310	Introduction of cataphract cavalry equipment into China.
311	Hsiung-nu capture Lo-yang. Collapse of Western Ts'in dynasty. 'Barbarian' kingdoms control northern China.
383	Northern attempt to conquer southern China defeated at Fei River.
387–534	Toba dynasty of Northern Wei in northern China.
420	Eastern Ts'in in south replaced by Liu-Sung dynasty.
502–557	Liang dynasty in south.
534–577	War in the north among successors to Northern Wei.
581	Yang Chien seizes power in Northern Chou and founds Sui dynasty.
589	Fall of Ch'en. Empire reunified under Yang Chien.
612–614	Sui campaigns against Koguryo in Korea.
618	Yang-ti assassinated. Collapse of Sui dynasty.
623	Central government restored under T'ang dynasty.
630–648	T'ang conquest of the Tarim Basin.
661–665	T'ang protectorate over the Western Turks.
660–668	New war in Korea.
c. 670	Tibetans overrun Tarim Basin.
690–705	Interregnum under the Chou dynasty of Empress Wu.
736–755	War with Tibet. T'ang authority established briefly as far west as the Pamirs.
751–752	T'ang armies defeated on three fronts by Nan-chao, Arabs and Khitans.
755–763	Rebellion of An Lu-shan.
808	Sha-to Turks settle in north-western China.

874–884	Rebellion of Huang Ch'ao.
907	Last T'ang emperor deposed by Chu Wen. Khitans found Liao dynasty in Manchuria.
c. **920**	Naphtha bombs and flamethrowers in use in southern China.
936	Liao occupy north-eastern China.
960	Chao K'uang-yin establishes Sung dynasty.
1004–1119	Wars between Sung and Tanguts in the north-west.
1038	Yuan-hao proclaims Tangut Western Hsia dynasty.
1044	First mention of gunpowder in a Sung military manual.
1068–86	Unsuccessful military reforms of Wang An-shih.
c. **1125**	Metal-cased explosive bombs developed.
1125	Liao dynasty overthrown by Jurchen.
1127	Fall of K'aifeng to Jurchen. Establishment of Kin dynasty. Sung retreat to Lin-an in the south – the 'Southern Sung'.
1161	Major Kin invasion defeated by Sung navy.
1227	Fall of Western Hsia to Mongols.
1235	Kin dynasty destroyed by Mongols.
1260	Accession of Kubilai as Mongol khan.
1266	Capital of Mongol Empire moved to Tatu.
1267–72	Siege of Hsiang-yang.
1268	Kaidu's revolt. Break-up of Mongol Empire.
1271	Kubilai proclaims the Yüan dynasty.
1276	Fall of Lin-an to the Yüan.
1279	Death of last Sung emperor. China reunited under Kubilai.
c. **1288**	Possible date of earliest known handgun.
1294	Death of Kubilai.
1307	Japanese attack Ch'eng-yuan. Beginning of more than two centuries of Japanese seaborne raids.
1332	First known accurately dated cannon.
1351	Outbreak of Red Turban revolt. End of effective Yüan government.
1356–68	'Ch'un-hsiung' era of 'competing leaders'.
1356	Chu Yuan-chang defeats Yüan at Ts'ai-shih and captures Chin-ling.
1360–63	Ming–Han war.
1363	Ming defeat Han at Lake P'o-yang.
1365	Ming defeat Wu at Hsin-ch'eng.
1368	Yüan Emperor flees from Ta-tu. Ming dynasty proclaimed by Chu Yüan-chang.
1370	Ming victory over Mongols at Ting-hsi.
1372	General Hsu Ta defeated by Mongols near Karakorum.
1388	Offensive against Mongols resumes with victory at Lake Buyur.
1398	Death of Hung Wu Emperor.
1399–1402	Civil war. Victory of the Prince of Yen.
1405–33	Seven overseas expeditions under Cheng Ho.
1406–27	War in Annam.
1410–24	Yung Lo Emperor's campaigns in Mongolia.

1440–54	War in Lu-ch'uan.
1448–49	Revolt in Fukien.
1449	Ming defeated by Mongols at T'u-mu. Cheng-t'ung Emperor captured.
1464	Military reorganization under Ch'eng-hua Emperor.
1465–66	Native tribes rebel in Kwangsi.
1465–76	Cheng-hsiang rebellion.
1473–85	First phase of work on wall system in north-west.
1498	Last expedition to Mongolia under Wang Yueh.
1499–1502	Lolo rebellion in Yunnan.
1513	Arrival of Portuguese under Jorge Alvares.
1517	Mongols defeated at Ying-chou.
1525	Seagoing junks ordered destroyed in an attempt to isolate China from foreign influences.
_c._ 1540	Construction of modern 'Great Wall' system begun.
_c._ 1540–_c._ 1565	Heyday of _wo-k'ou_ piracy in south-eastern China.
1550	Siege of Peking by Altan Khan.
1567	Ban on overseas trade lifted.
_c._ 1583	Rise to power of Nurhachi, future founder of the Manchu state.
1593–98	War against the Japanese in Korea.
1618–19	Major Ming offensive against the Manchus defeated.
1626	Ming victory over Manchus at Ning-yuan. Death of Nurhachi.
1636	Manchus proclaim the Ch'ing dynasty.
1643–44	Short-lived Shun dynasty of Li Tzu-ch'eng.
1644	Death of last Ming emperor. Manchus capture Peking.
1661–1722	Reign of K'ang-hsi Emperor.
1664	Manchu conquest of Fukien. All of mainland China now under Ch'ing control.
1673–81	Rebellion of the 'Three Feudatories'.
1683	Fall of the pro-Ming Cheng regime in Taiwan.
1689	Sino-Russian border fixed by Treaty of Nerchinsk.
1696	Defeat of Galdan Khan. Eastern Mongolia becomes a Ch'ing protectorate.
1720	Tibet becomes a Chinese vassal.
1736–96	Reign of Ch'ien-lung Emperor.
1757	Imperial decree restricts foreign trade to Canton.
1757–59	Defeat of the Jungar Mongols and their Muslim allies.
1792	Gurkhas of Nepal defeated by a Chinese expedition.
1793	British embassy under Lord Macartney in Peking.
1817–27	Muslim 'Jihad' of Jahangir in the Tarim Basin.
1839	Outbreak of first Opium War with British.
1842	Treaty of Nanking opens more Chinese ports to Western trade. British seize base at Hong Kong.

Note: All dates before 841 BC are approximate. The above chronology is based on the 'Bamboo Annals' of the 3rd century BC, which is favoured by more modern scholars, as well as being easier to reconcile with external influences, than the dates derived from Ssu-ma Ch'ien, who would place e.g. the battle of Mu in 1122 BC.

PART 1

The Shang dynasty

Although later tradition describes a revolt of the Shang people against an even earlier dynasty, the Hsia, culminating in the battle of Ming T'iao in 1763 BC, it is only with the introduction of writing under the Shang that China emerges from prehistory. By the 15th century BC the valley of the Hwang Ho or Yellow River was dominated by a palace-based military caste which owed its supremacy to a monopoly of bronze-working techniques among a still mainly Stone Age population. There is no direct evidence for the origin of this new technology, but similarities in weapon types suggest that it diffused into northern China via Siberia and Manchuria. The Shang themselves, however, were certainly indigenous, as their styles of art and writing show. Their original centre of power may have been in modern Shantung, but they moved their early wooden palaces frequently, perhaps to avoid the notorious Hwang Ho floods, gradually drifting north and east down the valley. As they did so they brought an increasing number of neighbouring tribes under their rule. Shang culture as well as political influence spread over a wide area of northern China, but did not yet constitute a centralized state.

The *Shu Ching* or 'Book of Documents' describes a Shang sphere of influence stretching from the sea in the east to the sand deserts of the west, but only the area within a hundred miles or so of the capital was under direct royal control. Outside this were provinces ruled by Shang-influenced local nobles who often fought with each other or even with the king himself. Still further out were 'allied barbarians', mostly semi-nomadic Yi tribes which had not yet adopted Shang culture but were at least temporarily overawed; and, beyond them, the 'wild' nomads. It is likely, however, that the distinction between 'Chinese' and 'barbarians' was less clear than it later became, and that the Shang themselves were a pastoral people, relying as much on their herds of sheep, cattle and horses as on their crops.

War was a means of legitimizing the power of the new aristocracy, and the main aim of foreign policy was the sending out of expeditions to parade this power and gather tribute. Surrounding peoples were deliberately left unconquered to serve as an excuse for war and a reservoir of booty and prisoners;

BELOW Bone arrowhead from the early Shang dynasty, about 3¾ inches long (9.5cm). (British Museum 1973.6-20.3)

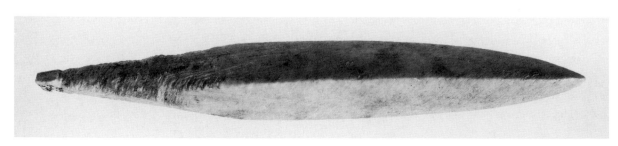

Shang dynasty bronze spearhead. (British Museum OA 1953.12-15.2)

the maintenance of a steady supply of captives was important to the Shang state, as its religion relied heavily on human sacrifice. This represents a primitive stage in the evolution of international relations, in which the resources of other communities at a lower technological level are exploited in a manner analogous to a hunting expedition. In fact hunting trips and military campaigns were organized in the same way, and the distinction between them was often blurred.

The Shang nobility was held together by a complicated clan system, royal power apparently alternating among the members of ten of these clans. This arrangement sometimes led to civil strife, but the period as a whole was one of gradual increase in state power. In about 1300 BC King Pan-k'eng moved the capital to Yin, where it was to remain until the fall of the dynasty. The palace-cities were by now on a considerable scale; it has been estimated that the defences of the 15th-century city of Ao would have taken 10,000 men 18 years to build.

By the 13th century BC, Shang influence had spread upriver to what is now Kansu Province, a region occupied by the people known as the Chou. The Chou adopted a compromise between the culture of the Shang and that of the steppe further west. They used bronze and may have had chariots before the Shang. Certainly their vehicles were better made, and they had more horses. At first they appear as Shang vassals, but by the 11th century BC their strength had greatly increased. In about 1040 BC their ruler, Wen, was given the title 'Count of the West' by the Shang king Shou Hsin, who trusted Wen to guard his rear while he was involved in a campaign in the south-east. Shou is described in Chou records as a depraved tyrant, but he may have been right to fear the growing power of Wen, who by now controlled two-thirds of the realm. At any rate, Shou imprisoned him, and Wen's son Wu led the Chou in revolt. The decisive battle was fought in 1027 BC in the wilderness of Mu. Wu occupied the central Hwang Ho valley, building forts at Hao and Lo to hold his conquests, and proclaimed the Chou dynasty. Later Chou propaganda depicts the Shang people as welcoming him as a liberator, but other data cast doubt on this. Shou had been killed, but his son led a revolt that took three years to suppress, and fighting

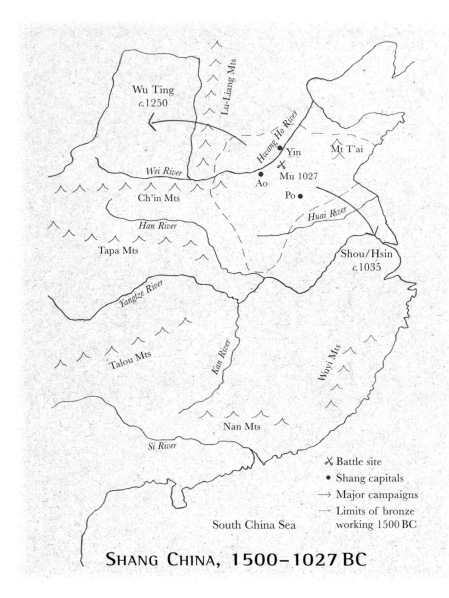

SHANG CHINA, 1500–1027 BC

continued in the east for generations. Eventually a Shang successor state, Sung, was allowed to survive on the lower Hwang Ho, although it soon adopted Chou military methods.

The Shang army

Shang expeditions mentioned on excavated oracle bones averaged 3,000 to 5,000 strong, but in emergencies forces of up to 30,000 could be raised. Evidence for the appearance of Shang warriors can be gleaned from the pictographs used in inscriptions, as well as from a few surviving statuettes and excavated items of

Shang warriors, 1500–1000 BC. At bottom right is a soldier of the *shu*, or royal halberdiers, reconstructed from the pictographs used in inscriptions to denote warriors. At bottom left is a captive from the Huai Valley who is about to be sacrificed. In the centre is a Shang nobleman, and at the back is an axeman carrying an axe designed for the decapitation of human sacrifices. (Angus McBride © Osprey Publishing Ltd)

armour. Weapons included bows, spears and the *ko* or dagger-axe – a primitive weapon consisting of a blade mounted at right angles to a three- to six-foot (approx. 0.9–1.8m) shaft and usually used one-handed together with a shield. Conventional axes were known, but were less popular. Spears were around seven feet (approx. 2.1m) long, and had bronze blades; the jade spearheads often found are too brittle for combat, and presumably had a ceremonial function.

Bronze knife, about 24.5cm (9 ½ in) long, probably used by a Shang charioteer. The design of the handle suggests Central Asian influence. (British Museum 1973.7-26.30)

The composite recurved bow was known, usually made of strips of bamboo glued or bound together with silk and averaging four feet (approx. 1.2m) long. Arrows were of reed or bamboo, tipped with bronze or bone; the metal did not completely replace bone for this purpose until very late in the Shang period. Knives and daggers, often very ornate, are common in aristocratic graves. These also were originally made from bone, often that of human sacrifices, but by the 13th century BC bronze was more usual. Nobles could wear armour; in the early Shang this mainly consisted of breastplates made from pieces of shell tied together, but again bronze became popular later. Bronze helmets, usually decorated with monstrous faces cast in relief, were rarer, and the rank and file probably did without any protection except for a leather shield stretched over a bamboo frame.

The chariot, probably an import from Central Asia, first appeared at around the time of the foundation of Yin, but was always restricted to the aristocracy. A 12th-century BC inscription listing the spoils of a campaign in the west gives an idea of the likely proportions: 1,570 prisoners, 15 pieces of armour, but only two chariots. Shang vehicles were drawn by two horses, although four are occasionally found in burials. The crew consisted of an archer, a driver, and often a third man armed with a spear or dagger-axe. Only the harness decorations, part of the yoke and the axlecaps of the chariots were bronze, the rest being wood, lashed or pegged together. Wheels were up to five feet (approx. 1.5m) in diameter with 18 or more spokes; the cab of the vehicle was low and open-fronted, enclosed only by rails. Horses were small and large-headed, reminiscent of the wild Przewalski breed of Mongolia, and were controlled by a bit and bridle made of rope.

A final possible constituent of Shang armies was the war elephant. Elephants of the Indian variety were wild in central China until the first millennium BC, and were certainly captured alive on occasion. A very old tradition ascribes the use of elephants to a minister of the legendary King Yao on a campaign against the southern tribes; and a later legend has the minister Shun conquering a wild brother known as Hsiang ('Elephant') by kindness. It is likely that these stories were based on a genuine memory of the use of the beasts in war, in which case it must have originated with the Shang, the first dynasty to fight in the central

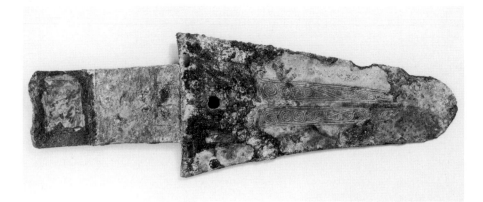

Bronze weapons, such as this Shang dagger-axe blade from north-eastern China, survive much better than their later iron counterparts, and so their original appearance can be reconstructed in great detail. Note the intricate pattern on the blade. This piece is about 24cm (9½in) in total length. (British Museum W.G. 940)

and southern regions where they were found. The tactic probably did not catch on because of the rapid decline due to the hunting of the wild elephant, which is difficult to breed in captivity, and its limited usefulness against foes well equipped with missiles.

Armies were recruited and equipped on an organized basis. Weapon and chariot manufacture was under royal control, and officials were responsible for various aspects of raising an army. Despite the immense social gap between the nobles and the peasantry, the latter were not slaves, and were called up to fight when necessary. Many would, however, have to make do with stone or bone weapons. Four grades of troops are known from inscriptions. The *ma* were the chariot warriors, supported by separate bodies of *she*, or archers, the most numerous infantry type, and *shu*, close-combat troops with spears or dagger-axes. In addition there were guard units, but it is not known how they were equipped. The infantry were not necessarily all peasants; before 1300 BC the nobles fought on foot, and some guard units may have continued to do so later.

Excavated burials provide some details of unit organization, although we cannot tell how universal they were. At Hsiao T'un the burial of a chief was accompanied by his household troops, sacrificed to protect him in the afterlife. These were divided into five units, each consisting of a chariot, five crewmen or escorts, and 25 infantry. Other burials confirm that chariots were organized into units of five and 25, but five crew per vehicle seems too many, and it is likely that two or three of them escorted the chariot on foot while the other infantry were deployed separately in battle.

Details of how expeditionary forces were supplied are lacking, but they covered impressive distances on occasion. Shou Hsin's campaign in the east probably reached the lower Yangtze and covered over 1,000 miles, while in the 13th century BC, Wu Ting penetrated the Inner Mongolian steppe to subdue the Ti and Wei barbarians.

The Western Chou

From the start, the Chou dynasty was faced with formidable military problems. After the war against the Shang there were threats from barbarians in the south and west as well as from the dynasty's own vassals, many of them local chieftains who had simply transferred the shaky allegiance that they had previously owed to the Shang. Traditionally the Chou are seen as the inventors of the feudal system in China, but in fact they merely legitimized an existing situation. Four great feudal duchies, Yen, Lu, Ch'i and Sung, were set up under native leaders dignified with Chou titles. Elsewhere, land grants were made to the Chou and Shang nobility; a total of 71 fiefs was established, 55 going to members of the Chou royal clan. This was a shortsighted policy that ensured the temporary loyalty of those who had sided with the conquest, but left the king with insufficient land to maintain an effective royal army. The Chou rulers had to rely on contingents provided by their vassals, the most powerful of whom were the least likely to be loyal.

At first all went well, the Chou emphasizing ritual and culture as a unifying force, and Chinese influence spread much further than under the Shang. The second and third kings, Ch'eng and K'ang, continued the struggle to contain the Shang and consolidate royal power, while their successors, Chao and Mu, led long expeditions into the south, where what was to become the state of Ch'u, whose rulers claimed descent from the Hsia dynasty, was precariously held in subjection. Chao's death by drowning on one such campaign was a major setback, and by the 9th century BC the pretensions of Ch'u were casting doubt on the Chou claim to be the only legitimate rulers of the Chinese world. By that time, the system was beginning to fall apart.

Civil war racked the realm after a coup in 841 BC, and in 771 BC the Jung barbarians from the west overran the old Chou homeland. Most of the great vassals refused to mobilize against the Jung, and Hao was sacked and the court forced to flee east to a new capital at Lo-yi. Their old lands were soon recaptured, but the kingdom remained divided; and although it was briefly reunited in 750 BC, from then on its authority was merely nominal. Over 170 effectively independent states, led by former vassals, held the real power.

In 707 BC, King Huan attempted to assert his authority over a minister who held the fief of Cheng, but at the battle of Hsu-ko his allies fled and the Cheng forces surrounded him. Huan was permitted to escape, although wounded with an arrow, but he lost his power and had to recognize the independence of his former subjects. Chou survived as a minor state until 256 BC, occasionally receiving lip-service from its neighbours but no longer of any political or military relevance.

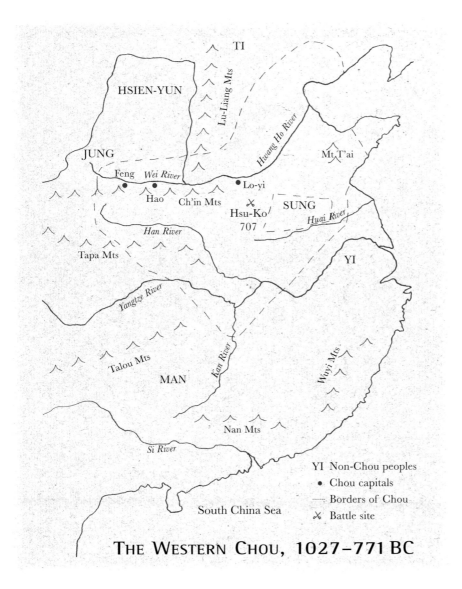

TI

HSIEN-YUN

Lu-Liang Mts

Hwang Ho River

JUNG

Mt T'ai

Feng   *Wei River*

Hao   Ch'in Mts   • Lo-yi

Hsu-Ko   SUNG

707   *Huai River*

Han River

Tapa Mts

YI

Yangtze River

Talou Mts   Kan River

MAN   Wuyi Mts.

Nan Mts

Si River

YI Non-Chou peoples
•   Chou capitals
      Borders of Chou
✗   Battle site

South China Sea

THE WESTERN CHOU, 1027–771 BC

The Western Chou army

Chou armies showed a great deal of continuity from their Shang predecessors, but new forms of weapons and equipment gradually evolved. The dagger-axe now had a haft up to 18 feet (approx. 5.5m) in length, and was used two-handed. It also began to develop more sophisticated features: the blade was extended down the haft to give an effective cutting edge, and the shaft itself had an asymmetrical cross-section to stop it twisting in the hand. The chariot was also further developed. Wheels became larger, with more spokes, and were dished outwards from the hub to the rim for extra strength. Four horses were usual, but rare two-horse burials are known from as late as the 7th century BC. Harnesses

23

Western Chou chariot, *c.* 800 BC. Reconstructed here from archaeological discoveries, with armour and horse-trappings from descriptions in the 'Rituals of Chou' and *Tso Chuan*, the four-horse chariot was the main shock weapon of the early Chou. (Angus McBride © Osprey Publishing)

were decorated with bronze frontlets and strings of cowrie shells, and the whole vehicle was often covered with bronze bells and ornaments to the extent that it was overloaded and unnecessarily cumbersome in battle. This suggests that the chariot was valued more as a psychological shock weapon than for its mobility. Swords had been unknown to the Shang, and were not to come to prominence until the 6th century; but the early Chou occasionally used bronze swords with blades about 18 inches (approx. 45cm) long. These may have been derived from Central Asia, but probably evolved from the indigenous dagger.

Otherwise weapons were similar to those of the Shang, battle accounts emphasizing chariot archery; but the Chou had their own distinctive styles of armour. These are described in the *Chou Li* or 'Rituals of Chou', which lays down guidelines for the palace armourers. One type, the *kia*, was a sleeveless coat of rhinoceros or buffalo hide formed on a wooden dummy, while another kind, the *kiai*, consisted of leather scales on a fabric backing. This was used for corselets and armoured trappers for chariot horses, which were also protected by tiger skins. Chou bronze helmets were similar to Shang types but less elaborately

Bronze frontlet, about 29cm (11½in) long, part of a set of armour for a chariot horse, Western Chou dynasty. (British Museum 1932.3-16.3)

decorated, and it is thought that the hood-shaped styles of the Han dynasty were metal copies of older leather versions.

The army consisted of contingents supplied according to strict rules by vassal states. Vassals of the first rank had to provide three armies; those of the second, two; and third-rank states, one. The size of these forces is not known, but a large army of the Western Chou could field up to 3,000 chariots and 30,000 infantry. The chariot-riding nobility were the mainstay of the army, but the common people also had a vital role. The 'Book of Changes', a work of divination dating from the early Chou, uses as a metaphor for the army the image of water hidden under the earth, referring to the military power represented by the peasantry, and emphasizes the need to deal fairly with the people in order to retain their loyalty. This conflicts with the traditional view that Chou warfare was essentially an aristocratic game, and implies that the later development of mass armies was a logical continuation of the Chou system.

Further evidence comes from the 'Book of Songs', where the peasants are described as undergoing a month's military training every year; and from the account in the 'Book of Documents' of the Chou army at the battle of Mu, where Wu ordered his men to advance slowly in ranks and halt at intervals to keep their order. These do not sound like chariot tactics, and the passage may point to a much more highly developed role for infantry than is generally assumed. Confucian tradition relates that the Chou organized farmers in their domains into a system known as *ching-t'ien* or 'well-field', according to which each unit of eight families grouped round a well had to provide one recruit for the army. The system must have existed, but the version we have is an idealization which was probably never rigidly adhered to.

The Shang system of small-unit organization was apparently retained. At Hsu-ko chariots were deployed in units of 25, each vehicle protected by 25 infantrymen in five ranks. Armies were generally divided into three divisions, left, right and centre, perhaps corresponding to the 'armies' that vassals were required to provide. In later periods the left took precedence, but early Chou generals were usually found in the centre.

The Eastern Chou

The period between 770 and 256 BC is known as the Eastern Chou after the capital at Lo-yi. It is traditionally divided into two sub-periods: the 'Springs and Autumns', after the annals of the state of Lu, up to 479 BC, and the 'Warring States' thereafter. A distinction is often drawn between the chivalrous, aristocratic warfare of the former period and the mass armies and ruthless professionalism of the latter. In fact the true picture was one of steady evolution, and plenty of examples can be found of ruthless generalship as early as the 8th century BC, and of individual heroics as late as the 3rd. Certainly there was never much respect for the rights of the smaller states, which began to be swallowed up by stronger neighbours from the 720s onwards, and where permitted to survive were usually impressed into one of the alliances led by the major powers. The hundreds of independent states were reduced by the 5th century BC to only eight of any consequence: Ch'in, Ch'i, Ch'u, Yueh, Yen, Han, Wei and Chao, the last three having been formed from the breakup of the old great power of the Hwang Ho valley, Tsin. There were many reasons for the success of these states, but it is significant that all were originally on the periphery of the Chinese world, and were able to expand outwards and increase their strength by assimilating barbarian peoples. The ruling house of Tsin, for example, was originally a clan of the Ti tribe, while Ch'i built up its power in the 6th century BC by incorporating the Yi of the Shantung Peninsula. Ch'in, Ch'u and Yueh in particular were so heavily under barbarian influence that it was a long time before their neighbours recognized them as Chinese at all; but from the time of their first appearance in history they had adopted local forms of the political and military institutions of the central states.

The Chinese/barbarian distinction was still very unclear, and tribes usually regarded as barbarian existed between and within organized states, living in towns and maintaining chariot forces like the true Chinese, and often supplying them with allies. The Ti, for example, fought with Ch'i against Wei in 640 BC, and with Tsin against Ch'in in 601 BC. After the 6th century BC, however, most

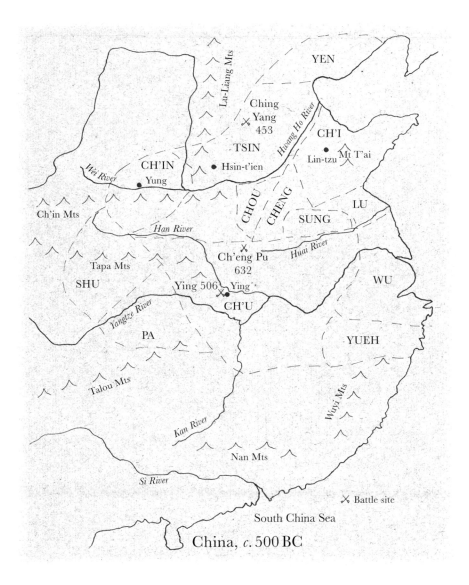

China, *c.* 500 BC

of these tribes were absorbed or banished to the arid borderlands, and the survivors appear in Chinese records mainly as enemies.

The 8th to the 5th centuries BC saw the greatest cultural differences between the states, but internally they were becoming more centralized as a civil service based on merit replaced the old nobility. A state's power was judged by the number of chariots it could field, and this provides us with a rough guide to the rise of the great powers: Tsin, for instance, which could muster 700 chariots in 632 BC, had 4,900 by 537 BC. Ch'i had only 100 in 720 BC, but over 4,000 at the beginning of the 5th century BC. The age was one of endemic warfare, increasing in scale and ferocity as the states widened their ambitions. By the 5th

Light axes were a popular sidearm in early China; this example, from its elaborate decoration, probably belonged to a noble charioteer. It dates from around 700 BC. (British Museum 1936.11-18.32)

century BC they were contending openly for mastery of 'All Under Heaven', as China was known at that time.

Originally, rulers had continued to be graded according to the rank system of the Western Chou, given here with the usual English translations: *Kung*, duke; *Hou*, marquis; *Po*, earl; *Tzu*, viscount; and *Nan*, baron. In 704 BC, however, the ruler of Ch'u took the title of *Wang*, king, and most of the big states eventually followed suit. The unofficial title of *Pa*, or hegemon, was given to five leading statesmen, the first being Duke Huan of Ch'i in the early 7th century BC, who at various times acted as Lord Protector on behalf of the Chou king and exercised a form of authority over the other states, but this authority was never much more than nominal.

The 7th and 6th centuries BC were dominated by a series of wars between the alliance headed by Ch'u on the one hand, and the northern powers of Tsin and Ch'i on the other. The cause was the determination of the kings of Ch'u to get a bridgehead over the Hwang Ho, but northern victories at Cheng-p'u in 632 BC and Yen-ling in 575 BC kept them in check. Meanwhile, central states such as Lu, Sung and Cheng made brief bids for power, only to sink back into obscurity. Their weakness stemmed from various causes. Sung, true to its Shang ancestry, never managed to centralize authority, and went to war under the divided command of two commanders-in-chief and a minister of war. It was defeated by Ch'u at the Hung River in 638 BC, and eventually abandoned military ambition and took the lead in a series of unsuccessful diplomatic initiatives designed to bring about peace. Cheng, at first the leader of the northern states, was eclipsed by the growing strength of Tsin during the 7th century BC, while Lu remained under the control of an ancient aristocracy more interested in ritual than in warfare.

In 506 BC, a new force erupted onto the scene. The state of Wu in the south-east was barbarian in origin, but had learnt Chinese military methods from a refugee Ch'u general, and had for several decades carried on a border

Bronze dagger-axe with tiger and phoenix design, Eastern Chou dynasty, 6th–early 5th century BC. (Topfoto/HIP/Museum of East Asian Art)

dispute with Ch'u, originally over some mulberry trees. In 506 BC a Wu army invaded Ch'u, won five battles and sacked the capital, Ying. Ch'u was temporarily neutralized, although its king was later restored with the help of a Ch'in army; and Wu embarked on a rampage ending only in its destruction in 473 BC by an even more barbarous southern power, Yueh. The Yueh, ancestors of the Vietnamese, remained a thorn in the side of Ch'u until their final defeat in 333 BC. However, these southerners were responsible for important innovations in the art of war, including the use of iron, which was probably transmitted via Wu from further south in around 500 BC.

The 5th century BC saw temporary stalemate, as the ambitions of each of the leading powers were thwarted in turn. Tsin, which had long suffered from instability, was defeated by its former allies at Ching Yang in 453 BC, a blow that led to its disintegration and to the foundation of the three new powers. However, economically and culturally it was an age of great progress, and the population of China increased from 12 million in 650 BC to as many as 40 million. Pressure on land became yet another factor driving the states into war.

Eastern Chou armies

It is not necessary to take too seriously the rules which are supposed to have governed conflict in the 'Springs and Autumns' period. For example, it was said that a state should not invade another while it was distracted by a revolt, or in the year in which its ruler died – but these were in fact favourite times for taking advantage of another's weakness. Defeated states were also not supposed to be annexed, but even the annals of the law-abiding state of Lu are full of instances of this happening. In fact there was no real difference between this and the supposedly more ruthless 'Warring States' era.

The 8th to the 5th centuries BC were the heyday of the chariot, which appeared in greater numbers than ever before or since, but infantry often succeeded in defeating them. For example, in Tsu in 613 BC a peasant revolt overthrew the ruler, and a force of 800 chariots sent by his allies to restore him was routed by the peasant army. It seems that chariots were less mobile than might be thought, and could easily be outmanoeuvred by infantry unless the

Blade for a chariot axle, 5th to 4th centuries BC. Although the Chinese chariot was not designed for breaking up infantry formations in the manner of the scythed Persian variety, such an attachment would deter infantrymen trying to climb aboard, and might damage the wheels of enemy chariots not so equipped. (British Museum 1965.7-28.1)

terrain was perfectly level and the going firm. The result was that the enthusiasm of the common people was more essential than ever for making war, and rulers were known to consult popular assemblies before deciding on policy.

From the late 6th century BC reliance on the chariot declined, in part because of the influence of states such as Wu, which never adopted them on a large scale, and by 540 BC charioteers are found dismounting to fight in mountainous terrain. For a while chronicles continued to emphasize chariot archery between noblemen, concentrating on individual heroes such as Lang Shin, a disgraced officer who in 624 BC redeemed his reputation by leading a suicidal charge of the Tsin charioteers against Ch'in at P'ang-ya, gaining the victory almost single-handedly. But by 500 BC, the sword was beginning to gain popularity, and from this time swords start to predominate over bows in battle narratives, sword and shield being apparently regarded as a superior combination for infantry fighting to the spear or dagger-axe. In 520 BC, a Ch'i army routed the troops of Hua by throwing away its long weapons and charging on foot with swords, a move that no doubt gained a moral advantage as it implied a greater eagerness to risk close combat. Even at this early date there does not seem to have been much objection to the use of deception, or to taking advantage of an enemy's misplaced sense of honour. The *Tso Chuan* relates how in 520 BC a certain P'ao of Hua missed the Tsin general Shing with an arrow, and was about to shoot again when Shing called to him, saying that it was unchivalrous to take two shots without allowing him to defend himself. P'ao lowered his bow, and was immediately shot dead.

Organization and tactics were highly developed. The traditional three divisions were still used, but this could be varied if necessary. At Che in 717 BC, three Cheng forces were used to pin the enemy frontally while a fourth worked its way round the flank; while in 540 BC Tsin fought in five bodies against the Ti. Infantry were deployed five deep, either with the chariots or as a body in the centre; and a remark in 'Wu Chi's Art of War', that tall men were given missile weapons and shorter men spears and halberds, implies that archers could be deployed behind the spearmen to shoot overhead. Tactical formations such as 'crane and goose' and 'fish-scale' are mentioned, the latter placing the chariots in line in front with infantry behind. All arms were subjected to a ferocious code of discipline: in 540 BC, for instance, a Tsin nobleman was beheaded for refusing to fight on foot when ordered.

Continuous warfare accelerated developments in weapons and equipment. The chariot still carried three crewmen – a driver, an archer on the left, and a man armed with spear or dagger-axe on the right. Wheels now had up to 26 spokes, and the old nine-foot (approx. 2.8m) chariot pole, a source of structural weakness, was shortened to six feet (approx. 1.8m). Cabs were covered with leather to protect the crew, and a canopy or parasol began to appear, although

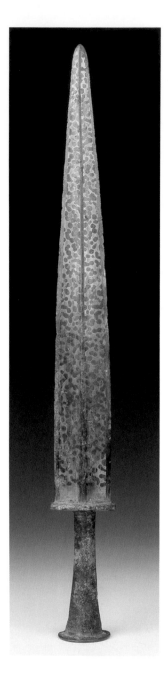

Bronze sword of the 3rd century BC. Such short and relatively primitive weapons were typical of the Eastern Chou period. (Topfoto/HIP/Museum of East Asian Art)

this may have been removed in battle. Four horses were now standard. Some chariots were also equipped with serrated bronze blades about a foot (approx. 30cm) long on the axle caps. Paradoxically, despite the increase in vehicle numbers, archaeological finds of bronze chariot-fittings are much rarer from the Eastern Chou than from earlier centuries; this may reflect the fact that chariots were now state property and were reused rather than buried with their owners, but it is also likely that they had become more functional and less hampered with excessive decoration.

Armour and bows were similar to earlier types, but the dagger-axe continued to evolve, and by the 4th century BC the addition of a spear-blade to the end of the shaft had turned it into a true cut-and-thrust weapon or halberd. Spears and dagger-axes fell into two groups, one about nine feet (approx. 2.8m) long, the other around 18 feet (approx. 5.5m). Swords were still of the short, stabbing type; blades were still bronze, but from the 5th century BC iron began to appear, the states of Ch'u and Han being known for their weapons of low-grade steel. Iron smelting technology, however, remained very primitive until the 2nd century BC, and the metal could not replace bronze for most military purposes.

Another development of this period was the crossbow, ascribed to Ch'in Shih of Ch'u in the 6th century BC. The maximum range of this weapon was said to be 600 paces, but its advantage over the conventional bow lay in its penetrating power at short range; its slow rate of fire made it at first most popular for defending towns. By 340 BC, however, it was in use in pitched battles and may have contributed to the decline of the chariot, which as a large, slow-moving target protected only by leather must have been very vulnerable.

Two peculiarities of southern warfare in this period are of interest: the use of convicts and of elephants. Wu pioneered the employment of condemned criminals as suicide troops at Ke-fu in 518 BC, when 300 were lined up in the van and launched in an attack on the Ch'u army before it was properly deployed. At Tsui-le in 496 BC the Yueh went one better when, unable to break the Wu line, they sent three ranks of convicts out between the armies. These unfortunates were threatened with reprisals against their families, given swords, and ordered to cut their own throats. The Wu troops, transfixed by this gruesome sight, were taken unawares and overrun by the Yueh. Southern warfare in general was waged with a savagery unknown to the northerners; casualties were far higher, and the total collapse of Wu and Yueh can probably be attributed to the excessive strain on their manpower. Before its overthrow by Yueh, Wu was completely exhausted by its campaigns, and the *Tso Chuan* describes how the bones of its warriors covered large areas of the border with Ch'u 'like weeds'. In 506

BC, in a desperate attempt to save Ying from the Wu army, Ch'u deployed a force of elephants of unknown strength, but the ploy was unsuccessful and the city fell soon afterwards. It is usually said that the elephants had torches tied to their tails, but this interpretation is uncertain. Probably they were led by men with torches, who then used them to stampede the frightened animals into the Wu ranks. There is no mention of men actually riding them, and whatever the outcome the experiment was not repeated.

Methods of raising an army varied from one state to another. Duke Huan of Ch'i introduced in the 670s BC a formal system that gave him an advantage over the often haphazard levies of his rivals. Every family provided one militiaman with obligation to serve whenever required, the families being grouped into three provinces of five districts each. This system provided three armies, each of five divisions. Three armies were usual for the larger states, a survival from the organization of the Western Chou, but smaller ones fielded only one or two. Lu, for example, reduced its establishment from three to two, briefly increased it again to three, but was unable to sustain this burden and reverted to two. This implies that armies were of a universally standard size, but details are lacking.

Military expeditions were of two types: *fa*, a formal march with drums beating, and *ch'in*, a stealthy raid or surprise attack. The latter was a favoured way of augmenting supplies by stealing the harvest from a neighbour's fields, but by the 5th century BC most states had grain surpluses and this type of campaign became less common. Promotion and merit were originally gained by bringing back the heads or ears of dead enemies, a practice particularly popular in Ch'i and Ch'in, but in most states this custom was discouraged by the 4th century BC as it made the maintenance of order on the battlefield impossible. Prisoners were still sometimes sacrificed and their blood smeared on the drums as a way of invoking divine aid. The consultation of oracles before battle was another time-honoured tradition, but by the end of the period a sceptical attitude, derived from Confucian influence, was gaining ground.

The 4th and 3rd centuries BC

During the 4th century BC, while the central and northern states squabbled over the remains of Tsin, further developments were taking place on the frontiers. In the south-west, new semi-barbarian powers were arising. Shu and Pa, pastoral territories inhabited by tribesmen known for their wild songs and dances, became organized under dynasties founded by exiles from Ch'u; but the most ominous cloud on the horizon was the rise of Ch'in. This state had its origins in a fief in Kansu granted by the Chou to a minor aristocrat in 897 BC so that he could raise horses for the royal armies. Its early history was a long series of wars

Bronze spearhead with *t'ao-t'ie* pattern – an animal-like mask of uncertain significance. Western Chou–early Eastern Chou dynasty. (Topfoto/HIP/Museum of East Asian Art)

Eastern Chou warriors, 700–400 BC. This illustration depicts one of the elite guards or shock troops of a ruler's household hunting with an infantry archer. (Angus McBride © Osprey Publishing)

against the Jung tribes, but in 623 BC a decisive victory was won, and by 400 BC the Jung had been absorbed into the growing state. Gradually, as the chaos further east allowed it to expand, Ch'in crept eastwards, despite a serious defeat by Tsin in 576 BC, and in 350 BC set up its capital at Hsienyang in an area known as the 'land within the passes'. This, the upper valley of the Wei River, was a natural stronghold which enabled Ch'in to build up its power in security. It was said that a force of 20,000 could hold the passes indefinitely against a million men.

Ch'in was a culturally backward land, playing only a minor part in the events of the 8th to the 5th centuries BC; the turning point came with the reforms of Lord Shang, a brilliant minister who, after the middle of the 4th century BC, set out to convert Ch'in into a totalitarian state. The people were warlike but manpower was limited, so Shang started irrigation schemes to increase the amount of agricultural land, and for the first time allowed land to be bought and sold. Peasants from all over China therefore flocked to Ch'in in search of land of their own. Every man was a soldier, and 20 grades of military and civil nobility were introduced, based solely on the number of heads cut off

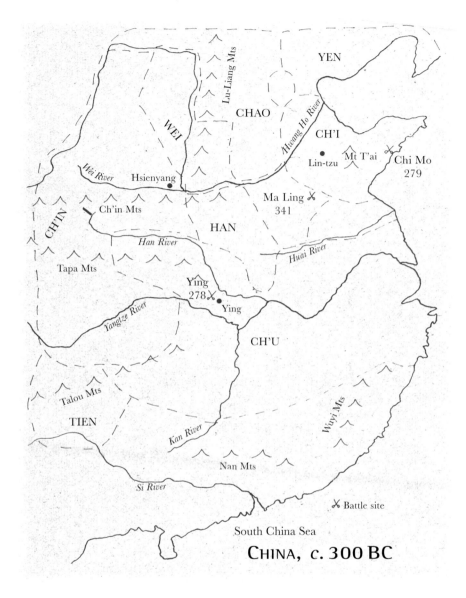

CHINA, c. 300 BC

in battle. The result was that everyone was not only willing, but eager, to fight. Ch'in was also helped by its relative primitiveness, freedom from tradition and willingness to adopt new ideas. It was also used to employing aliens from other states in the army and government, and so was able to attract the best talent from many sources.

Shu and Pa, conquered in 316 BC, were the first victims of Ch'in expansion. Ch'u was then drawn into a long war in which neither side seemed able to gain a decisive advantage, despite the capture of the Ch'u king Huai in 299 BC and the sack of Ying in 278 BC. *Chan-Kuo Ts'e* (the 'Intrigues of the Warring States')

Bronze spearhead with rhombus and recessed lattice diaper pattern, Eastern Chou dynasty, 5th century BC. This type of weapon is associated with the eastern states of Wu and Yueh and is an example of the kind of prestige pieces that circulated among rulers of different states. (Topfoto/HIP/ Museum of East Asian Art)

describes the problems caused for Ch'u by Ch'in bases far up the Yangtze from which rafts, each carrying 50 men with supplies for three months, could float downstream to Ying in only five days 'like a swooping hawk', long before troops could be deployed to meet them. One result of this war was the spread of Chinese military systems still further south and west. In the 290s BC, the Ch'u general Chuang Chiao, who had been sent to subdue the barbarians of Yunnan, finding his way home blocked by a Ch'in invasion, remained in Yunnan with his army and set up the state of Tien. This remote region remained isolated and was never conquered by Ch'in, but it adopted many items of Chinese technology, such as bronze armour and the crossbow.

War broke out in the north-east in 285 BC, when Yen took revenge for intervention in its internal affairs by invading Ch'i, defeating its armies and overrunning its territory. Ch'i resistance centred on the city of Chi Mo, from which the hero T'ien Tan led a campaign that eventually liberated the country. From then on, however, the history of the 3rd century BC is that of a monotonous series of victories by the Ch'in forces, aided by continuing quarrels among their victims. As Ch'en Chen of Wei put it, 'our states boil one another alive, and Ch'in need not even supply the faggots'.

In 260 BC, at Ch'ang-p'ing, the Chao army was surrounded and allowed to surrender on terms, but the Ch'in soldiers, eager for their quota of heads, killed the prisoners in cold blood. In 238 BC, King Cheng, the future Ch'in Shih Huang Ti, the First Emperor, came of age and took over direction of the campaigns, aided by his minister Li Ssu. In 228 BC, Chao was finally destroyed, and although a reverse was suffered at the hands of Ch'u in 226 BC, three years later Ch'u fell to General Wang Chien. The other states followed in quick succession, the last being Ch'i in 221 BC; and by the end of that year the Chinese people were united for the first time in over five centuries. No depth of treachery seemed too low for Ch'in: Huai of Ch'u, for instance, was kidnapped and imprisoned while visiting Ch'in under a safe conduct to discuss peace terms.

States involved in this kind of total war had to conscript every man available, and many of their armies were huge by pre-modern standards. Ch'in forces up to 600,000 strong are mentioned, and although this must be an exaggeration, 'Sun Tzu's Art of War' considers armies of 100,000 as commonplace, and accompanies these figures with a detailed analysis of costs, suggesting that they are more than just a guess. In fact, careful estimates of an enemy's strength carried out in the temples had largely replaced the use of oracles by the 4th century BC, so at least roughly

A bronze head for an arrow or crossbow bolt, late Eastern Chou. (British Museum W.G. 943)

accurate figures must have been available. *Chan-Kuo Ts'e* contains a discussion on this question in which armies of only 30,000, such as were usual in earlier times, are dismissed as inadequate for 3rd-century BC conditions.

Such multitudes could not be adequately supplied overland in the absence of proper roads, and although water transport was used where possible, the *Sun Tzu* recommends feeding them by foraging in enemy territory. The effects of plunder on this scale must have been disastrous, and it is not surprising that famine and disease began to appear. The *Sun Tzu* remarks that 'an army which does not suffer from one hundred diseases is said to be certain of victory'.

At about this time the study of war became an important theme in the writings of Chinese philosophers; and the works of Sun Tzu, a follower of Confucius, illustrate different attitudes to such questions as recruitment and maintenance of morale. In a debate at the court of the king of Chao in 260 BC, Sun Tzu and Lin Wu-chun put forward two approaches to the problem of dealing with the Ch'in invasion. The latter advocated reliance on strategy and the hiring of mercenaries, but Sun Tzu somewhat naively argued that it was sufficient to gain the support of the common people by enlightened policies, believing that an aggressor's troops would not fight against a virtuous ruler. Both, however, agreed on the need for strict discipline, condemning many contemporary commanders who disregarded this as no better than bandits.

Armies of the 4th and 3rd centuries BC

The chariot continued to be employed as a shock weapon until the end of the period, but it was nearing the end of its career and no further significant development took place. By 300 BC, cavalry was starting to take over many of its roles. Horse-riding by individuals is attested as early as the 6th century BC, but the first Chinese cavalry units were not raised until 307 BC when Wu Ling of Chao forced his men to adopt the dress and equipment of the Hu barbarians. This was initially regarded as a betrayal of Chinese culture, but its advantages were obvious; and it soon spread among the northern states, where the terrain was open and the threat from mounted steppe nomads greatest. The first horsemen were recruited from conscripted peasants and nomad mercenaries, but by the end of the 3rd century BC mounted combat was respectable even for a Chinese gentleman. Chao, Ch'in, Wei and Yen were the leading cavalry exponents of the early 3rd century BC, Ch'in and Wei in particular being unpopular with their neighbours because of their use of undisciplined Hu tribesmen.

4th–3rd-century BC bronze fittings inlaid with gold and silver from an Eastern Chou crossbow. (British Museum OA 1934.2-16.1,2)

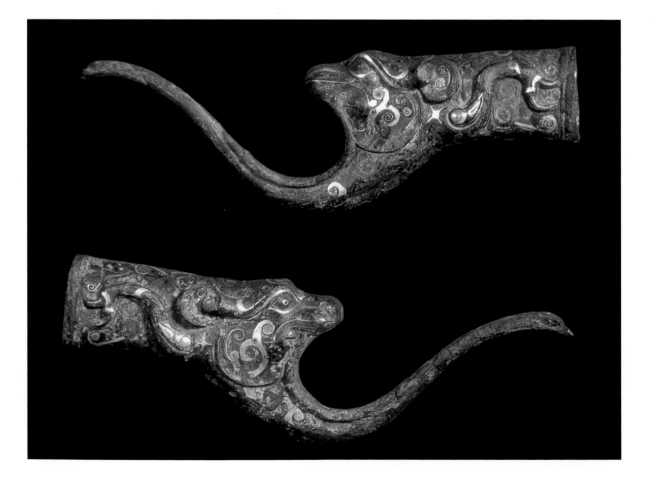

The horse of the period was still the small Mongolian breed, and partly for this reason early cavalry was mainly light, equipped with the bow and noted for mobility rather than close-combat skills. By the end of the 3rd century BC, however, at least a few horsemen wore armour. It is not certain whether mounted crossbowmen were in use this early. It is usually thought that they had to await the development of a belt-hook device for cocking the weapon, which otherwise had to be drawn by standing on the bow and pulling up with both hands; but Han armies had them by 170 BC, and the use of a light crossbow that could be cocked with the arms alone is not impossible.

By this time the sword was overwhelmingly the most popular weapon for close combat. Armour, now common for at least elite infantry units, was still often of leather, but metal protection was beginning to appear. The Ch'in terracotta warriors depict several styles of body armour, formed from plates riveted or laced together, in colours that suggest iron, bronze and probably leather. Similar coats of iron plates dating from the mid-4th century BC have been excavated. It used to be thought that Ch'in owed its military supremacy to its adoption of iron weapons, but recent research does not bear this out. Iron swords and spearheads were in fact more common in Ch'u, and Ch'in bronze-casters were able to make blades at least as good as the brittle cast iron of the time. Ch'in swords could be coated with a chromium alloy to improve their sharpness, and the technique may have been known elsewhere. The state of Han was noted for the excellence of its arms and equipment, particularly bows, crossbows, swords and halberds. *Chan-Kuo Ts'e* describes its troops as all equipped with iron facemasks and thumb-rings, which implies that all were trained as archers.

The system of organization by fives was still in force, an infantry squad sometimes being formed from three spearmen supported by two archers or crossbowmen, but missile troops could also be deployed separately. A larger unit consisting of a chariot, three crewmen and 72 infantrymen accompanied by a baggage wagon and 25 grooms, cooks and servants may have been administrative rather than tactical; by the 3rd century BC we read of officials specifically responsible for administration and supply.

A division of the army into five bodies was now usual, denoted by a system of flags: *Left Wing*, Green Dragon; *Right Wing*, White Tiger; *Vanguard*, Red Bird; *Rearguard*, Black Tortoise; *C-in-C with Bodyguard*, Great Bear constellation.

Elite infantry guard units were now popular; those of Ch'u were armoured crossbowmen who were trained for seven years and could march 100 miles (approx. 160km) 'without resting'. Other elite formations were the *ch'i* or 'extraordinary forces', whose main function was surprise attacks. They were selected from the strongest and bravest men, often by drafting one from each five-man squad. 'Wu Ch'i's Art of War' suggests other sources for shock troops, such as men who have disgraced themselves and wish to make amends by acts

General, crossbowman and swordsman from the 4th and 3rd centuries BC. The crossbow is based on an example found at Hsienyang. (Angus McBride © Osprey Publishing)

of courage. The *ch'i* units would not have been distinctively uniformed, as they were relied upon to deceive the enemy after the ordinary troops had pinned him. Sun Tzu's advice is to 'use the ordinary forces to engage; use the extraordinary to win'.

Wu Ch'i has some interesting information on the characteristics of the different states' armies. Ch'in forces were brave but lacked discipline, as everyone fought for his own profit. They were best dealt with by luring them into

Bronze trigger mechanism for a crossbow with gold inlays, Eastern Chou dynasty, 4th–3rd century BC. The secret of this precision mechanism was for centuries a vital advantage for the Chinese in their struggles with the barbarians who, although they often captured examples, were never able to duplicate the workmanship involved. (Topfoto/HIP/Museum of East Asian Art)

a pursuit and ambushing them. This is supported by other sources which describe Ch'in soldiers as charging fanatically, even throwing off their armour in a kind of berserk rage.

Ch'u, on the other hand, was not highly regarded: the land was rich, but the people were lazy and lacked stamina. Sun Tzu's comments on Ch'u are similar; he remarks that they were defeated by Ch'in not because they lacked good armour and weapons, but because they did not know how to use them. This may have been partly due to the unhealthy malarial climate, but in the revolt of 209 the men of Ch'u were regarded as worth ten of any other troops. Ch'u was the victim of a lot of unfair prejudice, its inhabitants being disparaged as semi-barbarians or 'monkeys with hats on'.

Yen soldiers are described as 'stupid and honest', knowing nothing of strategy and preferring the defensive; while the army of Ch'i was unreliable, as the government was corrupt and inspired no loyalty. Han, Wei and Chao were well organized but war-weary, and their officers were badly paid and so of poor quality. It should be remembered that these comments are not valid for all periods, and of course contain an element of bias, but they are a useful corrective to the idea that all Chinese were alike. Regional differences were reduced by the 3rd century BC, however, by the practice of incorporating prisoners of war into the captor's forces. Whole armies were sometimes added to the strength of a state in this way, and where possible would be transferred to a distant frontier to reduce the risk of them defecting again.

The Ch'in Empire

Ch'in expansion did not stop in 221 BC, and between then and 209 BC many remote regions were brought into the Chinese sphere of influence for the first time. In 213 BC, Emperor Shih Huang Ti invaded the lands south of Ch'u, his armies reaching the sea near present-day Canton. The Liaotung Peninsula in Manchuria was also occupied; and in 215 BC General Meng T'ien inflicted a major defeat on the newly formed nomad confederation of the Hsiung-nu on the borders of Chao. The Great Wall was built by linking up a series of walls that the northern states had been erecting since the 5th century BC, but was on a far grander scale than anything previously attempted. It covered 3,000 miles of the steppe frontier far to the north of the present wall, and was completed under the command of Meng T'ien by 300,000 troops and impressed labourers. The sufferings of these conscripts, and the savagery with which Ch'in law was imposed, led to discontent, and when the First Emperor died in 210 BC his successor was unable to hold the state together. The aristocracy of the former states had been deported en masse to Hsienyang, but many now escaped to add their authority to the revolts that broke out everywhere.

The Ch'in commanders had committed a strategic error by spreading their troops thinly throughout the empire in isolated garrisons, and the insurgents were able to defeat them in detail and to equip themselves with captured weapons and armour. In 209 BC, General Chang Han armed a force of labourers who were working on the First Emperor's tomb and used them to beat off Ch'en She's rebels from a town near Hsienyang, but such makeshift levies were not enough. Rebels from Ch'u took a leading role in the uprisings, and in 207 BC massacred a large Ch'in army at Hsin-an. The following year they destroyed the capital and extinguished the dynasty.

The empire fell into anarchy; but gradually two of the rebel forces collected the others around them and carried on the war against each other for mastery of China. The Ch'u army was led by a southern aristocrat, Hsiang Yu, while his main rival, Liu Pang, was a man of lowly birth commanding a force known as the Han, after his fief in Han-chung in the far west. The Han armies were strengthened by contingents from Shu, Pa and Ch'in, the latter won over by lenient treatment in contrast to Hsiang Yu's brutality.

The war dragged on for several years, complicated by numerous betrayals and defections among the allies, and at one point, after a defeat at P'eng-ch'eng in 205 BC, Liu Pang was a fugitive without an army; but his ability and determination were ultimately successful. Three years later, reinforced by drafts from Ch'in, he invaded Ch'u. At Kai-hsia, Hsiang Yu was encircled by an army four times the size of his own; he managed to escape with 800 cavalry, only to

OPPOSITE Liu Pang, who became the first emperor of the Western Han dynasty, taking the name Gaozu (Han Kao-ti) (247–195 BC). (© Stephen Turnbull)

be hunted down and killed. Liu Pang took the title of Han Kao-ti, proclaiming the Han dynasty which was to rule for 400 years.

The Ch'in army

Most of our evidence for the Ch'in army comes from the terracotta figures from the First Emperor's tomb at Hsienyang, which presumably represent the palace guard. If the huge numbers reported for Ch'in armies are even approximately correct, few can have been as lavishly equipped as these elite troops. Troop types depicted are both armoured and unarmoured infantry, armed with bows, crossbows, spears and halberds; cavalry, whose armament is unknown; and four-horse chariots. Swords have not been cast on the figures, although we know from many other sources that they were in common use, and the statues were probably equipped with real ones that were later stolen. Swords by now had blades up to three-and-a-half feet (approx. 1.1m) long, and we are told that King

Hsiang Yu is surrounded by the armies of his rival Liu Pang at the battle of Kai-hsia in 202 BC. (© Stephen Turnbull)

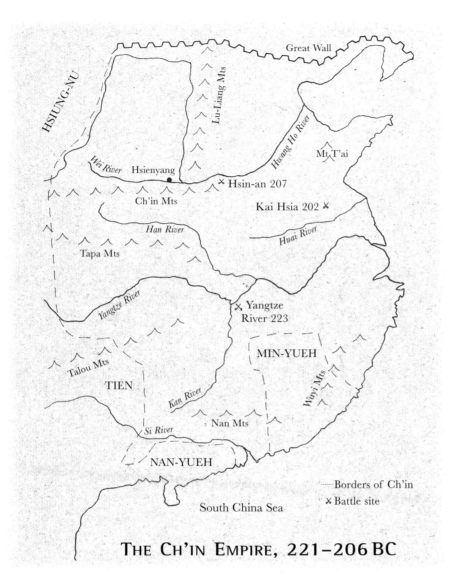

Great Wall

Lu-Liang Mts

Hwang Ho River

Mt T'ai

HSIUNG-NU

Wei River   Hsienyang

× Hsin-an 207

Ch'in Mts

Kai Hsia 202 ×

Han River

Huai River

Tapa Mts

Yangtze River

× Yangtze
River 223

MIN-YUEH

Talou Mts

Wuyi Mts

TIEN

Kan River

Nan Mts

Si River

NAN-YUEH

South China Sea

⸻⸻ Borders of Ch'in
× Battle site

THE CH'IN EMPIRE, 221–206 BC

Cheng had difficulty fighting off an assassination attempt in 227 BC because the length of his sword made it difficult to draw.

The pottery army has certain limitations as a source for the Ch'in: the weapons were taken by rebels soon after the burial, and the lack of shields may be attributable to the same cause. Alternatively, it is possible that shields were not carried when on guard duty, as opposed to in battle, although some figures appear to have been carrying something in each hand, perhaps a weapon and a shield. It is hard to believe that the troops would have faced the crossbows of their enemies without the benefit of shields, and reliefs of the Han period do show them in use by Ch'in soldiers.

However, the figures are a unique guide to styles of dress and armour, and it is possible to deduce something of Ch'in unit organization from the formations in which they were buried. The first pit contains an infantry unit of approximately 6,000 men. Most are close-formation armoured troops, wearing a variety of armour styles and probably armed with spears and halberds up to nine feet (approx. 2.8m) long. The officers are carried in six chariots accompanied by crewmen armed with similar weapons, and escorted by small groups of armoured or unarmoured infantry. In front of the unit are deployed about 200 skirmishers, probably crossbowmen. Other unit types are a group of 64 three-man, four-horse chariots; a unit of 19 chariots accompanied by eight horsemen and 264 armoured infantry; and a detachment of six chariots and 108 cavalry.

Tactical and strategic doctrine

A number of ancient Chinese works on military science survive. The best known are those attributed to Sun Tzu, who supposedly lived about 500 BC but which may be 4th century BC; and Wu Ch'i, traditionally a work of the 380s BC but in fact a compilation containing much 3rd-century BC material. However, 182 such books were known in the early Han period, and *Tso Chuan* describes Sun Shuh of Ch'u as quoting a manual called 'The Art of War' as early as the battle of Pi in 595 BC. Written works containing a formal system of strategy and tactics were therefore not, as is sometimes assumed, an invention of the 'Warring States' era.

The *Sun Tzu Ping Fa*, or 'Sun Tzu's Art of War', was by far the most influential of these books, and can be considered to contain the essence of Chinese thinking on the subject. It was not, however, without its critics. The philosopher Han Fei Tzu, whose ideas influenced King Cheng of Ch'in, felt that it placed too little emphasis on the role of discipline in controlling troops, and that its humane concern with the limitation of war was hypocritical. The Confucians, on the other hand, were horrified by its advocacy of deceit and covert operations. Yet to a modern reader it is remarkable for its rational approach and lucid exposition of the critical factors in warfare.

According to the *Sun Tzu*, the first requirement for a campaign is a mathematical calculation of the respective strengths of the combatants, with weighting where appropriate for factors such as the ability of commanders and the social cohesion of states. If it was decided to embark on war, it was essential to carry the fighting into enemy territory. This had three advantages: it enabled troops to live off the land without antagonizing one's own people, it disrupted the enemy's mobilization plans, and it reduced desertion by one's own men,

OPPOSITE Southern warriors, 600–300 BC. A Ch'u spearman is fighting a Wu convict who is one of the 'suicide warriors' employed in 518. Behind them is a shaman whose role was to inspire the army. (Angus McBride © Osprey Publishing)

Figure of a crossbowman
from the terracotta army
of the First Emperor of
Ch'in. A unique source for
historians, the discovery
of this buried army in
1974 revolutionized our
understanding of the
Ch'in army. (Topfoto)

whose best hope of safety in a hostile country was to stay with the army. This implies that commanders were often unsure of the reliability of their troops; and Sun Tzu frequently returns to this subject, suggesting that the army be deliberately led into 'death ground', a desperate position where retreat is impossible, in order to induce it to fight.

Sun Tzu goes on to describe the terrible effects of a long war and to emphasize the need for speed in strategic operations. Pitched battles were to be avoided when possible and fortified cities to be bypassed, it being preferable to subvert an enemy by deceit, including the use of spies and secret agents. This type of operation was made easier by the fact that an inhabitant of one Chinese state could usually pass himself off as belonging to another. Knowledge of the enemy commander's character was vital for this sort of trickery, so that his personal weaknesses and vices could be used against him.

If battle is inevitable, Sun Tzu again stresses the importance of knowing the enemy, of reconnaissance, and of familiarity with the correct use of terrain. The *Kuan Tzu*, a 4th-century BC work, is even more emphatic on this latter point, and on the necessity for the detailed study of maps. The Shang may have had maps cast on bronze vessels, and by the Eastern Chou they were in widespread use, painted on silk. A magnetic compass, consisting of a piece of lodestone swinging freely on a wooden board, was also available by the 5th century BC at the latest.

Battle tactics revolved around the use of the 'ordinary' and 'extraordinary' forces. The main themes throughout the period are operations against the flanks and rear, and direct frontal attacks by deliberately enraged troops. All the surviving manuals discuss ways of assessing the state of the enemy from the appearance of his formations and the noise his men are making, and explain the need to judge the correct moment for a charge. Whatever the exact plan used, all sources stress the primacy of the offensive in ancient Chinese warfare, although field fortifications were often used as a base from which an attack could be launched, and many commanders entrenched their camps at night when in hostile territory. Sun Tzu therefore devotes a chapter to the use of fire as a method of attacking the enemy in his camp, either by means of incendiary arrows or by burning dry grass.

It is difficult to say how far the precepts of the manuals were consciously adopted, and it is unlikely that they were actually consulted on campaign. Before the invention of paper in the 1st century BC they were inscribed on strips of bamboo tied together with leather, and even the relatively short *Sun Tzu* would have needed a cart to carry it. Nevertheless, many battle narratives show the application of the principles they advocate; and, as *Tso Chuan* shows, officers would know at least some passages by heart. It is therefore no exaggeration to speak of a coherent body of doctrine on the art of war from at least the Eastern Chou period.

OPPOSITE The Ch'in
Imperial Guard,
221–206 BC. Shown
here are a crossbowman,
halberdier and skirmisher,
all based on figures in the
terracotta army from the
tomb of the First Emperor.
(Angus McBride © Osprey
Publishing Ltd)

Command and control

The system for selecting commanders was of course vital to the conduct of warfare. During the Shang and Western Chou dynasties it was usual for the king himself to lead the armies, and noble birth was a prerequisite for command in most states until much later. Command was often hereditary within a family, but there were exceptions from an early date. Wu's second-in-command at Mu in 1027 BC was the son of a butcher, raised from the ranks because of his exceptional ability, but this was unusual. More typical was the case of Ts'ao Mei, who served Duke Chuang of Lu between 693 BC and 662 BC. This desperate character led the army to three successive defeats, but was retained as general because of his personal strength and courage. He later achieved notoriety by taking Duke Huan of Ch'i hostage during a peace-making ceremony. Even in the 3rd century BC a display of personal heroics was considered appropriate for a commander, but was no longer a necessity. Sun Pin, who had had his feet cut off after being falsely convicted of a criminal offence, was able to direct his armies from a litter in the rear.

By the 5th century BC, generals of peasant origin were becoming as common as those from the nobility. This paralleled the replacement of the aristocracy in civil office, and led to the rise of a professional military class that often had no loyalty to a particular state and would offer its services to the highest bidder. Wu Ch'i, for example, was born in Wei, studied war in Lu and then went to Ch'u, where he reformed the army. Sun Pin, also a native of Wei, led the Ch'i army to its greatest victory against his home state. It was considered disastrous for a ruler to interfere in the conduct of a campaign once he had appointed a general to carry it out, and the *Sun Tzu* warns against this temptation.

Methods for controlling troops on the battlefield were highly developed. A large variety of flags was used, both for signalling and to raise morale; divisions and commanders were distinguished by flags, and each unit was identified by smaller banners of a different colour. Movements to the right or left were indicated by flags, while drums signalled the advance and bells the retreat. Four beats of a drum signified 'prepare for action', and five the commencement of a march. Bronze bells, struck like a gong from the outside, were often carried in chariots. Wu Ch'i mentions horse-borne and 'ordinary' drums, presumably carried on foot. Drums and gongs were also used for psychological warfare, inspiring their own side and terrifying the enemy, and the generation of the maximum amount of noise was considered essential to a successful charge. It is difficult to tell at what date this system developed, but flags and drums are mentioned at the beginning of the Western Chou and seem to have had the same functions as later. Coloured banners were also used as national recognition symbols; for example, the Chou army at Mu carried white ones, while the Ch'in Empire adopted black, and the Han in the succession wars used red.

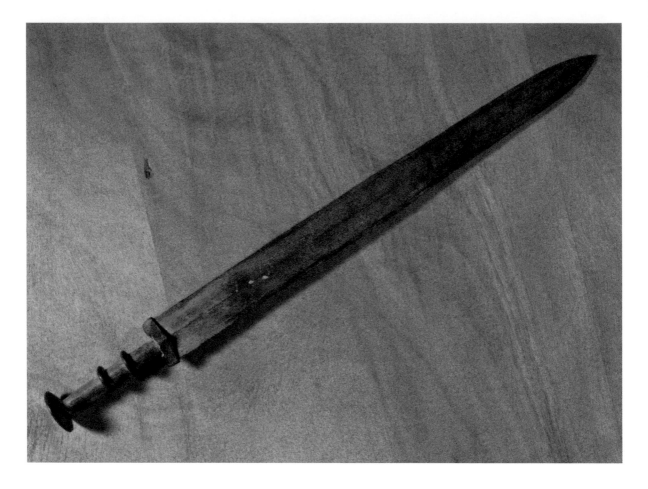

Bronze sword of a later type, 3rd century BC. Well balanced for cutting and stabbing, this type – here about 46cm (18in) long – was to develop into the long sword of the Ch'in period. (British Museum 1921.4-6.2)

When discussing signalling, Sun Tzu remarks on the difficulty of hearing the human voice in battle, or of seeing much once the dust was raised. A device used to overcome the latter problem was the *ch'ao-ch'e* or 'crow's-nest' chariot, which was invented during the Eastern Chou. This consisted of a chariot with a high chassis and reinforced wheels, with a small tower on top. *Tso Chuan* describes the king of Ch'u climbing on such a vehicle to observe the Tsin deployment in 575 BC. It seems that the tower held only one man, as the king had to shout his observations to an officer below for interpretation.

Chinese troops were strictly controlled and drilled from an early date. The good order of the Chou army at Mu has already been mentioned, and the account in *Tso Chuan* of the Ch'u army of 595 BC also bears witness to a developed system of drill. The troops could all manoeuvre at once in response to signals, and were trained to deploy in emergencies without specific orders. The introduction of marching in step has been associated with Wu Ch'i around 380 BC, but may have taken place much earlier. A music manual of the 1st century BC describes a military dance of 'ancient times' in which the dancers advanced 'keeping together with perfect precision, like a military unit', the pace being regulated by the beat of a drum. Such dances were used as early as the Western Chou as training for war.

Fortification and sieges

The walled cities of the Shang represent the earliest Chinese fortifications. The walls were built by pounding earth with wooden rammers until it became as hard as brick; at Ao, they were 60 feet (approx. 18.3m) thick at the base and 25 feet (approx. 7.6m) in height. This technique was used until Ch'in times, but refinements were added later. By the 6th century BC, lookout towers were being built above the walls, which could be faced with stone or brick. The area enclosed by the walls was traditionally square or rectangular, with a gate in the middle of each side; but the growth of towns in the Eastern Chou period led to the building of suburbs outside the walls, and these on occasion became the scene of furious battles. In some cases a series of concentric walls was erected at different times to enclose these suburbs.

The 'Book of Songs' describes methods used for assaulting towns in the Western Chou. Scaling ladders were available, including types that could be wheeled up to the walls, and protective mantlets were used to shield men attempting to tunnel through them. Starvation and assault by escalade remained the most popular ways of taking cities, although Kaou-yu in Lu was captured in 546 by Tsin troops creeping in through the storm-drains. By the 4th century BC, however, assaults were regarded as a last resort.

The defence had by then been strengthened by the invention of large artillery crossbows which were stationed on the walls. Some of these were cocked with pulleys and windlasses and had draw-weights of 400 pounds (181kg). In about 350 BC the 'Book of Lord Shang' described how the population of a beleaguered city was divided into three 'armies': the able-bodied men guarded the ramparts, the women dug ditches and built earthworks, while the very young, old and infirm looked after the livestock. During the 4th century BC, a new element was introduced into the defence by Mo Tzu, a philosopher who preached justice for the weak and was prepared to put his ideals into action. His works covered the techniques of defence and his followers, known as Mohists, intervened on numerous occasions on the side of small states under threat. Among their inventions were kites for signalling, improved pulleys and counterweight mechanisms, and a type of primitive resonance box made from a pottery jar with a leather membrane over the mouth. These were buried in deep shafts within the walls, and by listening to the vibrations that they amplified it was possible to discover the direction and distance of enemy mining operations. Besiegers' tunnels, when located, were dealt with by burning noxious substances such as

dried mustard in a furnace and blowing the smoke down the tunnels with oxhide bellows. Mo Tzu was able to prevent at least one war by demonstrating to the aggressor some of the techniques he was prepared to use in support of the victim.

Another aspect of Chinese fortification was the building of long walls to protect a state's territory from attack. According to the 'Book of Songs' the Chou built a wall against the northern barbarians in the 8th century BC, and by the 5th the practice was widespread, as a protection not only against barbarians but against Chinese neighbours. Han, Wei, Chao, Ch'i, Yen, Ch'in, Chong-shan and Ch'u all had walls in the 4th century BC, some of which still survive in part despite the Ch'in Empire's demolition of internal barriers. Wei was defended against Ch'in by two parallel walls 540 feet (approx. 166m) apart, the outer being more than 20 feet (approx. 6.2m) thick. Square watchtowers were erected a bowshot beyond the outer wall. The walls and towers are now about 12 and 30 feet (approx. 3.87 and 9.2m) high respectively, but would originally have been considerably higher. The walls were made of rammed earth, the towers being strengthened with timber, and incorporating signal beacons to give warning of attack. All these constructions were crude compared to later versions, and few were continuous along the whole length of the borders; but the Ch'in wall started in 215 BC was a much more formidable obstacle, and at least in part

OPPOSITE The statue of the infantry general of the terracotta army. No other figure so far excavated has equalled his height. (Topfoto)

Gold- and silver-inlaid bronze ornament for a chariot yoke in the shape of an ox-head, 5th–4th centuries BC. (British Museum 1934.2-16.3)

seems to have taken the battlemented form familiar to us today, with room for vehicles to drive along the top. Even this barrier was probably guarded along most stretches only by outposts and patrols, however.

Significant battles of Ancient China

Mu, 1027 BC

Wu of Chou, leading an army of 3,000 nobles and their retainers, augmented by barbarian allies and 800 Shang defectors, met the Shang king, Shou Hsin, at Mu. The Shang force was considerably larger than that of the Chou. Wu therefore instructed his men to advance slowly and in strict formation: 'do not exceed four or five strokes, six or seven thrusts, then halt and line up'. The next morning the Shang attacked, but their front rank was thrown into confusion and fell back, disordering those behind. Despite the claims of Chou propaganda, the battle was hard-fought, but the Chou were victorious and showed no mercy, shedding enough blood 'to float a log'. This battle made Wu master of most of the Hwang Ho valley.

Che, 717 BC

The southern Yen invaded Cheng in support of one of their allies, bypassing the town of Che. Three Cheng divisions were sent to occupy the enemy by skirmishing as they advanced, while a fourth body, under the earl's sons Man-pi and Tse-yuen, manoeuvred itself into their rear. The two princes entered Che undetected, and led the citizens in an attack that took the Yen by surprise and defeated them.

Cheng, 713 BC

The northern Jung, a foot-fighting barbarian tribe who were 'light and nimble, but had no order', invaded Cheng and were confronted by the earl. The Cheng charioteers feared that a swift attack would overrun them, so the earl's son Tu proposed a plan. The main body of the army was divided into three and withdrawn into positions for an ambush, and a detachment was sent forward to make a feint attack. This group pretended to flee and the Jung pursued in a disorderly mob. General Chu Tan ambushed the first body of barbarians to come within reach, and surrounded them. Tu had correctly judged the character of the enemy, for the rest of the Jung fled, making no attempt to help their comrades.

Ch'eng-p'u, 632 BC

Duke Wen of Tsin faced an invading army under Tzu-yu of Ch'u. The two men were personal enemies, and Tzu-yu led the chariots of his left wing with the aim of killing Wen. The Tsin left pinned the Ch'u right with a feint attack while their own right withdrew behind a screen of chariots dragging branches to raise dust. When Tzu-yu was well separated from his centre, the Tsin right and centre closed in on him from two sides with chariots and infantry. The Ch'u commander was killed and his army routed.

Pi, 595 BC

The Ch'u and Tsin armies faced each other for several days while the charioteers skirmished; the battle developed by accident when a force of Tsin chariots came out to rescue two of their skirmishers and the Ch'u charged them. Ch'u chariots advanced on both flanks, driving back their opponents when their reserve of 40 vehicles was committed, and the Tsin army began a general retirement. By chance, the king of Ch'u was with his left wing when it began to pursue, and from this time the left took precedence in Ch'u, a practice later followed by other states.

Yen-ling, 575 BC

Ch'u once more confronted Tsin at Yen-ling, but the condition of the Ch'u army was poor. It contained many 'wild tribes of the south' who were badly disciplined, and the two ministers commanding it hated each other. The Tsin officer Meao Fun-hwang pointed out that the best Ch'u troops, those of the royal clan, were in the centre, and suggested an enveloping attack on both flanks while the Tsin centre stood on the defensive, protected by a marsh. This plan was successful and the Ch'u army was defeated.

P'ing-yin, 554 BC

Tsin beat a superior Ch'i army by deception. Deploying in close terrain, the Tsin soldiers set up banners in marshes and defiles where there were no troops, to make their line look longer than it was, and sent out patrols of carts dragging branches, and chariots with one crewman in each, the others being dummies. The Marquis of Ch'i, observing from Mount Wu, was convinced that he was outnumbered and decided to withdraw. The retreat was detected by the Tsin commander because of the activities of crows in the deserted camp, and he ordered a pursuit. Ch'i attempted to hold the pass of P'ing-yin against him, but the rearguard was taken prisoner and the main body harried back to Ch'i.

Ma Ling, 341 BC

Leading an expedition from Ch'i to aid Han, which was being attacked by Wei and Chao, Sun Pin took advantage of the fact that the Wei regarded Ch'i troops as cowardly and unreliable. As he advanced into Wei he ordered his men to light fewer campfires each night, deceiving the enemy general, P'ang Chuan, into thinking that the Ch'i were deserting en masse. P'ang Chuan therefore made a forced march with light troops to cut them off before they could escape, and marched into a trap. In a defile at Ma Ling, Sun Pin had deployed 10,000 infantry with crossbows – the first time that this weapon is mentioned in open battle. The Wei force came within range as darkness was falling, as Sun Pin had predicted, and volleys of bolts drove them back in rout. P'ang Chuan committed suicide – an additional source of satisfaction to Sun Pin, since he had been responsible for the latter's imprisonment and mutilation.

Yangtze River, 223 BC

Following the defeat of an earlier expedition, King Cheng of Ch'in sent the veteran Wang Chien to conquer Ch'u with an army said to number 600,000. Nevertheless, Wang Chien moved cautiously, and on arrival at the frontier near the Yangtze River built a fortified camp and waited, feigning hesitancy. The Ch'u warriors were overconfident after their previous victory, and believing that the enemy was afraid, their frontier army began to relax, many men drifting away homewards. Seeing this, Wang Chien launched a sudden attack and scattered the Ch'u forces. The king of Ch'u was captured and his state annexed by Ch'in.

The Ching-hsing Pass, 204 BC

Han Hsin, sent to force the Ching-hsing Pass, which was held by a large Chao army, first ordered out a division of 10,000 men which deployed in view of the Chao lines with its back to the River Ti. He then marched out in front of the troops with his commander's flag and drums, tempting the enemy to attack. Believing that the Han were trapped, the Chao sallied out from their fortifications. Han Hsin then fled back to his division on the riverbank, which, being in 'death ground', put up a desperate fight and held the attack long enough for the trap to be sprung. Two thousand Han cavalry had been sent through little-known defiles to arrive on the Chao flank, and at a given signal they rode into the deserted fortifications and set up the red flags of Han on the ramparts. Seeing this, and unaware of the small size of the force in their rear, the Chao panicked and turned back. Han Hsin followed up and routed them.

OPPOSITE Western warriors, 300–200 BC. Depicted here are a Chao horseman and a Tien warrior, who is based on a bronze figurine from Yunnan. The Chinese had been in contact with cavalry on the steppe since before 500 BC, but did not field their own for another two centuries. (Angus McBride © Osprey Publishing)

PART 11

The Western Han, 202 BC–AD 25

The new empire established by Han Kao-ti was largely modelled on the centralized Ch'in system, with its north-western heartland divided into 'commanderies' under governors appointed by the court. However, victory in the civil war against Hsiang Yu had been achieved only with the help of several powerful allies, who were then rewarded with semi-independent 'kingdoms' in the north, south and east. The strategic keys to northern China were the natural strongholds formerly occupied by the states of Ch'in in the west and Ch'i in the east, so Kao-ti established his imperial capital in the former and made his son Liu Fei king of Ch'i. When the emperor felt secure enough, he began gradually to replace the other kings with his own relatives; eventually, in subsequent reigns, the kingdoms were absorbed piecemeal into the structure of the empire. This was not achieved without bloodshed: as late as 154 BC the king of Wu led a major revolt in the south-east in protest at curbs on his independence. Kao-ti himself died from an arrow wound received in battle against Ch'ing Pu, the king of Huai-nan, in 195 BC.

At first, however, the most serious military threat to the Han was posed by the recently formed rival empire of the Hsiung-nu. This nomad confederation, based in Mongolia, was always to have an ambivalent relationship with the Chinese. Many of the contacts between the steppe herders and the settled farmers to the south were peaceful, as each produced goods for which the other desired to trade – in particular, horses, of which the Chinese were always short – but the temptation for both empires to define the vague frontier between agricultural China and the pastoral steppe in their own favour was irresistible. Furthermore, the Hsiung-nu provided a haven for disaffected Chinese subjects, including in Kao-ti's reign such high-ranking personages as Liu Hsin, king of Han, and Lu Wen, king of Yen. The nomads had taken advantage of the chaos after the fall of Ch'in and plundered northern China, and in 200 BC Kao-ti led a Han army into the steppe in pursuit of the raiders. At Mount Pai-teng, near P'ing-ch'eng in modern Shansi, the emperor was ambushed and surrounded for a week by thousands of Hsiung-nu cavalry. He avoided capture only with difficulty, and thereafter adopted a policy of buying off the nomads with tribute and diplomatic marriages rather than attempting to suppress them by military means.

This strategy was not entirely successful in preventing further raids, but it was not until 133 BC that the 'Martial Emperor' Wu-ti, confident of the empire's growing strength and tempted by the explorer Chang Ch'ien's reports of the wealth to be gained from trade with the far west, reversed the policy and authorized aggressive campaigns into central Asia. The first Chinese move was a failed attempt to capture the unsuspecting Hsiung-nu ruler or *Shan-yu*, followed by a cavalry attack on nomads who had come to trade at markets along the

PREVIOUS PAGE Huang Ch'ao's peasant army attacks Ch'ang-an, the T'ang capital, in 874. (© Stephen Turnbull)

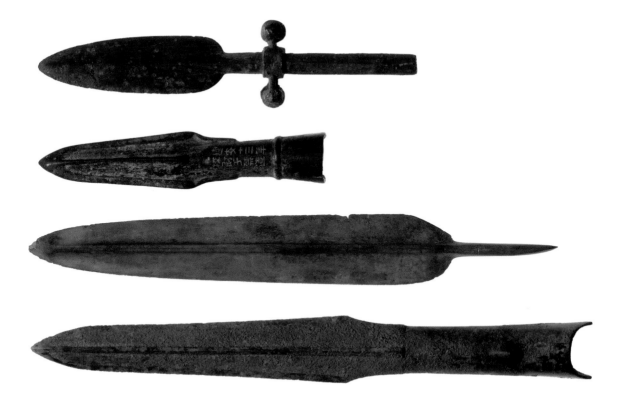

frontier. The latter seems to have taken the enemy by surprise, and in 127 BC the Ordos region – a strategic base of great importance in the loop of the Yellow River – was brought under Han control. It was immediately organized into two new commanderies and settled with 100,000 Chinese colonists. Between 121 and 119 BC two outstanding generals, Wei Ch'ing and Huo Ch'u-ping, took their cavalry further west, overthrowing five subordinate Hsiung-nu kingdoms in two great converging sweeps; and a line of earthworks was built to extend the Ch'in defence line further into the steppe. For the next 18 years, there were no recorded Hsiung-nu raids into China.

After the capture of Turfan in 108 BC, advances were made still further west, with the aim of controlling the already flourishing Silk Route trade with the Middle East, and of detaching the Hsiung-nu from their allies among the city-states of the Tarim Basin region. The most ambitious of these campaigns was the 'War of the Heavenly Horses'. The kingdom of Ta-yuan or Ferghana (west of the Pamirs, in modern Uzbekistan) was at the very edge of the known world at this time, but reports reached the Han court that its ruler possessed a herd of blood-sweating 'heavenly horses' of exceptional quality. Good mounts for cavalry were always in short supply in China, so an envoy was sent to demand

Bronze weapons were still in widespread use at the beginning of the Han dynasty. These spearheads probably date from the 4th or 3rd centuries BC. (British Museum 1894.7-27.3)

63

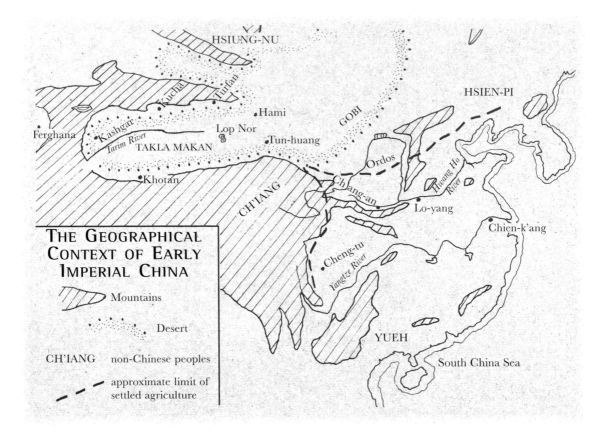

THE GEOGRAPHICAL CONTEXT OF EARLY IMPERIAL CHINA

⬚ Mountains

··· Desert

CH'IANG   non-Chinese peoples

--- approximate limit of settled agriculture

some of the animals as tribute. The king of Ta-yuan refused, and in 104 BC Li Kuang-li was sent from the border post of Tunhuang with 6,000 steppe cavalry and 20,000 Chinese to enforce the demand. The route lay along the edge of the inhospitable Takla Makan Desert, and supplies soon ran short. After a march of over 1,000 miles, Li arrived in Ta-yuan with the exhausted and starving remnants of his army and was forced to withdraw. He blamed the supply situation on the fact that his army had been too small to force the local city-states to cooperate, and was sent west again with reinforcements which brought his strength up to 60,000. Surprisingly, the extra manpower did solve the problem: most towns submitted to the overwhelming show of force and provided food, and those that did not were stormed. Li still lost half his force, but reached Ta-yuan with enough men to defeat the king and set up a puppet ruler in his place. The Han army returned in triumph with 3,000 horses. The Tarim Basin states were so overawed by the victory that they came over to the Han en masse, and garrisons were established throughout the Western Regions.

Wu-ti's reign also saw advances in other theatres. In 113 BC an army was sent south to take Fan-yu (modern Canton), which had previously been part of

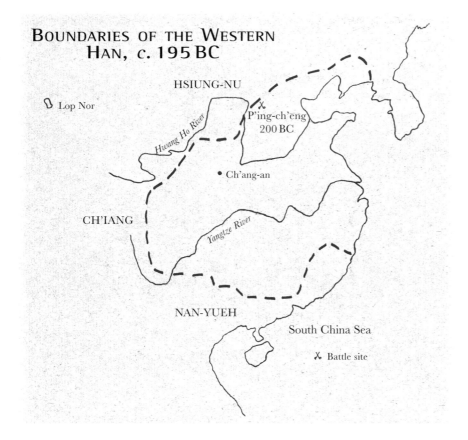

BOUNDARIES OF THE WESTERN HAN, c. 195 BC

HSIUNG-NU

Lop Nor

P'ing-ch'eng
200 BC

Hwang Ho River

• Ch'ang-an

CH'IANG

Yangtze River

NAN-YUEH

South China Sea

X Battle site

the independent state of Southern Yueh, and in 110 BC Eastern Yueh, on the coast south of the Yangtze, was also brought under control. The existence of a trade route to India via the south-western kingdoms of Tien and K'un-ming, in present-day Yunnan, had been known since about 130 BC, but the K'un-ming blocked all attempts at exploration, and it was not until 109 BC that the area was occupied by a Han army. Tien had planned to resist, supported by other local tribes, and the Chinese had gone to the lengths of building an artificial lake to train troops in naval warfare in anticipation of battles on Lake K'un-ming, but in the event the area fell almost without a fight. Like the south-east, the far south-west was brought permanently into the sphere of Chinese civilization, although the local tribes retained their warlike traditions and sporadic revolts remained a problem.

There were signs, however, that the Han armies were overextended, and that the resources built up during the decades of peace were being depleted. A perpetual horse shortage became a major problem in the 1st century BC. The Hsiung-nu inflicted two serious defeats in 99 and 90 BC – the last of which saw Li Kuang-li's capture – and raids resumed along the northern frontier, although

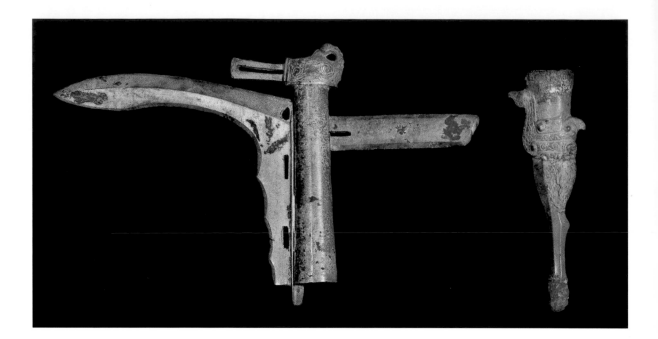

Bronze halberd-blade and butt-ferrule; late Warring States or early Western Han. Weapons of this type, often with an additional spear-point, equipped the bulk of the close-combat infantry of the early Han. (British Museum 1949.5-18 1,2)

the Western Regions were mostly quiet. After the death of Wu-ti in 87 BC, internal power struggles distracted the Han, but fortunately the Hsiung-nu were similarly split at this time. Gradual colonization began to replace punitive expeditions as the instrument of control in central Asia after 61 BC, and under Yuan-ti (49–33 BC) the expansionist policy was virtually abandoned. However, despite the reluctance of Confucian officials at court to authorize more expensive adventures, in 36 BC another Chinese expedition penetrated west of the Pamirs (see the battle of *Kang-chu*, page 146).

This campaign was the last great strategic advance of the Western Han in central Asia. In AD 9, Wang Mang, a nobleman who had acted as regent on behalf of several young emperors, proclaimed himself the founder of the Hsin dynasty. The Hsiung-nu tried to intervene, but Wang mobilized 300,000 men along the northern frontier and the nomads backed down. The new emperor began a series of radical social and political reforms, but was thwarted by forces beyond human control. The Yellow River changed its course, causing widespread flooding and famine, and the eastern coastal region became a refuge for desperate peasants, many of whom turned to banditry. By AD 18 they were organized into a movement known as the Red Eyebrows – from their habit of painting their foreheads red – and were allied with local gentry campaigning for the restoration of the Han. With the government distracted, the Tarim Basin cities revolted and the Hsiung-nu moved in to fill the vacuum.

In AD 22 the rebel movements in the south came under the control of Liu Po-sheng, a distant descendant of Han Kao-ti. After several setbacks, the Han

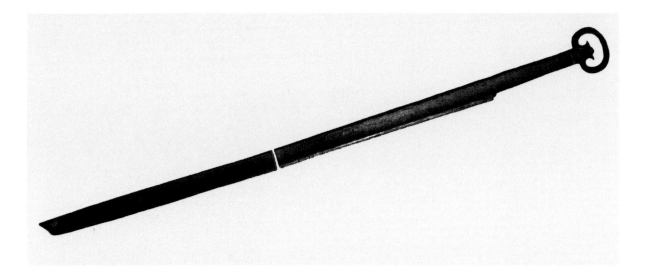

armies routed the Hsin forces at K'un-yang, and in October of AD 23 the Red Eyebrows captured Chang-an and killed Wang Mang. In AD 25 the Later, or Eastern, Han was established at Lo-yang, the 'Eastern' capital (as opposed to Chang-an, the 'Western' capital, from where the dynasty had ruled until Wang Mang's usurpation) by Liu's brother, who became Emperor Kuang-wu-ti, but the Red Eyebrows remained in possession of Chang-an. Finally running short of supplies, they wandered further west into barren steppe country, where a combination of bad weather, hunger and attacks by local warlords defeated them. Early in AD 27, the rebels surrendered.

Bronze sword, Western Han. The ring-pommel is characteristic of Han swords. (British Museum 1911.4-7.25)

The Eastern Han, AD 25–189

One enduring legacy of the reign of Wang Mang was the adoption of the concept of the 'mandate of heaven' as part of the imperial ideology. Previously the legitimacy of the regime had rested ultimately on military power, but from then on the influence of the Confucian intelligentsia led to a greater emphasis on the emperor's responsibility for the maintenance of the traditional order of society. This coincided with a growing disdain among the gentry for military affairs and a movement favouring a return to the policy of the Chou dynasty, which had allegedly attracted and tamed the barbarians by its obvious cultural superiority. Nevertheless, Kuang-wu-ti was quickly forced to rely on his army to enforce his authority against local officials who had set themselves up during the civil war as independent rulers. The most dangerous of these were Wei Ao in Kansu, who was suppressed in AD 34, and Kung-sun Shu in Szechwan, who held out until the end of AD 36. Even then the empire was not at peace, for

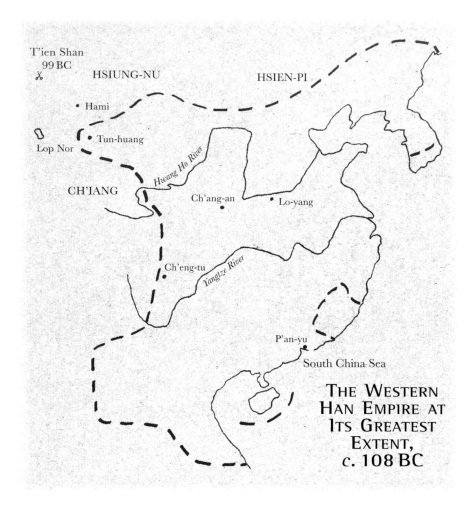

T'ien Shan
99 BC

HSIUNG-NU

HSIEN-PI

• Hami

Lop Nor

Tun-huang

CH'IANG

Hwang Ho River

Ch'ang-an

Lo-yang

Ch'eng-tu

Yangtze River

P'an-yu

South China Sea

THE WESTERN
HAN EMPIRE AT
ITS GREATEST
EXTENT,
c. 108 BC

Hsiung-nu raids had resumed in the north and new fortifications had to be built along the frontier. In AD 49, however, the Hsiung-nu Empire split into two groups, and the Shan-yu of the southern horde made peace with China and was allowed to settle along the upper Yellow River as a buffer against his hostile northern rival.

In AD 73 the Han embarked on another phase of conquests in Central Asia, with the reoccupation of Turfan and the fertile supply base of Hami. The Chinese and the southern Hsiung-nu united to attack the northern horde, and in AD 89 a Han army, under Tou Hsien, crossed the Gobi into Mongolia and routed the hostile tribes at Mount Ch'i-lo. At the same time, the Tarim Basin was being returned to Han control following the campaigns of Pan Chao, who with very few resources achieved his aim through a combination of diplomacy and actions of the utmost daring. On one occasion he led 40 men to attack the camp of a much larger Hsiung-nu delegation to a wavering city-state, setting fire to

Han dynasty iron sword
in a lacquered scabbard,
3rd–2nd century BC.
(Topfoto/British Museum)

their tents while his archers picked off the barbarians as they ran out and other soldiers beat drums furiously to simulate a bigger force. The next morning he presented the local ruler with the head of the Hsiung-nu ambassador, and the city submitted. Pan Chao was honoured with the title of 'Protector General of the Western Regions' in AD 92, and in 97 he sent out the famous expedition of Kan Ying with the aim of making direct contact with the Roman Empire. Parthian opposition caused this attempt to fail, but it illustrates how far China's sphere of influence then extended towards the west.

The Northern Hsiung-nu were also under attack from two of their subject tribes, the Wu-huan and Hsien-pi, based in eastern Mongolia and Manchuria. The former became allies of the Han from AD 49 onwards and provided cavalry for Chinese armies until the 3rd century, but the Hsien-pi were more difficult to control. Originally encouraged to attack the Hsiung-nu with the promise of a reward for every head taken, they demanded ever more expensive 'gifts' until, by the late 1st century, they were being bought off at ruinous cost. After AD 91 they took over much of the northern Hsiung-nu territory, and in the mid-2nd century they were united under T'an-shih-huai into a confederation said to have fielded 100,000 warriors. Although T'an-shih-huai's empire did not survive his death in AD 180, the Han never found a way of dealing successfully with Hsien-pi raids. Ultimately an offensive policy against the steppe warriors could never be successful, as many officials recognized, because of geographical and climatic factors. Yen Yu had analyzed the problem in Wang Mang's reign, explaining that lack of food and firewood, combined with the short life expectancy of the oxen that carried the supplies, prevented any campaign being sustained for longer than 100 days. Even such short expeditions into the steppe had to include long and vulnerable supply-trains (on one occasion '100,000 oxen, over 30,000 horses and tens of thousands of donkeys, mules and camels'). Under such conditions it was very difficult to bring the mobile nomad bands to battle if they wished to avoid it – a lesson in futility that was likened to 'fishing in the Yangtze without a net'.

Early in the 1st century AD the Ch'iang tribes of the west added to the pressure on the empire by beginning to move into the Kansu corridor, which had been occupied by the Han, partly in order to prevent the Ch'iang linking up with the Hsiung-nu. This nightmare became reality early in the 2nd century AD, and by AD 140 effective control of large areas of the north-west had been lost to marauding bands of Ch'iang, Hsiung-nu and disaffected Chinese. This cut communications with the Western Regions, and meant that they too were lost. Settlers had been sent into the area in the hope of sinicizing the barbarians, but the effect of contact seems often to have been the reverse. The Ch'iang fought on foot and were not well organized, but they appear to have been exceptionally great in number, and by about AD 190 the whole empire is said to have lived in fear of them.

Elsewhere on the frontiers, the Eastern Han was also unable to maintain the gains of its predecessor. In AD 106 the Korean kingdom of Koguryo drove out the Chinese garrisons, and although a Han expedition in AD 132 regained some of the losses, Koguryo was never fully subdued. In AD 43 General Ma Yuan, aided by a supply fleet sent along the coast, had reoccupied Vietnam, capturing the Trung sisters, who had revolted three years earlier. But the rebellion had dealt Han authority a serious blow, and the war cost them dearly, with half of the troops sent from the north becoming casualties. In the 2nd century AD problems on other frontiers had their repercussions in the south, as peasants fleeing from the Ch'iang poured into the sparsely populated lands south of the Yangtze, provoking the local tribes to continual revolt. After AD 137 there was unrest throughout the south, and it spread to the north on the death of Emperor Shun-ti.

About this time there first appeared groups known as *yao* or 'supernatural' rebels – men motivated by millenarian prophecies to establish a new dynasty. The most important of these, the Yellow Turbans, launched a rebellion in AD 184 which was to play a major role in the downfall of the Han. The court commanded loyal officials to suppress the revolt, but after temporarily defeating the Yellow Turbans in AD 185, the officials retained their private armies and began to meddle in politics. When Emperor Ling-ti died in AD 189, power fell into the hands of Tung Cho, a warlord allied to the Ch'iang, who first established a puppet emperor and then expelled him from Lo-yang. Loyalist officers formed a coalition that defeated Tung Cho in AD 191, but it was too late to restore order. Although the Han dynasty persisted officially until AD 220, the unity of the empire was at an end.

Recruitment

The army of the Western Han consisted of three main elements: conscripts, convicts and volunteers. Conscription was prescribed for men within an age range which was normally from 23 to 56 but varied according to circumstances. Most spent their first year of service in training and a further year with the armies at the capital or in the provinces, or with the frontier garrisons. Selected former soldiers formed a local militia, the *pen-ming*, available in emergencies. Conscripts served mainly as infantry; cavalry was provided by volunteers from noble families or by non-Chinese auxiliaries.

Conscription was extended to both the commanderies and the semi-autonomous kingdoms of the empire, but probably not to the *shu-kuo* or dependent states, which were formed in frontier regions once local rulers had accepted Han overlordship. The earliest known dependent state was formed from a group of Hsiung-nu in 121 BC, and after 109 BC *shu-kuo* cavalry are frequently referred to in Han armies. It was logical to employ barbarian troopers in the northern steppes, to which their equipment and tactics were already adapted, but the Wu-huan were especially highly regarded, and they were deployed throughout the empire from the mid-1st century AD. A similar policy was employed by the Eastern Han with regard to the tribes of the south, where the climate was unhealthy and imposed unacceptable attrition on units recruited in northern or central China. The army sent to suppress a revolt in I-chou in AD 48, for example, was mainly drawn from the nearby commandery of Pa.

Various grades of convicts also served with Han armies; most were labour troops, but some apparently did fight, although there is no evidence that they

The group of bronze horsemen and carriages found in the tomb at Wu-wei, Eastern Han dynasty. (Topfoto)

Han chariot. The four-horse chariot continued in use with Han armies until the 1st century BC, but although it was considered a vital constituent of the armed forces, its role was increasingly usurped by the cavalry, and its main function by Han times was probably as a transport for high-ranking officers. (Michael Perry © Osprey Publishing Ltd)

formed a fanatical assault force as they had in some earlier Chinese armies. Standard convict dress was a red robe and iron neck-collar, and their heads were shaved as a symbolic alternative to decapitation.

Other sources of troops were exploited on occasion, and although conscription provided the bulk of their manpower, Han forces could be very diverse in origin. A well-known example is provided by an account of an army sent against the Ch'iang in 61 BC, which comprised serving prisoners; amnestied convicts; conscript infantry; a unit of volunteer marksmen; another unit of orphans whose fathers had died on active service; 'barbarian' cavalry; Chinese cavalry from six western commanderies; and Ch'iang cavalry from one of the dependent states.

The quality of Han armies also varied, as a decree of 90 BC shows: in giving reasons for not undertaking a new campaign in the north-west it cites badly maintained defences, ill-disciplined officers and troops of poor morale. The loss of two armies to the Hsiung-nu in 129 BC was blamed on lack of time to train the newly raised conscripts. Li Kuang-li's armies of 104 and 101 BC were mostly raised from 'young men of bad reputation', and skilled bowmen amnestied from prison for the purpose.

Mounted archer and lancer from the Han cavalry. (Michael Perry © Osprey Publishing Ltd)

There is little reliable information on the numbers of troops available to the Han, although from population censuses it can be deduced that it must have been in the hundreds of thousands. Huge armies are sometimes mentioned, such as the '50,000 cavalry and several hundred thousand infantry' sent against the Hsiung-nu in 119 BC. However, a comment in the *Han Shu*, to the effect that the troops levied for one campaign were 'altogether more than 40 thousand and were called a hundred thousand', suggests that large round numbers may often represent nominal unit sizes rather than an exact count.

Organization

A characteristic of the Han command system was a reluctance to concentrate power in too few hands; an army was often commanded by two generals – 'of the Left' and 'of the Right', or 'of the Front' and 'of the Rear' – whose

One of a set of bricks from Szechwan depicting a mounted archer practising the rearward shooting technique known in the West as the 'Parthian shot'. (British Museum 1909.12-14.3)

personal rivalry could be relied upon to prevent collusion against the throne. A field command was usually an ad hoc appointment for a specific purpose, often reflected in the title given to the recipient – such as 'General Charged With Crossing the Liao' for a campaign in Korea. Penalties for failure were severe: a defeated general risked execution, as did subordinates who returned after their commander had been killed. Junior officers were tested annually for their skill at archery, and were rewarded according to the number of hits scored on a target.

Records from the north-western garrisons give an outline of unit organization at lower levels: a *hou kuan* or company usually consisted of five *hou* (platoons), each with several *sui* or sections of an officer and four to ten men. Five-deep deployment seems to have been the norm for infantry. Above the *hou kuan* were the sector headquarters or *to-wei fu* for garrison troops, and the division or *ying*, under a *chiang-chun* or general, the highest permanent position. *Hsiao-wei*, often translated as colonel, was a lower rank used for temporary appointments. Units were distinguished by names, either relating to the place where they were stationed, or honorific or exhortatory, such as *P'o-hu* or 'Smash Foe'. Imperial Guard units existed with titles such as the 'Brave as Tigers' and 'Feathered Forest' cavalry. Although emperors like Wu-ti practised riding and archery and wore the uniform of the Imperial Guards, after Kao-ti they seldom participated personally in operations.

In the Later Han the system of conscription continued, but gradually permanent standing armies came into existence which enhanced the political power of their commanders. After AD 89 the title of *Ta Chiang-chun* or Commander-in-Chief was a political appointment that carried the responsibilities of a regent. The permanent guard at the capital, Lo-yang, was known as the 'Northern Army' and comprised one unit of Wu-huan and Hsiung-nu horse-archers and four of Chinese, totalling 4,000 men. The 'Army of the Western Garden' was created in AD 188 as a counterweight to the Northern Army, but consisted of little more than the private forces of a collection of warlords.

Weapons

The armies that founded the Han were mainly footsoldiers, with a small proportion of cavalry and chariots, and forces within the empire tended to remain dependent on infantry. However, the campaigns on the Central Asian steppe from the mid-2nd century BC were often carried out by all-cavalry forces. Weapons and armour were similar to those used by the Ch'in. Infantry were often protected with leather or iron lamellar armour. They wore caps or iron helmets, and were equipped with spears or halberds, swords, and bows or crossbows. The crossbow is the most frequently mentioned weapon in the sources, and was often given the credit for the Han army's superiority over its enemies. There were various grades of crossbow of different draw-weight. The heaviest required a pull of over 350lb (159kg) to cock them, and were suitable only for static positions, where they could be fixed on revolving mounts. Strong men capable of loading the larger weapons were known as *chueh chang*, and were highly valued specialists. Many accounts testify to the effect of massed crossbow volleys in beating off cavalry attacks. In sieges, and occasionally in the field, missile troops were drawn up behind men carrying spears or shields, but separate deployment seems to have been the norm. Lighter crossbows were also used by Han cavalry, who were prepared to fight dismounted if necessary, and one source implies that both crossbow and halberd could be carried. Some crossbows were very small, and probably intended for one-handed use. (It may have been one of these which Hsiang Yu concealed on his person and used to wound the future Emperor Kao-ti in 203 BC.)

Like the infantry, cavalry also used halberds, spears, swords and bows. The mounted archer is a common theme in Han art, and it is often difficult to tell whether it is a Chinese trooper or a steppe nomad auxiliary who is being depicted. Nomad troops were highly valued for campaigns in the open terrain of the northern frontier, where their horse archery could be devastatingly effective. Ssu-ma Ch'ien describes a skirmish in which three Hsiung-nu eagle hunters, by circling and using their bows from a distance, defeated a party of about 30 Han cavalry, killing most of them.

Some riders wore armour, but horse armour is not attested until the very end of the dynasty. A relief from I-nan, possibly late Han, appears to show two cavalry figures with shields, but this was uncommon, perhaps because weapons such as halberds, bows and crossbows required the use of both hands. The

RIGHT Pottery model
of a watchtower, Han
dynasty. (British Museum
1929.7-16.1)

four-horse chariot was still in use under the Western Han, but it disappeared during the 1st century BC.

Defences

The Han inherited from the Ch'in not only the hostility of the Hsiung-nu but the policy of building fortifications to keep the nomads at bay. The 'Great Wall' mentioned in several Han treaties was not necessarily, however, the original Ch'in one. The dynasty temporarily lost the Ordos region – within Shih Huang-ti's wall – to the Hsiung-nu after 200 BC, and had to build new defences further south and eventually extend the line further west into the region of modern Kansu, which had never been occupied by the Ch'in. Wall building was a fairly quick and simple operation – a single man was said to be able to erect 18 feet (approx. 5.5m) of rampart per month – and the walls were probably no more than low earth banks, using loose stones or even bundled twigs as a core, which acted more as boundary markers and lookout posts than as serious fortifications. Rectangular brick watchtowers were placed at intervals of slightly less than a mile, and banks of raked sand outside the defences were used to reveal any nocturnal incursions. A system of signalling between the towers by means of red and white flags, smoke or bonfires was in operation by about 160 BC.

Garrison life

Thanks to the records excavated at Edsin-gol, we know something about conditions in the forts on the northern frontier. Most of the troops were conscripts, but some seem to have been stationed there for many years, perhaps acting as paid surrogates for men who wished to avoid military service. Garrison life was often dull, relieved only by expedients familiar to many later generations of servicemen: training, inspections and the liberal use of whitewash – of which 13 coats have been distinguished on one excavated wall. Professional standards were generally high, and supply and medical services very advanced for the time. However, the bureaucracy could be stifling; the sheer bulk of the files which accompanied an army HQ could be inconvenient on the march, especially since until the 2nd century AD they were painted onto wooden strips. Returns had to be made of the most trivial matters, and one surviving inspection report mentions, among other things: 'in two small woodpiles the stacking was not alternated … two water storage jars missing … wall unswept … dogs not kept in kennel …'.

Maps were also important: when the Ch'in dynasty fell, Hsiao Ho braved the chaos of the sack of Hsienyang to collect all the maps and registries of Ch'in and hand them over to Kao-ti, who was thus 'able to inform himself of all the strategic defence points of the empire'.

Garrison units were supported by military-agricultural colonies which grew food for the combat troops. The aim was both to push forward the agricultural frontier at the expense of the Hsiung-nu, and to supply the garrisons at no cost to the rest of the empire. Colonies were established in fertile oases beyond the frontier, to act as supply bases for mobile operations. The first were probably set up in the late 2nd century BC, at Lun-t'ai and Ch'u-li on the southern slopes of the T'ien Shan, but the most important was at Hami, at the eastern end of the Tarim Basin. Hami frequently changed hands between the Han and the Hsiung-nu, but was finally abandoned to the nomads in AD 153.

The Three Kingdoms and the Ts'in, 189–316

The period that followed the collapse of effective Han authority is generally referred to as the 'Three Kingdoms', after the rival successor states of Wei, Wu and Shu. Largely due to the influence of the later work known as the 'Romance of the Three Kingdoms', it has passed into folklore as an era of chivalry and adventure – a sort of Arthurian age. The reality, however, was rather more sordid.

The generals who had overthrown Tung Cho soon began quarrelling among themselves. To add to the chaos, the Yellow Turban rebels remained under arms, joined by numerous other bandit groups, until decisively defeated in AD 192 by the most famous of the contending warlords, Ts'ao Ts'ao, who abducted Tung Cho's puppet emperor, Liu Hsieh. The Korean commanderies came under the control of the marquis of Liaotung, who attempted to invade China and restore Han authority but was beaten off by another warlord, Yuan Shao. In 200 Ts'ao, his armies strengthened by surrendered rebels and barbarian auxiliaries, including many Hsiung-nu, crushed Yuan in turn, but failed to reunify the empire. Ts'ao's attempt to take Szechwan was thwarted in 208 at the battle of the Red Cliffs, and Liu Pei, a member of the Han imperial family, set up the independent state of Shu – often known as Shu Han – in the south-west.

On Ts'ao's death in 220, his son Ts'ao P'ei deposed the figurehead emperor and founded the Wei dynasty; Liu Pei riposted by proclaiming himself the rightful Han emperor. Meanwhile Wu, in the south-east, also declared itself independent under Sun Ch'uan.

Pottery figures showing spear-throwers have been found at various 3rd- and 4th-century sites in north-western China. This one is from the 3rd century and may represent a Ch'iang tribesman. (Topfoto)

Wei in the north was by far the most powerful of the Three Kingdoms, with roughly 60 per cent of the total population, but the task it faced was formidable. Wu was able to shelter behind a series of river obstacles, and its marshy and semi-tropical terrain was unsuitable for the northern cavalry. Its ally, Shu, was efficiently organized under its chief minister, Chu-ko Liang (AD 181–234) – next

THE THREE KINGDOMS, c. 220 AD

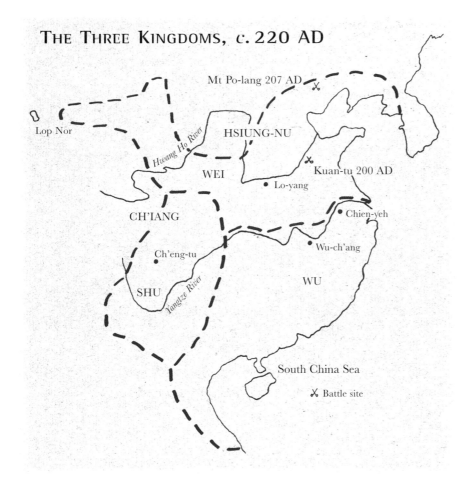

Mt Po-lang 207 AD

Lop Nor

HSIUNG-NU

Hwang Ho River

WEI

Kuan-tu 200 AD

Lo-yang

CH'IANG

Chien-yeh

Ch'eng-tu

Wu-ch'ang

Yangtze River

SHU

WU

South China Sea

Battle site

OPPOSITE Infantry of the Eastern Han. Depicted here are an archer (right), a Vietnamese auxiliary (left) and an armoured infantryman. (Michael Perry © Osprey Publishing Ltd)

to Ts'ao Ts'ao probably the most famous figure of the age. Shu even managed to bring some of the tribes further to the south under intermittent control, but in the long term could not overcome the Wei superiority in manpower. In 263 three Wei armies, allegedly totalling 180,000 men, converged on the Shu capital, Ch'eng-tu. Driven back from the frontiers, the Shu forces, under Chiang Wei, held a line of mountain passes and blocked the advance of the enemy main body, but in an epic march through supposedly impassable terrain the Wei general, Teng Ai, crossed the mountains undetected, defeated the Shu reserve army in two battles, and captured Ch'eng-tu. Chiang Wei was undefeated, but decided to surrender.

Two years later the Wei dynasty was replaced in a coup d'état by the Ts'in (founded by Ssu-ma Yen), which continued the struggle against the south-eastern state. Wu was finally conquered in AD 280 and the empire was once again united, but the Ts'in regime – known to later historians as the Western Ts'in to distinguish it from its successor based in the south-east – was built on shaky foundations. Its northern power-base, ravaged by war, was not as prosperous as it had been, and the army was under the control of a group of wealthy and powerful imperial princes whom Ssu-ma Yen had placed in command of large numbers of troops in an attempt to offset the risk of another officer seizing power as he had done. An ill-advised demobilization after the fall of Wu antagonized the princes and added to the disorder caused by bands of unemployed ex-soldiers, some of whom sold their weapons to the Hsien-pi or Hsiung-nu. After Ssu-ma's death in 290, open civil war broke out among the members of his family.

The beginning of the end for the Western Ts'in came with this period of internecine fighting, known as the 'Troubles of the Eight Princes' (AD 291–306). The non-Chinese groups which had been settled in the north and west since late Han times – Hsiung-nu, Hsien-pi, Chieh, Ch'iang, Ti and related peoples – saw their opportunity and began to move east into the Yellow River plain, setting up independent states within the empire. At this point the old Han practice of marrying imperial princesses to Hsiung-nu leaders came home to haunt the Chinese. A Hsiung-nu chief – a descendant of one of these princesses – adopted the Chinese name of Liu Yuan and announced his claim to be the rightful heir to the Han Empire. In 311 an army under his son, Liu Ts'ung, sacked the Ts'in capital at Lo-yang, and in 316 Ch'ang-an also fell, marking the formal end of the Western Ts'in. A successor state, the Eastern Ts'in, was set up south of the Huai River, but northern China was effectively abandoned to the barbarians.

Military developments of the Three Kingdoms period

The Three Kingdoms era is traditionally seen as one of the high points of the art of war in China, and many of the examples of successful stratagems found in later books and commentaries feature the exploits of men like Ts'ao Ts'ao, Chu-ko Liang and Teng Ai. In army organization and tactics, however, there was much continuity with the Han. Many of the generals who rose to power following Tung Cho's coup relied heavily on non-Chinese auxiliaries; the core of Yuan Shao's army, for example, was provided by Wu-huan allies.

In general, shock cavalry seems to have been increasingly emphasized, especially in Wei, although the proportion and numbers of horsemen mentioned suggest a decline in the overall numbers available with the loss of Chinese control over the extreme north-west.

Weapons were mainly lances and bows, although the relative proportions of each are not known. Horse-archery was not restricted to the nomad-influenced armies of the north: Shu Han had a 'Flying Army' of mounted bowmen, and a king of Wu in AD 258 is described as carrying a bow on horseback. One tomb painting shows a Wei- or Ts'in-period rider with both lance and bow, but this was probably not usual. Many cavalrymen wore armour, as did a minority of horses. The earliest reference to horse armour seems to date from AD 188, but the first archaeological evidence is a tomb model of 302, showing a simple chest protector of what seems to be quilted material. The ten sets of horse armour owned by Ts'ao Ts'ao, the *ma-kai i-ling* mentioned in a memorial of 226, and the armour of the horses captured from Wu in 251, may therefore have been no more than partial frontal barding. Ts'ao Ts'ao's forces were initially very short of armour, but battle accounts imply that it was in widespread use for both cavalry and infantry.

Native infantry were armed much as they had been in Han times, although a series of tomb figurines which appear to be throwing spears suggests that this practice – uncommon among Chinese troops – was adopted by some in this period. They may be foreign auxiliaries such as the Ch'iang, who are described as fighting on foot with bows, spears and swords, and as scattering easily, which implies skirmishing tactics.

Specially picked units of 'dare-to-die' shock troops were common, and the ancient tactic of making infantry discard their long weapons and charge with swords and shields alone was still in use. At a battle between Wei and Wu in 253, the Wu commander even made his men remove their armour to storm a position on top of a dam, presumably because the weight might have slowed them down when climbing the slope. The Wei soldiers laughed at this, but were routed by the Wu swordsmen.

Most footsoldiers, however, were probably archers or crossbowmen, and battle accounts describe their missiles as 'falling like rain'. Although deployed in separate units, crossbowmen and close-combat troops could be used in mutual support. Yuan Shao, for example, defeated enemy cavalry with a formation consisting of 800 infantry with shields, flanked on each side by crossbows.

The use of field defences such as wagon laagers, earth ramparts or lines of felled trees became very widespread, and many battles took the form of assaults on fortified lines or camps. The most extreme example was probably a dummy 'wall' of rush matting erected by Wu along the Yangtze to deter a Wei crossing. Siege equipment mentioned by Ssu-ma Kuang includes artillery, movable towers and artificial mounds erected to enable besiegers to shoot over city walls, and scaling ladders. Walls were still constructed of rammed earth and were often damaged by heavy rain. Naval operations were also common on the rivers, especially the Yangtze, which formed the main Wu line of defence.

The Wei state established by Ts'ao Ts'ao was well organized, and supported large regular forces, possibly as many as 400,000. Ts'ao kept the army under central control, permitting his relatives to retain only small bodyguard units. Food production was a major problem after the damage done to agriculture in the civil wars, so he set up families of colonists, which grew crops, stored up supplies in time of peace and provided manpower in time of war. Allied cavalry

OPPOSITE Typical costume and equipment of the Three Kingdoms. Depicted here are an armoured cavalryman, a north-western rebel and men carting typical Chinese wheelbarrows, a tool likely invented during the Han period. (Michael Perry © Osprey Publishing Ltd)

LEFT This figure represents a horseman, and may give an idea of the appearance of the Ch'iang cavalry who fought for the Han and later overran the north-west. (British Museum 1912.12-31.54)

was recruited from the Hsiung-nu, Hsien-pi and Wu-huan, many of whom were settled within Wei territory. There were also guard units, notably the 'Tiger Cavalry', employed as Ts'ao Ts'ao's personal bodyguard. The Ts'in inherited the Wei system after AD 265, until Ssu-ma Yen deliberately abandoned the centralized system of command and placed members of his family in control of private armies.

The armies of Wei's southern rivals, Wu and Shu, were similarly equipped in most respects, but they did not have access to mounted nomad allies, and the southern tribes were too unruly to be a reliable source of recruits. Shu armies did employ some Ch'iang and Ti tribesmen, however. Until his death in 234, Shu was effectively controlled by Chu-ko Liang, who is famous for solving the problem of supplying his troops in the mountains of the south-west by substituting wheelbarrows for the usual ox wagons. The survival of Shu, with perhaps a quarter of the manpower of Wei, has often been ascribed mainly to Chu-ko's efficiency at organizing the state for war.

The barbarian invasions, 316–589

For the next hundred years after the fall of Ch'ang-an, a bewildering succession of local warlords rose and fell in the north. These regimes are generally classified according to the nationality of the rulers, but in reality most of their armies were an unstable mixture of various races, usually with a core of nomad cavalry but often including many Chinese infantry. They based their power to varying degrees on the local agricultural population, generally employed Chinese noblemen as officials and adopted Chinese-style dynastic names. None of these regimes – not even those few, like the Former Liang (AD 317–376) and the Northern Yen (AD 407–436), which briefly flourished under native leaders – were established on any firmer basis than naked force, and few long outlasted the warlords who founded them. The Former Chao, established at Ch'ang-an by the Hsiung-nu, survived until AD 329, when it was replaced by the Later Chao, of the rival Chieh tribe. The Chieh were themselves overthrown in 331 by one of their Chinese generals, but the power vacuum thus created did not lead to a native reconquest. The Mu-jung clan of the Hsien-pi, moving in from Manchuria, occupied the north-east from Shansi to Shantung and set up the Former Yen state, which in its turn fell in 370 to the Former Ch'in.

Led by a general of Ti origin, Fu Chien, the Former Ch'in dynasty succeeded in unifying northern China between AD 350 and 376, and in 383 attempted to invade the south. Defeated by the Eastern Ts'in at the Fei River, Fu Chien lost the respect of his warriors and his empire collapsed. The north remained in chaos and the native Chinese, their lands ravaged by incessant warfare, fled south in increasing numbers or turned to the consolations of Buddhism.

Eventually, by about AD 430, a regime arose that succeeded in harnessing the abilities of both the barbarian horsemen and the Chinese farmers and administrators. Originating in Mongolia, the Toba were a branch of the Hsien-pi based at Ping-ch'eng in northern Shansi. By 139 they had reunified northern China under a dynasty known as the Northern (or Toba) Wei, and by an intelligent policy of sinification managed to promote a measure of long-term stability, although fruitless attempts to conquer the south continued until 516.

In 493 the Wei emperor Hsiao-wen-ti moved south to Lo-yang, where the ruined capital of the Ts'in was rebuilt. On the Mongolian steppes at the beginning of the 5th century new powers had arisen – the Juan-juan and a

Turkish tribe, the Kao-ch'e – and the Toba were obliged to take on the role of a traditional Chinese dynasty, sending expeditions into the steppes to counter nomad attacks. In 429 they inflicted a major defeat on the Juan-juan, advancing as far as the T'ien Shan and bringing back hundreds of thousands of captives. Eventually, however, the Wei became overstretched by the demands of both northern and southern fronts, and by the 6th century had resorted to strengthening the northern frontier with six great fortresses built along the edge of the steppe. These were carefully sited to deny water and grazing to nomad armies exhausted after the crossing of the Gobi Desert. One minister even proposed building a huge wall like that of the Ch'in, which had long since fallen into disrepair, but the proposal was not implemented.

Other barbarian regimes also adopted Chinese fortification methods, though not always profitably. The Hsiung-nu of Hsia in the far north-west bankrupted themselves to build a great triple system of defences for their capital, Tung-wan, which nevertheless fell easily to the Toba 14 years later.

Much of the prosperity of the north was restored under the Northern Wei regime, but tensions between the new sinicized elite and the traditionalist Toba garrisons of the frontier led to the 'Revolt of the Six Garrisons' in 523, which severely destabilized the state.

In 534 the Wei split into two mutually hostile polities: the Eastern Wei, under Kao Huan, a former garrison commander, and the smaller and more traditionalist Western Wei, under the able minister Yu-wen T'ai, based at Ch'ang-an. A series of wars led to the defeat of the Easterners – an outcome attributed to the more efficient organization of the western state and the high social status of its army. In the 550s internal coups replaced the Eastern and Western Wei with the Northern Ch'i and Northern Chou respectively, but hostilities continued. Northern Ch'i, which controlled the fertile Yellow River valley, was far richer than its rival, but seems to have placed little emphasis on military readiness and to have supported an inordinate number of Buddhist monks and nuns. It adopted a defensive policy towards the northern tribes, building over 1,000 miles of walls between AD 550 and AD 556. The Northern Chou, on the other hand, ruthlessly confiscated church property and imposed taxes on the monks in order to fund a mobile army. They also recruited large numbers of Chinese to supplement their Hsien-pi troops. In AD 577 they eliminated the Northern Ch'i and once again brought northern China under the control of a single power, and one more reliant on its native subjects than any previous barbarian regime.

During this period it was fashionable in the north to mock the Chinese of the south as unmilitary rustics who 'rode facing backwards on water-buffaloes' and depended mainly on rivers and other natural obstacles for their defence. Yu-wen T'ai referred scathingly to 'the southerner, the aged Hsiao Yen [emperor of the

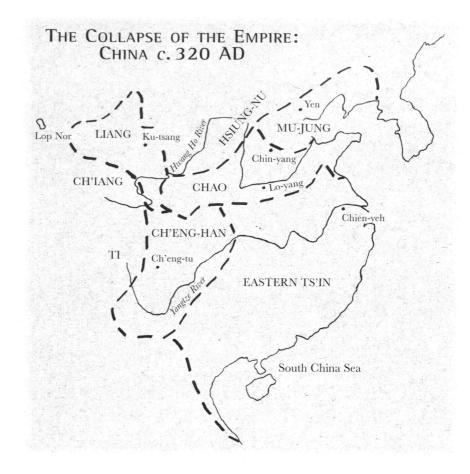

THE COLLAPSE OF THE EMPIRE:
CHINA c. 320 AD

Liang, AD 502–549], who concerns himself solely with ritually approved clothes and caps, with rites and liturgical music'. It is true that the southern elite was less militarized than the barbarian aristocracy of the north, but the natives were by no means always passive victims. On occasion they did undertake offensive operations, and considering that the population of the north outnumbered them by about six to one, they achieved some creditable feats. The Eastern Ts'in recaptured Szechwan from the Ti in 347 and made several attempts to conquer the north between 351 and 365, but the state was weak because of the internal divisions which plagued it – between the original Chinese settlers and the recent immigrants from the north, between various aristocratic clans vying for power at court, and between the regime and the peasant societies (successors to the Yellow Turbans), which instigated several major uprisings. The most significant of these was the revolt of Sun En, who from 399 to 403 occupied an island off the east coast and launched shipborne raids up the Yangtze, allegedly with up to 100,000 men.

Early in the 5th century, however, with the Toba preoccupied by the Juan-juan in the north, the southerners undertook an ambitious offensive under Liu

Yu. In 410 the Southern Yen of Shantung, a Hsien-pi state, was conquered, and between 415 and 417 Liu invaded the north-west and destroyed the Later Ch'in based at Ch'ang-an.

In 420 Liu overthrew the Ts'in and established his own dynasty, the Liu-Sung, which ruled successfully for 50 years but in 479 met the same fate as

Shown here are a cataphract cavalryman and an armoured archer of the Northern dynasties. (Michael Perry © Osprey Publishing Ltd)

89

its predecessor at the hands of another general, Hsiao Tao-ch'eng. His Southern Ch'i was replaced in 502 by the Liang. This continual infighting prevented any further serious attempts to wrest the north from the Toba, but the Ch'i and Liang continued to be successful in repelling all attacks.

In 529, with the Wei distracted by civil war, a southern expeditionary force of 7,000 men, under Ch'en Ch'ing-chih, against great odds won several victories and briefly occupied Lo-yang. This bold stroke was not followed up, however, and the Liang puppet ruler was quickly driven out. In 548 the Liang invited a disaffected Wei general, Hou Ching, to bring his army south, but this resulted in disaster when Hou besieged the Liang capital at Chien-k'ang and sacked it. In 552 a Liang prince in Szechwan tried to secede, but instead fell under the control of the Western Wei. The south was permanently weakened, and the Liang state was split into a Toba puppet regime – the Later Liang – on the middle Yangtze, and the independent Ch'en state downstream. Foolishly, Ch'en joined Northern Chou in its final campaign against Northern Ch'i, taking as its reward the territory north of the Yangtze as far as the River Huai, but in 577 the Chou drove the Ch'en armies out again, inflicting on them an irreversible defeat.

Another detail from the attack on Ch'ang-an, showing spearmen. (© Stephen Turnbull)

By 580 the Northern Chou dynasty was supreme in the north, and in the south only Ch'en remained a rival. Despite the troubles of the previous three centuries, the resources of northern China – with about 85 per cent of the total population – still far outweighed those of the south, and when in 581 a half-Chinese officer, Yang Chien, seized power in Northern Chou after a brief civil war, he found most of the work of reunification already done. Styling himself the first emperor of the Sui dynasty, he organized a massive logistical operation to overwhelm Ch'en. Canals and ships were built for transportation, grain stores were located at strategic points, and eight separate columns were sent to converge on the lower Yangtze. The river itself was cleared by a fleet of huge war-junks manned by Szechwanese marines and equipped with 'striking arms' – heavy iron spikes on the ends of long wooden shafts, which were released to fall onto the decks of enemy ships. At least ten Ch'en war-junks were smashed to pieces by this new weapon, and the Yangtze came under Sui control. The south submitted without further significant resistance. In 589, for the first time since the beginning of the 4th century, China was united under a single ruler.

Armies of the invasion period

The 4th century AD is significant in Chinese military history for the introduction of cataphract equipment for cavalry, and for the first widespread use of stirrups. Whereas in western Asia the rise of fully armoured charging cavalry long pre-dates the invention of the stirrup, in China the two innovations seem to have occurred at about the same time. What little evidence we have suggests that the latter may have been an indigenous development, while complete horse armour appears to have spread from a point of origin in the north-east. The Hsiung-nu in north-western China first obtained panoplies in 312 by capturing them from the Hsien-pi, who had migrated from Manchuria and probably introduced the cataphract horse into China proper. The earliest depiction in art is from the tomb of Tung Shou, a Ts'in warlord buried in what is now Korea, which dates from 357.

It appears that cataphract cavalry spread through China fairly quickly – illustrations from the period 385–94 were found in a tomb in Yunnan in the far south-west – but the tactics best suited to their capabilities took some time to evolve. At one 4th-century battle the Mu-jung Hsien-pi are said to have chained together 5,000 mounted archers to form a solid block which repulsed a series of Hsiung-nu charges. Although the iron chains may be merely a metaphor – it is difficult to imagine a commander going to the trouble of having them forged and then carried along on campaign, or the tribal nobility agreeing to submit to such indignity – it suggests that static shooting formations came into vogue for a time, when nomad cavalry had become too heavily armoured to skirmish.

Toba Tao, the emperor of the Northern Wei dynasty 424–451. A classic image of a leader of the 'barbarian invasions of 316–589'. (© Stephen Turnbull)

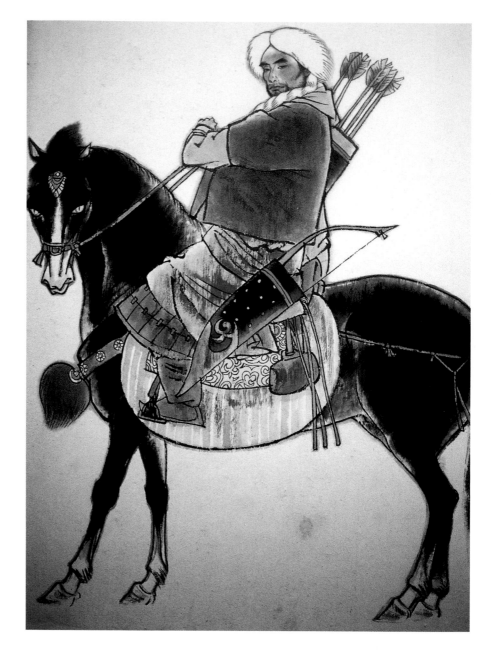

Other horsemen wielded lances, swords and halberds, as well as bows, but horse-archery remained an important aristocratic accomplishment. Some heroes, such as Ch'en An in 323, are described as wielding lance, sword and bow, apparently simultaneously. Not until the 6th century do we hear of what may have been massed lancers, in a series of encounters in which armoured horsemen overthrew far more numerous enemies. (See the battles of Yeh and Sha-yuan, pages 149–50.)

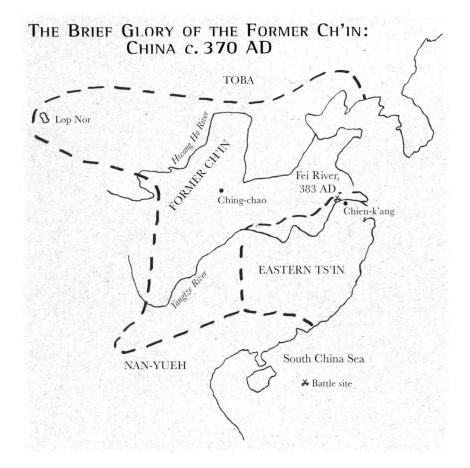

THE BRIEF GLORY OF THE FORMER CH'IN:
CHINA c. 370 AD

TOBA

Lop Nor

Huang Ho River

FORMER CH'IN

Ching-chao

Fei River, 383 AD

Chien-k'ang

EASTERN TS'IN

Yangtze River

NAN-YUEH

South China Sea

⚔ Battle site

In the 4th century such heavy cavalry was characteristic of the Hsiung-nu and Hsien-pi states, although many poorer tribesmen were no doubt still equipped as light horse-archers. Some early armies consisted entirely of cavalry, but all the barbarians eventually recruited native Chinese infantry; the first to do so was the Hsien-pi Former Yen between 337 and 370. The Ch'iang and Ti provided their own infantry, armed with spears, swords and bows, but they were said to lack steadiness. The Ti Empire of Former Ch'in, which briefly dominated the north from 376 to 383, supplemented these with Chinese conscripts, who proved no more reliable. Native cavalrymen were also incorporated into northern armies by the 6th century, supplied by the richer aristocrats, who could afford to provide their own equipment.

Better infantry were raised by the Northern Wei, who set up the 'Three Leaders' system, under which native hamlet, village and district officers were responsible for taxation and conscription. They also re-established the old Han system of frontier garrisons supported by agricultural colonies. At the beginning of the 5th century the nomadic Toba were forcibly settled on the land by

Emperor Tao-wu-ti but continued to supply heavy cavalry, backed up by a central reserve of 100,000 horses pastured on imperial grazing grounds along the Yellow River. Less sinicized Hsien-pi tribesmen provided guard units with traditional Chinese names, like the 'Forest of Wings' and 'Tiger Guards' based in Lo-yang.

Outside the regular Wei army and answerable only to the emperor in person were the Ehrchu, a Chieh tribe of Central Asian origin, possibly descended from the Yueh-chih whom the Han had met in Sogdiana. The 'iron-clad' Ehrchu owned enormous horse herds and fought as armoured cavalry. There were also nomadic Juan-juan and Kao-ch'e auxiliaries, and, by the mid-6th century under the Western Wei, representatives of the new great power in central Asia – the Turks.

Tomb figurines of the 6th century from the north often depict guardsmen on foot in unwieldy-looking armour which is clearly unsuitable for wearing on horseback. They carry oval or rectangular shields, and often long swords. Chinese infantry of this period are usually depicted in art with sword and shield

6th-century guardsmen, Northern Wei or successors. This style of armour is believed to represent leather. Note the cords which appear to hold a separate breast plate in position but are probably a device for transferring some of the weight of the armour from the shoulders to a belt around the waist. (British Museum 1952.10-28.15)

or with bow, although the crossbow also remained in use. Such footsoldiers were the core of the armies of the native southern dynasties; although cataphract cavalry were known in the south, the lack of good horse-breeding areas restricted their numbers. Despite their nominal control over the far south, the Eastern Ts'in, Liu-Sung, Southern Ch'i and Liang could not rely heavily on the tribesmen of that region; although some progress was made towards assimilation, the presence of Chinese colonists driven from the north during the invasions of the 4th century was a source of unrest, just as it had been under the Han. At one battle in 554, the Liang employed a handful of elephants, but this was an isolated incident.

Naval warfare continued to be important in the south. Paddle-wheel ships, worked by a treadmill inside the hull, were first used in battle in 418, terrifying the enemy as they advanced with no visible means of propulsion.

Traditionally, the origin of the oriental martial arts is traced to the visit of a Buddhist monk of Indian or Persian origin, Bodhidharma, to the Shaolin Temple in the territory of the Northern Wei, about AD 520. Bodhidharma was a historical figure, but the tradition cannot be substantiated from official histories and appears to contain many mythical elements. Nevertheless it is not unlikely that a synthesis between certain Buddhist disciplines and the practices of native Chinese secret societies gave rise to an ancestor of modern unarmed fighting techniques at about this time.

The art of war in the early imperial age

The regimes that followed the Han recruited their civil and military officials from the hereditary aristocracy (the bureaucracy open to talent was an innovation of the Sui and T'ang era). The Toba, for example, awarded rank to anyone who raised the appropriate number of men at his own expense. Even under the Han, military command was primarily an aristocratic privilege, although at the end of the dynasty, Ts'ao Ts'ao was singled out for praise because he 'recognized men of talent and promoted them, irrespective of humble origin'.

We know less about the routine procedures of the Han mobile armies than about the frontier garrisons, but it is evident that the same high standard of professionalism applied to many of their commanders, and that noble birth did not exempt them from the usual harsh system of punishments. Some latitude, however, was permitted to successful generals. Li Kuang was criticized for being lax about discipline and record-keeping, but his critics had to concede that the Hsiung-nu were more afraid of him than of his stricter colleague, Ch'eng Pu-chih.

Armoured horse, groom and swordsman from the Liang dynasty. The horse armour is made in five main sections – the chanfron for the head, neck guard, chest and shoulder guard, flank pieces and crupper. (Michael Perry © Osprey Publishing Ltd)

By the Han era the tradition of military doctrine epitomized by Warring States writers such as Sun Tzu and Wu Ch'i had already been supplemented by hundreds of other works, many of them attributed to famous figures of the remoter past. The practice of writing down and codifying the art of war was still very much alive in the period covered here. It may be possible, however, to detect a move away from the psychological approach of the Warring States, based on deception, to a more typically bureaucratic attitude under the Han: the 'Three Strategies of Huang Shih-kung', a work probably of Western Han date, states, 'The basis of complete victory in battle is military administration.' Huo Ch'u-ping, the famous 'Swift Cavalry General' of the Western Han, was known for his contempt for the ancient texts.

When civil strife re-emerged after the end of the Han it was accompanied by a revival of older doctrines. According to the *Wei Shu*, Ts'ao Ts'ao 'followed in the main the tactics laid down in the *Sun Tzu* and *Wu Tzu* … by deceiving the enemy, he won victory; he varied his tactics in demonic fashion'. Ts'ao himself wrote a military manual which all his generals followed when on campaign, and

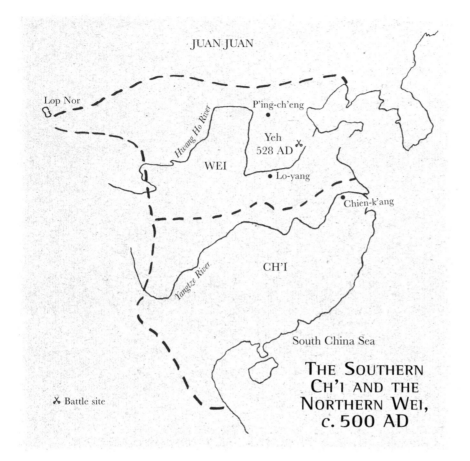

JUAN JUAN

Lop Nor

P'ing-ch'eng

Yeh
528 AD

WEI

Lo-yang

Chien-k'ang

CH'I

South China Sea

THE SOUTHERN
CH'I AND THE
NORTHERN WEI,
c. 500 AD

Battle site

he produced the earliest known commentary on *Sun Tzu*, while another commentary ascribed to Ts'ao's rival, Chu-ko Liang, has become part of the canon of Taoist writings. Although Ts'ao was the best-known practitioner of this style of warfare, ambushes, surprise flank attacks and similar stratagems were very common tactics.

Even under the Han, however, there persisted an even older tradition – that of personal heroics on the part of commanders. Instances of individual officers influencing the outcome of battles or obtaining promotion through acts of personal courage are recorded throughout this period. Three examples will suffice.

During the Wu revolt of 154 BC, Kuan Fu avenged his father's death in Wu captivity with a desperate foray into the rebel camp, accompanied by only a dozen or so mounted followers. Armed with a halberd, he killed or wounded 20 or 30 Wu soldiers and returned covered with wounds. Kuan became famous throughout the empire for this feat, and the Emperor Ching-ti made him a general.

Ssu-ma Kuang, a Sung historian, described Tien Wei's fearless courage in a battle against Lu Pu in AD 194:

Cataphract, Northern Wei. Figures of this type are very common and suggest that clothing was often worn over armour. The Ehrchu who sacked Lo-yang in 528 wore white in mourning for the young emperor, Hsiao-ming-ti. (British Museum 1936.10-12.292)

Ts'ao Ts'ao called for men to break into the enemy line, and ... Tien Wei of Ch'en-liu led out a group of volunteers ... Wei said to his men, 'When the enemy are ten paces away, then report it.' The other men said 'Ten paces!' He said again 'Tell me when it's five paces.' The others were frightened and shouted at once, 'They're here!' Holding a halberd, Wei rose up and roared defiance. Whenever he struck there was none who could stand against his blow. Pu's forces retreated.

The *Chou Shu*, the official history of the Northern Chou dynasty, records the actions of a leading general of the Western Wei, Ts'ai Yu, at an encounter in AD 538:

Ox wagons were the usual means of transporting military supplies. This is a late-6th-century tomb-model. (British Museum OA 1925.10-15.3)

[he] dismounted and fought on foot, and killed several men with his own hands … the enemy surrounded him ten or so deep and called to him, 'You appear to be a brave knight, sir. If you would but put aside your armour and surrender, can you believe you would be without riches and honours?' Yu cursed them … The Eastern Wei men did not dare to press him but called up one with heavy armour and long sword to advance directly and seize him … The enemy slowly advanced and when ten paces away Yu finally shot him right in the face … The enemy then withdrew a bit and Yu slowly led a retreat.

Commands in battle were transmitted as in earlier times by flags, gongs and drums. Three Kingdoms armies frequently used large numbers of flags and banners to accompany feint manoeuvres and give the impression of a much larger force. Military music was important throughout the period, and attacks were accompanied by a roar of drums in an attempt to inspire the attackers and demoralize the enemy. It was sometimes thought possible to judge the chances of success of an army by the quality of its music. The Northern Wei had flute music, 'the sound of which turned cowards into heroes, and made swordsmen long for action', and some martial songs of the Liang, adapted from northern tunes, have been preserved.

The Sui dynasty, 589–618

Yang Chien, who became the emperor Wen-ti, the first ruler of the Sui, had enjoyed a distinguished military career before he came to the throne, having served under the famous minister of the Western Wei, Yu-wen T'ai. Like most of those who founded dynasties, he was a member of an old aristocratic family, and traced his descent both from the native Chinese gentry and the Hsien-pi tribal chiefs who had migrated from the north-east some three centuries previously.

Yang Chien's conquest in 589 of the last rival Chinese state, Ch'en, did not bring lasting peace to the empire. He at first attempted to conciliate the independent-minded southerners, but his destruction of their old capital at Chien-k'ang sparked rumours that the entire population was to be deported to the north-west. Scattered revolts broke out, and the emperor reverted to his natural authoritarian style, ordering generals Yang Su and P'ei Chu to bring the south to heel – a task they carried out with great ruthlessness. Furthermore, the loyalty of the people was soon strained by the enormous public works – including the Grand Canal complex and the rebuilding of thousands of miles of walls in the north-west – which were undertaken using forced labour. Fear of further trouble led to a decree of 590 effectively placing the military outside the capital under the control of local civil officials, and in 595 to the confiscation of privately held weapons. In 598 there was even an attempt to ban all boats over a certain length from the rivers of the south, in order to prevent them from being used to aid rebellion.

In foreign relations, just as at home, Wen-ti was guided by a desire to emulate the achievements of the Han. Like their predecessors, the Sui were faced with a threat from the northern steppes, where the T'u-chueh or eastern Turks – heirs to part of the Turkish Empire which in the mid-6th century had briefly controlled the whole of Central Asia – remained powerful despite serious internal divisions. Wen-ti's policy was to exploit these divisions by supporting rival Turkish factions, and in this way he managed to stave off several potential crises without resorting to all-out warfare. In the south, Chiao-chou (in what is now northern Vietnam) had escaped from Chinese control in the 4th century. An army under Liu Fang reconquered it in 602, but an attempt to advance further south into the kingdom of Champa was less successful. Liu sacked the Champa capital and returned with some valuable loot, but his army was severely

OPPOSITE Sui guardsman (left), infantryman in 'cord and plaque' armour (centre) and an unarmoured infantryman who might be Sui or T'ang. (Michael Perry © Osprey Publishing Ltd)

M Perry

weakened by disease on its way home. The court soon lost its enthusiasm for such expeditions, and Champa retained its independence.

Yang-ti, who succeeded to the Sui throne in 604, was even more ambitious. In 607 he led an army to the far west, receiving the submission of the T'u-chueh as well as the kings of Turfan and Hami, while his general Yu-wen Shu inflicted a major defeat on the T'u-yu-hun in the Tarim Basin. At the T'u-chueh court, however, the triumphant emperor made a disturbing discovery: an ambassador from Koguryo, an independent kingdom in northern Korea, was already in residence. Alarmed at the thought of an alliance between these two potentially hostile powers, Yang-ti sent emissaries to Koguryo to demand its formal submission. When this was refused, he began to prepare for war.

This was to be one of the most ambitious campaigns ever undertaken by a Chinese dynasty, using all the resources of a newly unified and self-confident

Figures representing heavy cavalry on armoured horses are common in 6th- and 7th-century tombs. This example, dating from the Sui or early T'ang period, is wearing a variant of the popular 'cord and plaque' armour. (British Museum 1938.5-24.48)

empire. First, a northern branch of the Grand Canal had to be completed to enable supplies to be brought to the frontier from as far away as the Yangtze valley; then a huge army – said to number a million men – was raised. All this, however, was to prove too much for a state not yet fully recovered from centuries of disunity and civil strife.

It was not until 612 that the emperor was able to lead his army across the Liao River on a specially built bridge and into Koguryo. The Koreans, however, were aware of the defensive advantages provided by their terrain and climate, and made the most of them. On the far side of the Liao the Chinese found forested mountains, the few routes through which were blocked by a chain of fortified towns. These resisted throughout the summer, and in the autumn, rains forced Yang-ti to retreat. In 613 he tried again, but a revolt at home obliged him to detach troops to suppress it, and his weakened army was no more successful than it had been the previous year. The following summer he pushed across the Liao yet again, bypassing the fortresses and reaching the capital city of P'yong-yang, but few supplies could get through and the troops began to desert in droves. The king of Koguryo offered to submit, and the Sui were glad of an excuse to withdraw, but the Korean ruler failed to turn up at court on the agreed date. A furious Yang-ti proposed to attack a fourth time, but the enormous cost of keeping the army in the field for so long had strained the empire beyond endurance. The emperor returned home to a country seething with rebellion. It was too late for repression, as by now the nobility as well as the common people were disaffected. In 617 two of his grandsons were set up as rival emperors, and in the following year Yang-ti was assassinated.

The T'ang, 618–907

Li Yuan, the duke of T'ang, saw in the events of 617 an opportunity to increase his own power. He made an alliance with the Turks, who supplied him with men and horses, and moved against the Sui from his base on the northern frontier, capturing the imperial capital, Ch'ang-an. The next year, after the death of Yang-ti, he deposed the new Sui emperor and proclaimed himself founder of a successor dynasty – the T'ang. At first this was only one of perhaps a dozen rival regimes set up in different parts of China, but from the beginning the T'ang had a number of advantages over its rivals.

Li's power base in Kuan-chung in the north-west – the 'land within the passes', which had also been the cornerstone of the Ch'in and Han regimes – possessed a large and thoroughly militarized population, as well as natural defences that made it very difficult to attack from the east. The support of his northern neighbours, the T'u-ch'ueh, was also of vital importance. Furthermore,

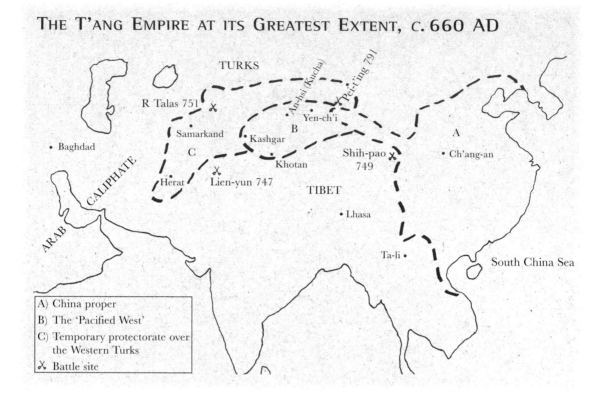

THE T'ANG EMPIRE AT ITS GREATEST EXTENT, C. 660 AD

TURKS

R Talas 751

An-hsi (Kucha)

Pei-t'ing 791

Samarkand

Kashgar

B

Yen-ch'i

A

Baghdad

C

Khotan

Shih-pao
749

Ch'ang-an

Herat

Lien-yun 747

TIBET

Lhasa

Ta-li

South China Sea

A) China proper
B) The 'Pacified West'
C) Temporary protectorate over
   the Western Turks
X Battle site

Li's enlightened treatment of Sui officials and other rivals who joined his cause, and his willingness to enrol captured enemy troops in his own armies, brought in a steady flow of willing defectors. According to the traditional account, however, the T'ang's greatest asset was Li's younger son, Li Shih-min, who is portrayed not only as the man who encouraged his indecisive father to revolt, but as a precocious military genius and dashing cavalry leader who from the age of 15 led the T'ang armies to a series of stunning victories. On the evidence of the official T'ang histories, Li Shih-min is a leading candidate for the title of greatest general in Chinese history, but we must be wary of an element of bias in the records. The official accounts of this period were, after all, drawn up under the close supervision of Li Shih-min himself, after his accession to the throne.

Late in 618 a rival emperor, Hsueh Chu, defeated the T'ang and threatened Ch'ang-an. The imperial capital was saved only by Hsueh's sudden death. The next major challenge came from two warlords of the Yellow River plain, Wang Shih-ch'ung and Tou Chien-te, but after Li Shih-min's victory over Tou at Ssu-shui in 621, they surrendered. At this point a new Turkish Qaghan broke with the T'ang and invaded the north with 150,000 men, but this too was defeated. Organized opposition to the spread of T'ang power throughout China ended in 624 with the defeat of Fu Kung-shih on the lower Yangtze.

OPPOSITE Another view of the 'cord and plaque' style of armour, on a 7th-century figure of an infantry soldier. (British Museum 1912.12-31.3)

In 626 Li Shih-min forced his father to abdicate and took the throne for himself. He ruled until 649 as Emperor T'ai-tsung, one of the most militarily successful reigns in Chinese history, and one which became a classic model for later rulers. As peace strengthened the economy and the Turks' own internal troubles reduced the threat from that quarter, the T'ang began to contemplate the enlargement of the empire. In 629 the Turkish Qaghan was defeated, and 100,000 of his surrendered subjects settled on the northern frontier. In 634 the T'u-yu-hun in the far west were similarly crushed. During the 630s the cities of the Tarim Basin became Chinese vassals, and following a revolt in 644–48 the protectorate of An-hsi ('the Pacified West') was set up, with its headquarters at Kucha, to bring this area and its trade routes to the West under firmer control. Subsequently, emissaries began to arrive in China from as far afield as Sassanid Persia and Constantinople.

In 645 T'ai-tsung intervened in a dispute between his Korean vassal Silla and the old enemy, Koguryo. Despite a major victory in the field at An-shih, the T'ang failed against the frontier defences just as the Sui had, and another long-drawn-out war was prevented only by T'ai-tsung's death. But the much stronger economy of the T'ang Empire was able to withstand the strain, and it continued to expand on other frontiers. The year 640 had brought the Chinese into contact with a new power in the west: Tibet. The Tibetan ruler, Srong-btsan-sgam-po, demanded a Chinese princess in marriage – implying diplomatic recognition – and after a brief invasion of Szechwan this was granted. The Tibetan Empire remained China's most powerful rival until its collapse in the mid-9th century.

T'ai-tsung's successor was dominated by his consort, the Empress Wu, who is traditionally accused of ruining the empire with intrigue and extravagant spending. Nevertheless, for a time the military successes of the T'ang continued unabated. In 657 the Western Turks overran the Tarim Basin but were defeated in a great battle near Lake Issyk-kul. Their lands were divided up into Chinese protectorates that extended as far north as Lake Balkhash and as far west as Herat, so that for a few years the T'ang Empire reached – in theory – more than half-way across Asia. No Chinese administration was ever installed in these new lands, however, and in 665 they broke away, never to be recovered.

In 660 the T'ang once more invaded Koguryo, in alliance with Silla. The plan was to land a seaborne force in the small south-western Korean kingdom of Paekche, then attack Koguryo simultaneously from there and from the north. Unfortunately Japanese forces became involved on the side of Paekche, inciting the people to revolt and pinning down the Chinese troops there. In 663 the T'ang navy defeated the Japanese at the battle of Kum River, enabling the two-pronged attack to go ahead, but it was another five years before Chinese and Silla forces finally took P'yong-yang and established a T'ang protectorate over Koguryo. Even then success was only temporary. In 676 a rebellion drove out the T'ang

Pottery figures of this type, representing a mounted archer, are among the most popular military subjects from the T'ang period. Note the simple bowcase, designed to carry an unstrung weapon. (British Museum 1910.6-14.5)

aided by Silla forces, which then proceeded to take most of Korea for themselves. One repercussion of this war was the creation in Manchuria of the P'o-hai state, which survived until it was conquered by the Khitan in the 10th century.

Meanwhile the Chinese Empire had met with setbacks in Central Asia. The Tibetans had conquered the T'u-yu-hun, and in 670 they overran the Tarim Basin. Two expeditions sent from Ch'ang-an to expel them met with disaster. In 680 Tibetan troops took the fortress of An-jung in Szechwan, which left them in control of the Szechwan and Yunnan border regions, while in the north after 682, a newly reunified Eastern Turkish state began raiding the frontier. The war in the west continued intermittently for several decades, with Tibetan invasions being either bought off or defeated in battle. The Tarim Basin was recaptured in 692, and a serious Tibetan incursion into north-western China in 700 was only repulsed after six hard-fought battles.

The war of 736–55 against Tibet saw T'ang forces once more penetrating as far west as the Pamirs. In 747 Kao Hsien-chih – a Korean general in T'ang service – outflanked the enemy by taking the provinces of Wakhan and Balur in what is now northern Pakistan. This western adventure soon brought China into conflict with the other great imperial power in Asia – the Muslim Arabs. In 751 Ferghana, nominally a vassal of the new Abbasid caliphate, asked Kao for assistance in a dispute with its neighbour, Tashkent, which was being backed by the Arabs. A Muslim force met the T'ang army at the Talas River – the only major battle ever to be fought between a Chinese and a Middle Eastern army. After an indecisive five-day struggle, Kao's Qarluq Turkish allies changed sides and Kao was forced to retreat through the White Stone Mountains. A mob of fleeing Ferghanan troops blocked the pass, and many of the trapped Chinese were captured. T'ang power in the far west was permanently broken by this defeat.

Two other major defeats occurred in 751: Nan-chao, a new power in the south-west, routed Hsien-yu Chung-t'ung's Szechwanese forces, while in the north-east a T'ang army, under the Sogdian general An Lu-shan, was lost to the Khitans, a Manchurian tribe descended from the Hsien-pi. Nan-chao established a disciplined army on Chinese lines and campaigned widely throughout south-eastern Asia, at various times allied to the Tibetans and the T'ang. The war with Tibet continued until 755, when China was thrown into disarray by the rebellion of An Lu-shan, who led a mixed army of Chinese, Turks and Khitans south from his stronghold on the north-eastern frontier. Government bungling led to the loss of Ch'ang-an, and the emperor was forced to abdicate. The rebellion was not suppressed until 763, after years of fighting had devastated much of northern China. In some respects the panic measures taken by the government to contain the revolt were even more damaging in the long term than the war itself. The north-western frontier was left defenceless when the garrisons were called home to protect the capital, and the decentralization of military power which was to cripple the later T'ang was encouraged by the setting up of local military commands throughout the provinces. After peace was restored, amnestied rebel commanders of dubious reliability were given imperial offices and remained in power over much of the north-east.

The series of disasters did not end there. In 763 a Tibetan army captured Ch'ang-an and installed a puppet emperor. Though he was soon driven out, the loss of the imperial horse pastures at nearby Lung-yu was more permanent.

Another spate of rebellions engulfed the north between 781 and 786, and thereafter the T'ang tended to concentrate its remaining military power in the capital, leaving the defence of the rest of the empire to provincial authorities. It is a tribute to the enormous prestige of the dynasty, however, that this did not lead at once to full-scale separatism. In fact the early 9th century saw several successful attempts to bring provinces that showed too much independence back under government control; the best known among them is the Huai-hsi campaign of 815–17.

By the 850s the general level of lawlessness and banditry was rising as the military effectiveness of the armies declined. The Che-tung rebellion of 859 was an ominous sign, since for the first time under the T'ang it involved a mass rising of discontented peasantry, and in the 860s bloody Nan-chao invasions of the southern province of Annam added to the dynasty's troubles. Huang Ch'ao's revolt in 874–84 marked the final stage in the decline of imperial authority. Two provincial warlords who played a vital role in suppressing Huang Ch'ao – Chu Wen and Li K'o-yung (the latter a member of the Sha-t'o Turkish tribe, which had been settled within the empire since 808) – took the opportunity to set up independent bases, from which they carried on a bitter struggle for power. The emperors were quickly reduced to mere puppets of the warlords, and the last campaign undertaken by the T'ang central government was an unsuccessful attempt to bring Li K'o-yung to heel in 890. Finally, in 907, Chu Wen deposed the T'ang emperor, slaughtered his ministers and proclaimed his own Liang dynasty. The regime that had brought China to the peak of its military prestige had come to an ignominious end.

T'ang infantry figure wearing an elaborate version of 'cord and plaque' armour. (British Museum 1912.12-31.4)

Sui and T'ang armies

The basis of both Sui and early T'ang armies was the *fu-ping* militia system, which had its origins in the Chinese troops conscripted by the Western Wei under Yu-wen T'ai in the 550s. The army of the Sui conquest was ethnically mixed, consisting mainly of Chinese *fu-ping* soldiers and Hsien-pi tribesmen. One modern study shows that out of 60 high-ranking officers, at least 40 per cent were non-Chinese, and 87 per cent had served under the previous dynasty – the Hsien-pi Northern Chou. The *fu-ping* was not a mass levy, but drew its manpower selectively from old hereditary military families and others charged with providing troops in lieu of liability for forced labour. Initially, military service therefore carried high social status for the families involved. These families were concentrated overwhelmingly in the north, especially in Kuan-chung, where society had already been militarized by the long series of wars of the previous three centuries, and where loyalty to the regime was strongest.

The *fu-ping* system continued in use under the T'ang, which maintained some 600 militia units, each containing between 800 and 1,200 men who were liable to serve between the ages of 21 and 60. While the Sui had subordinated these units to the local civil administration, the T'ang controlled them centrally, via a bureaucracy answerable to the *ping-pu* or Ministry of the Army. Units contained both cavalry and infantry, and were subdivided into *t'uan* of 200 men, *tui* of 50, and *huo* of ten. Officers were permanently employed, but the rank-and-file had to report for duty and training at the capital on a rotation system, depending upon how far away they lived. Those up to 500 *li* (about 160 miles) from the capital served one month in five, those over 2,000 *li* away, two months in every 18. A similar system provided men for three-year tours of duty in frontier garrisons. This arrangement functioned well at first because the *fu-ping* units were already concentrated on the northern frontier and in the vicinity of the capital, and it had a number of other advantages: it involved little government expenditure, since the men supported themselves for most of the year by farming; it ensured the existence of a reserve of trained troops available for call-up in war; and it kept the army divided into small units and concentrated at the capital where it could be supervised, preventing its generals from establishing strong power bases elsewhere.

There were, however, drawbacks, which became more obvious towards the close of the 7th century. The system was only suited to the provision of guards

Although much later in date, this model of a Tibetan lamellar coat gives an idea of the type of armour that was popular in Central and East Asia from the 7th century onwards. (The Board of Trustees of the Royal Armouries, no. XXVIA-18)

111

in peacetime, or to brief campaigns by field armies (*hsing-chun*) recruited for specific operations, not to the maintenance of static defensive positions on distant frontiers, nor to protracted wars like those in Korea. If the men were kept away too long agriculture would suffer, and their clothing and weapons, which they had to supply themselves at the outset of a campaign, would become worn out. Liu Jen-kuei's report on the state of the army in Korea in 664 complains that although the men had been told to make provision for being away from home for one year, they had already been in the field for two. T'ai-tsung had tried to ensure that soldiers were rewarded for good service and their families compensated if they died, but this policy had been neglected, and consequently the men were demoralized. Well-off families began to pay substitutes or evade service altogether, and by the time of the Empress Wu guards officers were being appointed not from *fu-ping* families but from among the relatives of court officials. The crisis in the system became obvious in 722, when the emperor planned a pilgrimage to Mount T'ai, but found that the units currently at the capital were so far below their paper strength that they could not provide an adequate escort.

From the beginning, however, T'ang armies were supplemented by troops from other sources. The 644 expedition to Korea, for example, included thousands of men from regions where the militias did not operate, and a remark attributed to T'ai-tsung suggests that many were volunteers: 'When we call for ten men we get a hundred; when we call for a hundred we get a thousand.'

Others, however, were conscripted as required from ordinary non-military families. There were also regular guard units, such as the Northern Army or Army of Fathers and Sons, which was originally formed from veterans of Li Yuan's campaign against the Sui, and the *San-wei* or cadet corps, consisting of aristocratic youths undergoing training as officers. The Sui had established 12 *chun*, or standing armies, to garrison the capital in cooperation with the *fu-ping* contingents, and the T'ang retained this system, adding a number of new units.

The process of replacing the *fu-ping* system with an enlarged standing army was gradual. In the late 7th century the frontier garrisons in remote regions began to be taken over by regular long-service troops known as *chien-erh*, many of whom were re-enlisted *fu-ping*. Then, in 710, a major reform began, aiming to make the frontier forces capable of withstanding invasions without the levied expeditionary forces to support them. Nine frontier commands were established, each comprising a number of garrisons and a *ching-lueh chun*, or 'defence army', under the overall control of a governor. These men were sometimes professional soldiers, but in less seriously threatened areas court officials were preferred, since they were considered more reliable. *T'un-t'ien* military-cum-agricultural colonies, where troops grew crops when not on active duty, were employed as a traditional Chinese solution to supply problems. From 737 it was decided to replace the

militia entirely with paid *chien-erh* regulars; they were recruited by calling for volunteers from the population in general. However *t'uan-lien*, or emergency local militias, were still raised from time to time in areas threatened by invasion.

Both the Sui and the T'ang also relied heavily on foreign auxiliaries. T'u-ti-chi, a chief of the Mo-ho people from Manchuria, became a vassal of Sui Yang-ti and sent troops – probably mounted archers – to his aid against Koguryo. T'u-ti-chi's son was later given the rank of duke by the T'ang for distinguished service against the Tibetans. Other Mo-ho fought for Koguryo against the T'ang in 645, but those captured by the Chinese were executed as traitors. Also prominent in Chinese service were Turks: in 605, 20,000 Eastern T'u-chueh served under Sui command against Khitan raiders, but a decade later Turkish support was instrumental in bringing the T'ang to power. T'ai-tsung

Eighth-century clay and wood model of a horse from Turfan, showing the typical T'ang saddle and saddle-cloth. (British Museum OA 1928.10-22.117)

attributed his success partly to the fact that whereas previous native Chinese emperors had cherished their own people at the expense of the 'barbarians', he had always valued both and treated them equally. Turks and related Central Asian cavalrymen continued to form an important part of the T'ang forces, and in the 8th century the cavalry of the allied Uighurs provided vital support to the dynasty on several occasions. Foreigners were even appointed to command armies, being thought to be more politically reliable than native Chinese – a belief the career of An Lu-shan showed to be somewhat naïve.

After An Lu-shan's revolt, the provincial governors' forces became virtually independent private armies, often fighting among themselves. New professional units were raised by the government to counter this tendency, but they too proved difficult to control. In the 9th century the *Shen-ts'e*, or 'Divine Strategy Army', was set up under the command of court eunuchs, and in 885 a new army 54,000 strong was established, composed largely of young men from Ch'ang-an. None of these forces was able to stand up to the battle-hardened veterans of the provincial armies. By the beginning of the 10th century, real power in the empire was held by two rival armies: that of Chu Wen, governor of Pian Province, in the south, and the Sha-t'o Turks of Li K'o-yung in the north. The Sui pioneered the system of civil service examinations, and this eventually provided China with a new ruling class, but until the end of the T'ang, high office – especially in the army – was largely the domain of aristocrats, and martial prowess was still often valued above academic training, with examinations placing emphasis on skill with the bow and lance. The career of Chang Wan-fu, a famous late-8th-century general, is instructive in this respect: his father and grandfather were both scholars with official degrees, but neither rose to high rank. Chang, therefore, 'took no pleasure in books but studied horsemanship and archery … he enlisted in the army to serve in Liao-tung and came home a general'. Youths from the old military families of the north-west trained with weapons from an early age, and the imperial family was no exception: Li Shih-min took the field in person until near the end of his life, and as late as the 780s the future emperor, Shun-tsung, took part in the wars of his father's reign, 'bow and arrows always in hand'. The T'ang ideal was *ju-hsiang, ch'u chiang* – a man who was equally accomplished at court or on campaign.

The main striking force of Sui armies was the heavy cavalry, equipped for close combat in typical 6th-century style, with lances, swords and often full armour for both men and horses. The leading military commander of the period, Yang Su, was noted for his enthusiasm for cavalry charges and aggressive tactics generally. Under the T'ang, the traditional Turkish combination of lance and bow was widely adopted even by ethnic Chinese cavalry, but probably did not replace the old-style charging cataphracts immediately. Certainly accounts of Li Shih-min's 'iron-clad' horsemen in battle are reminiscent of these earlier

T'ang figure in the classic pose associated with guardsmen. He appears to be wearing a long coat of lamellar armour. (British Museum 1925.12-19.1)

OPPOSITE Lokapala tomb guardian figure; late T'ang. It is not known whether such intricate designs were ever actually worn, but they are clearly an elaboration of the familiar 'cord and plaque' construction. (British Museum OA 1932.10-10.2)

tactics. It seems likely, however, that the use of the very heavy cataphract equipment declined as Turkish influence spread. Some T'ang expeditionary forces in Central Asia consisted entirely of cavalry – mostly Turks or similar allies, but also including both light and heavy Chinese horse-archers – and when infantry were taken along, they were frequently mounted on horses to increase their mobility over the huge distances involved. After the upheavals of the mid-8th century, the number and effectiveness of the cavalry declined dramatically. Repeated attempts to reverse this process failed, and by the end of the 9th century, native Chinese cavalry seem to have almost disappeared. It was considered worthy of note when Chu Wen, impressed by the performance of the Sha-t'o horsemen against Huang Ch'ao's rebels, raised 500 cavalry of his own.

Infantry in the 6th and 7th centuries was divided into *pu-ping*, or marching infantry, armed with spears, and *pu-she*, or archers. The crossbow, the principal weapon of Han infantry, appears to have been less common in this period than

the composite bow, although there are hints that it may have retained its importance in the south.

An 11th-century writer remarks that the T'ang had so little confidence in the crossbow that they equipped its users with halberds for self-defence. They then tended to succumb to the temptation to throw down their crossbows and charge, so that other men had to be sent to follow them and pick up the discarded weapons. One source gives the ratio of bows to crossbows in the ideal army as five to one. In fact this and other T'ang writings suggest that all soldiers – even those infantry who were primarily spearmen – were supposed to carry bows, but it is not clear how far this was achieved in practice.

As in earlier periods, sophisticated siege equipment was available, including artillery, towers and rams. T'ang armies on campaign protected themselves whenever possible with elaborate fortified camps. Tu Mu, a 9th-century writer, provides some interesting details on the construction of these works. Each division of the army had its own enclosed camp; these were linked together with walls and paths, and were sited 50 to 100 paces apart so that they could support each other with missiles. Small towers were built where the paths intersected, and topped with piles of firewood which could be lit as a warning of attack. Thus even if an enemy forced his way through the perimeter defences, he would find himself surrounded by smaller fortifications and illuminated by the fires, and could be shot at from raised positions on all sides. A recommended tactic was to deliberately allow an attacker to enter the complex, so that he could be trapped. Not surprisingly, Tu Mu comments that 'our only worry is that the enemy will not attack at night, for if he does he is certain to be defeated'.

The Five Dynasties and Ten Kingdoms, 907–959

This is the name traditionally given to the period of disunity between the fall of the T'ang and the Sung reunification – referring to the succession of nominally imperial dynasties established in northern China, and the de facto independent principalities which divided the south among themselves. The first of the northern 'Five Dynasties' was the Later Liang established by Chu Wen; this was overthrown in 923 by the Sha-t'o Turk Li Ts'un-hsu, who claimed to be restoring T'ang imperial authority with his Later T'ang regime. Li, however, failed to provide stability, and in 936 another Sha-t'o general set up his own dynasty, the Later Chin. Meanwhile, in 907, the Khitans had established a Chinese-style dynasty – the Liao – in Manchuria, and in 943–46 fought a successful war against the Later Chin, overrunning much of northern China. Faced with

Under the Later T'ang, lamellar coats like this one, derived from Central Asian traditions, largely replaced earlier types. This well-known figure from Mingoi in the Western Regions is probably of T'ang date. Round shields were also used on occasion by T'ang cavalry. (British Museum OA 1917/MAS 1061)

continuing popular resistance, the invaders withdrew, leaving the Sha-t'o commander Liu Chih-yuan with the only effective army in the region. Liu naturally lost no time in establishing himself at the head of yet another new dynasty – the Later Han. Finally, in 951, this short-lived state was replaced in a coup by one of its native Chinese officers, the founder of the Later Chou. It was this regime that was taken over in 960, after a mutiny of an army fighting the

The Sha-t'o Turks. Based on a painted scroll from the later T'ang dynasty, the horsemen in this procession are probably typical of the Sha-t'o aristocracy which ruled this and other northern states of the period. Their embroidered robes and head-dresses are mainly Chinese in style, though the rear rider is dressed more traditionally. Some Sha-t'o troops, however, were uniformed; Li K'o-yung's men wore black, giving rise to the nickname 'Li's Black Crows'. Armour could have been worn underneath the outer garments. (Michael Perry © Osprey Publishing Ltd)

Khitans, by a commander of the Palace Guard – Chao K'uang-yin, the first emperor of the Sung.

The forces of the Later Liang were organized into six armies, with additional units of both cavalry and infantry – apparently recruited from Chu Wen's personal followers in the civil wars at the end of the T'ang – based at the capital as guards. Chu's troops had originally been almost entirely infantry, but he subsequently raised several regiments of cavalry modelled on the mounted archers of the Sha-t'o Turks. The regimes that replaced the Liang were ruled by the Sha-t'o, and their military organization reflected their Turkish ancestry, although from Li K'o-yung's time onwards many Chinese were incorporated, forming the characteristic *fan-han* mixed armies. A proportion of Chinese families – originally one in ten, but later one in seven – had each to provide one soldier, while the rest supplied food and equipment. Apart from Chinese and the Sha-t'o themselves, their forces could also include Khitans, Tatars and other Mongolian and Turkish tribesmen. Despite their nomad ancestry, the Sha-t'o were not rich in horses, and often had to requisition them from their Chinese subjects; horses were expensive to maintain in China, and the Later

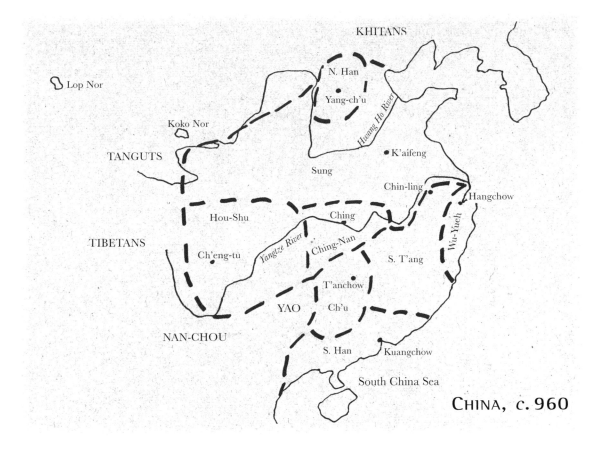

CHINA, c. 960

T'ang dynasty is said to have spent over two-thirds of its revenue on the cavalry, even though they were still a minority in the army. It was probably to preserve scarce horses that instructions were issued that cavalry were not to be mounted while on the march, unless the enemy was sighted.

At first the Sha-t'o warriors were notoriously uncontrollable, trading on their reputation for ferocity, but in 908 Li Ts'un-hsu introduced a strict code of discipline, setting out battle dispositions and regulations for the march, and prescribing prompt execution for malingerers. He also established a Chinese-style military secretariat. The Later T'ang and Chin retained the Six Armies of the Liang – including many of their native Chinese personnel – but kept a strong 'Emperor's Army' at the capital to counter any possible rebellion. The value of this was proved in 933, when the Six Armies plotted unsuccessfully to carry out a coup d'état. The Sha-t'o, who had never been very numerous, eventually disappeared by assimilation into the native Chinese population, and after 951 they ceased to play a distinct military role.

The Ten Kingdoms in the south were naturally less influenced by nomad traditions and seem to have relied largely on infantry – some of them armoured

– equipped with long swords. Naval warfare was also important. The Southern Han, based in the far south, was notable for its ultimately unsuccessful struggle to extend its control southwards into what is now Vietnam. This regime was also unique among Chinese states in maintaining a permanent corps of elephants. The animals are said to have been crewed by ten or more men each, although in view of the maximum loads quoted for modern Indian elephants, it is unlikely that they all actually rode in combat. The elephants were successful in battles against several local opponents, but in the Sung invasion of 970 they failed to stand up to crossbowmen, and were routed.

The Sung dynasty, 960–1279

The task of reunification upon which Chao K'uang-yin embarked in the 960s was on the surface more formidable than that which had faced the Sui founder at the end of the last period of fragmentation. The former Chou territories that Chao took over in the north formed the strongest single political unit, but continued migration into the Yangtze valley and further south had greatly increased the economic and manpower resources of those regions, which at that time were divided among six independent states. However, these regimes were prevented from supporting each other by mutual antagonisms. Chao cleverly took advantage of this. The small and unstable middle Yangtze states of Ching-nan and Ch'u fell first, followed by Shu in the west, which despite a popular uprising and subsequent hard fighting was under Sung control by the end of 966. In 970 the Southern Han was subdued, and five years later the Southern T'ang fell to a combined assault by the Sung and its coastal neighbour, Wu-Yueh. None of the victims had attempted to help each other, and Wu-Yueh, which had short-sightedly contributed to the Sung success, was now isolated and was forced to surrender in 978. The campaigns of conquest, now under Chao's successor Sung T'ai-tsung, were concluded in 979 by the defeat of the Northern Han, which was based in modern Shansi north-east of the Yellow River. This state was supported by the neighbouring Liao and put up strong resistance, only succumbing after a Khitan expedition was defeated by the Sung outside the city of T'ai-yuan.

However, the reunification of the empire had not been quite complete. The Khitans remained in possession of a small area around Yen-ching – the '16 Yen-yun districts' – which had been part of the T'ang domains. At first T'ai-tsung attempted to recover them by force, but in 979 he suffered a decisive defeat at the Kao-liang River near Yen-ching. In 1004 the Khitans retaliated with an invasion that threatened the Sung capital at K'aifeng, but after a drawn battle at Shan-chou the two powers finally made peace. This lasted for over a century,

The founder of the Sung dynasty, Chao K'uang-yin. (© Stephen Turnbull)

although occasional border disputes did arise – for example in 1074, when the building of fortifications on the Sung's north-eastern frontier provoked protests from the Liao. A more lasting military threat to the Sung, however, came from the north-west.

The Tangut people – variously described as related to the Hsien-pi and the Tibetans – had maintained a presence in the Ordos steppe since at least the 9th century. In 884 one of their chiefs, Toba Ssu-kung, received from the T'ang the title of 'King of Hsia' in return for help in suppressing Huang Chou's revolt, and although the Tanguts became effectively independent after the end of the T'ang,

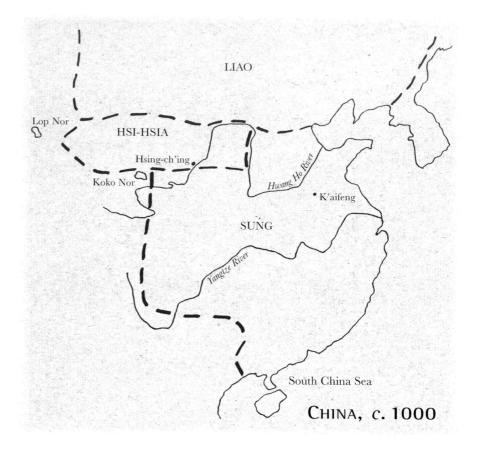

Toba's descendants remained on good terms with China, aiding the Sung in their campaign against the Northern Han.

The Ordos region was of great strategic significance, however, both as prime grazing land for cavalry horses and because it controlled the trade routes to the West. So when civil strife broke out among the Tangut clans in the 980s, the Sung could not resist the temptation to intervene. The first of a series of seven wars lasted from 982 to 1006, and succeeded only in uniting the Tanguts in opposition to the Chinese, who for lack of cavalry could make little headway on the open steppes. Conflict broke out again in 1040, provoked by Chao Yuan-hao's adoption of the title of Emperor of Great Hsia, thus claiming for his Hsi-Hsia, or Western Hsia, regime equal status with its Sung overlord. Hsi-Hsia invaded the Wei valley and inflicted heavy losses on the Chinese. The Sung won a moral victory in 1044, when Yuan-hao accepted nominal vassal status, but the truth was that the Tanguts had had to be bought off with large amounts of cash, silk and tea. The 'land within the passes', the strategic heart of previous Chinese empires, had become a devastated frontier zone.

The next clash, in 1070, was merely a bloody but indecisive border dispute, but 1081 saw another serious attempt to conquer Hsi-Hsia, which a Sung official rashly predicted would be 'as easy as breaking bamboo'. A force of 300,000 Chinese troops invaded the kingdom, in five columns. The city of Ling-chou was besieged, but the Tanguts broke the dikes that controlled the Yellow River and flooded the Sung camp, forcing a retreat in the depths of winter. This caused enormous losses. All-out war between 1096 and 1099 was another failure for the Sung. The last Tangut war, from 1114 to 1119, was linked to the Jurchen revolt against the Liao, in which the Sung supported the former and Hsi-Hsia the latter. In 1115 the Tangut cavalry won another great victory at Tsang-ti-ho, and the Chinese effectively gave up their attempts to subjugate them.

The Sung were also trying to restore the traditional boundaries of the empire in the far south, where in 939 the Vietnamese – at least nominally under Chinese control since Han times – had established the independent kingdom of Dai Viet. An invasion in 981 was unsuccessful, and another indecisive war was fought – mainly at sea – against the Ly regime in 1073–77. Apart from brief interludes, however, the region remained permanently outside Chinese control.

The turning point in the history of the Sung came early in the 12th century, with the Jurchen invasion. The Jurchen were a farming and cattle-raising people living north of the Khitans, and related to the Mo-ho and to the population of the former P'o-hai state. In 1114, under their chief Wan-yen Akuta, they revolted against their Liao overlords, and in the following year established their own Kin or 'Golden' dynasty. The Sung, under Emperor Hui-tsung, allied with them to attack the weakened Liao and regain the disputed 16 districts – a strategically inept decision, since the Khitan had long ago abandoned expansionist policies in

Excavated from Miran on the Silk Route, these lacquered leather lamellae are among the very few surviving examples of T'ang armour. (British Museum OA MAS 592)

China, and might have been a valuable buffer against wild tribes such as the Jurchen. The Liao dynasty was destroyed in 1125, and the Jurchen marched on into northern China. K'aifeng fell and Hui-tsung was captured, forcing the government to flee south and set up a new capital at Hangchow, to which they gave the prophetic name of Lin-an, or 'Temporary Peace'. Thus historians traditionally divide the dynasty into the Northern (969–1127) and Southern Sung (1127–1279), based at K'aifeng and Lin-an respectively.

The Jurchen did not stop at K'aifeng, however, but plunged on into the south, lured by the prospect of looting what was then the richest empire in the world. For a few years the Sung armies proved incapable of stopping the invaders, and the dynasty seemed doomed. While isolated units held out in parts of the north, the new emperor, Kao-tsung, was forced to take refuge with a fleet off the south coast. In this crisis the Sung navy saved the day, blocking the Yangtze crossings against returning Jurchen raiders and preventing further incursions into the far south while the army rebuilt its strength. The Chinese gradually gained the

Iron statue of a Sung soldier, dated 1098. (British Museum 1993.8-9.1)

initiative under the renowned general Yueh Fei, who in 1134–35 retook much of the lost territory. However, in 1141 a peace party at court persuaded the emperor to end hostilities, pay tribute to the Kin and leave them in control of the lands north of the Huai River. Yueh Fei spoke up against this and was murdered; as a result of his stand, he has been venerated ever since by patriotic Chinese.

In 1161 the Kin tried again to conquer the south, but were defeated at sea off Shantung, while a Sung river fleet prevented their land forces from crossing the Yangtze. Eventually the Jurchen troops mutinied and murdered their ruler, the bloodthirsty and widely hated usurper Hai-ling Wang. Hostilities continued intermittently until the 1220s, with a major outbreak in 1206–08, after which the Sung were forced to pay tribute yet again. By then, however, the Kin were themselves coming under pressure from another wave of invaders from the north – the Mongols.

When Chinggis Khan's armies appeared at the rear of the Kin and began to ravage the Yellow River plain from 1209 onwards, the Sung repeated their mistake of a century before and allied with the Mongols to destroy what could have been a valuable buffer state against the new menace. In 1217 they discontinued the payment of tribute to the weakened Kin, provoking another invasion. In 1219 a Sung counter-attack overran most of Shantung, and in 1222, compounding the error, the Sung general P'eng I-pin attacked Mongol-held territory in western Shantung and Hopei. P'eng was defeated and captured in 1225 at Tsan-huang, despite a desperate attempt to stop a Mongol outflanking move by setting fire to the hillsides at his rear. Two years later another general, Li Ch'uan, was also captured, but was taken into Mongol service as governor of Shantung.

There was then a period of peace between the Mongols and the Sung, while the Mongol invaders destroyed the last remnants of the Kin, but the war resumed in 1234. By this time the Mongols, immeasurably strengthened by the newly acquired manpower of northern China, were setting their sights on the conquest of the entire country. Thrown onto the defensive, the Sung were gradually encircled. In 1260 Chinggis's grandson Kubilai proclaimed himself emperor, founding a new dynasty which later became known as the Yüan. Within 19 years the Yüan had eclipsed the Sung and brought all China once again under one ruler.

Nomads, probably Mongols or Jurchen, from a 13th-century Sung painting, 'The Convoy of Wang Chao-chun'. (British Museum 1919.4-14.01)

Sung armies

Social and economic conditions in 11th-century China were very different from those which had prevailed under the T'ang. The opening up of the south had stimulated population growth, and encouraged an increase in wealth and social mobility. This has caused some to call Sung China the world's first 'modern' state. From then on an increasingly complex community could only be governed with the aid of the local scholar gentry, whose ethos was civil rather than military. Chao K'uang-yin, who feared the repetition of military coups of the kind that had brought him to power, made the best of this situation by pursuing a policy known as *chung wen ch'ing-wu*, or 'emphasizing the civil and downgrading the military', and by making his generals subject to on-the-spot control by civilian overseers.

The rank-and-file were mercenaries, serving for pay and rations, and recruited from among the lower orders of society – including petty criminals, vagabonds and amnestied bandits. This was not in itself a new phenomenon, but combined with the greater rewards to be gained from commercial activity, it contributed to the low status of the military. This was to be a feature of Chinese life from the Sung onwards. In fact this *yang-ping* system, introduced in the 960s, was intended not just to supply soldiers, but as a kind of social welfare scheme, defusing popular discontent by providing employment for the destitute. However, such people were seldom loyal to the dynasty, and were despised and exploited by their officers; by the 1040s they often received only one-tenth of their promised wages. Not surprisingly, mutinies were common, and deserters or 'military bandits' became a constant threat to law and order during the 11th century, especially in the north-east, where the Khitan wars had caused great hardship. In 1043, for example, the 'Winged Tigers' army defected en masse to rebels in Shantung whom they had been sent to suppress.

The *yang-ping* system proved to be extremely expensive. The population of the Northern Sung, at about 140 million, was twice that of the T'ang, and its armies were very large – 378,000 strong in 960; 900,000 in 1000; and 1,259,000 by 1041. By the latter date, with government income falling, the military absorbed 80 per cent of all expenditure.

All Chinese dynasties faced difficulties due to the fact that the bulk of the armies had to be stationed near the dangerous northern and north-western frontiers, where the climate prevented the growing of sufficient food to maintain them. The Sung, however, aggravated the situation by clinging to unrealistic dreams of expansion. The wars with Hsi-Hsia, in particular, were an unnecessary luxury for a state relying on an expensive mass army that could not forage for itself in enemy territory (as, say, a mobile cavalry force might have been able to do).

Another serious weakness of the Sung military system was the shortage of horses: as in T'ang times, this was a consequence of territorial losses in the north. Furthermore, the capital at K'aifeng was very exposed to raids by the Khitan cavalry sweeping unimpeded across the Yellow River plain, and although after the beginning of the 11th century relations with the Khitans were mostly peaceful, the latter were a potential threat that could never be ignored. The peace agreement of 1004 prohibited both parties from building walls or fortifications, but the Sung often ignored this stipulation. They strongly fortified the towns that lay between K'aifeng and the border, although they did not build long walls. Cheaper and perhaps less provocative expedients used to slow down possible cavalry incursions included the ploughing of fields across the expected invasion routes and the planting of extensive barriers of willow trees.

The army had some strengths, however. Training and drill were studied scientifically, and in the best units, at least, men were allocated to different duties on the basis of examinations in shooting and various athletic pursuits. Units of *sheng-ch'uan*, or 'picked men', were selected for special tasks such as night assaults.

Northern Sung swordsman and cavalryman. The swordsman is based on a ceramic pillow of Sung date and the cavalryman is based on a Northern Sung painting. Sung soldiers were distinguished by their long hair and leather boots. (Michael Perry © Osprey Publishing Ltd)

Soldiers of the *chin-chun*, or palace guard, were trained in unarmed combat, and held regular boxing matches between units to maintain standards. The government was well aware of the advantages of new technology, and encouraged invention with a system of rewards.

In the reign of Emperor Shen-tsung (1068–85), the minister Wang An-shih introduced a series of reforms. He established a system of local militias, or *pao-chia*, with the dual purpose of keeping order in the districts and forming a reserve for the regular army. Each unit of ten households was to contribute a man to undergo training. In 1073 a directorate of weapons was set up to supervise armaments manufacture and improve quality. Wang also attempted to solve the horse shortage by supplying animals to peasants in suitable regions. They were allowed to use the horses for agricultural work on condition that they looked after them and compensated the government if they died. However, these reforms were opposed by conservative elements at court, and do not seem to have been fully put into effect. Certainly they did not long survive Wang's resignation in 1086.

Chang Yu, a military writer of the late Sung period, describes a system of organization based on a squad of five, which implies that the traditional five-deep deployment was still in use. There were 50 men in a platoon, two platoons in a company, two companies in the next unit up, and so on up to an 'army' of 3,200. Chang Yu remarks,

> Each is subordinate to the superior and controls the inferior. Each is properly trained. Thus one may manage a host of a million men just as one would a few … officers and men are ordered to advance or retreat by observing the flags and banners, and to move or stop by signals of bells and drums. Thus the valiant shall not advance alone, nor shall the coward flee.

A wide variety of infantry weapons is illustrated in Sung manuals, including swords, spears and various types of polearm. The most important weapon, however, was the crossbow. The *Wu Ching Tsung Yao* of 1044 devotes considerable space to the crossbow – 'the strongest weapon of China, and what the four kinds of barbarian most fear'. It states that crossbowmen should be deployed in separate units and not mixed up with hand-to-hand weapons. Its readers are assured that 'when they shoot, nothing can stand in front of them', and that even an impetuous cavalry charge can be defeated by crossbows alone. Each man advanced to shoot, protecting himself with a shield, then retired to the rear of the unit to reload.

There were also crossbow specialists employed as long-range snipers: the Khitan general Hsiao T'a-lin was picked off by such a marksman at the battle of Shan-chou in 1004. Crossbows were mass-produced in state armouries, and improved designs were continually introduced, such as that presented to the emperor by Li Ting in 1068. This was made of mulberry wood and brass, and could pierce a tree at 140 paces.

Chao K'uang-yin employed tribal horse-archers such as the Hsi, a Manchurian people related to the Khitans, but his successors no longer had access to the northern and western regions from which such troops were recruited. Native cavalry employed halberds, swords and even fire-lances as well as bows. Illustrations in contemporary manuals prove that armour and barding for horses was known, and at least one 10th-century painting shows what are clearly dismounted cavalry in lamellar armour – like their T'ang predecessors.

Sung armies were overwhelmingly composed of native Chinese infantry, but in the mid-13th century a number of Mongol defectors – the *T'ung-shih Chun* – were employed. According to the Yüan Official History, they 'always fought in the front rank and were ready to give their all'. They were eventually captured by Kubilai Khan who, much to their surprise, did not punish them but incorporated them into his own army. In the same period, the Sung recruited from the She tribe from southern China. However these troops proved unreliable and prone to rebellion.

The development of artillery and gunpowder weapons is described in more detail below; the Sung came to rely heavily on such technology, and stone-throwers in particular were employed in very large numbers. In 979 the Emperor T'ai-tsung ordered 800 to be built, and in 1126 at least 500 machines were present at the defence of K'aifeng alone.

By Sung times the synthesis of native and Central Asian traditions had produced a style of armour which was to remain unchanged for centuries. This is a Ming statuette of Kuan-ti, the god of war. (British Museum SL.1174, Sloan collection)

The Liao, 907–1125

The Khitans had been a significant power in Manchuria since the 5th century, and had been successful in several wars against the T'ang governors on the north-eastern frontier. It was not until 907, however, that they achieved a centralized state under Yeh-lu A-pao-chi, who set up the Liao dynasty on the Chinese model and also brought Mongolia and most of northern Manchuria under his control.

Infantry combat, depicted on a ceramic pillow from the Northern Sung. (British Museum 1936.10-12.106)

The core of the Liao army were the regular *ordo* troops, who fought as heavily armoured cavalry on armoured horses, equipped with lance, bow, sword and mace. Each soldier also provided a 'forager' and an 'orderly', and additional bows, spears and halberds (presumably used to equip these retainers in battle). The foragers were also armoured, and certainly carried weapons of some sort, and the orderlies may have done so. It is likely that this organization translated directly into the standard battlefield deployment in three lines, with unarmoured horsemen in the first, armoured cavalry in the second, and men on armoured horses in the third. The *ordo* regulars would have provided an elite reserve in the third line, while the orderlies and foragers formed respectively an advanced skirmish line and its better-equipped supports. However, there were also tribal Khitan and allied troops outside the *ordo* system, who may have fought in their traditional nomad fashion as mounted skirmishers.

The settled populations – Chinese, and men from the conquered state of P'o-hai – provided infantry levies, who were often employed on labouring duties. The P'o-hai were seldom trusted with arms, as they were bitterly opposed to Liao rule and frequently revolted. Some Chinese, however, served in formed and trained bodies, providing good-quality swordsmen, crossbowmen and artillery units. Chinese artillery was used in siege warfare, sometimes supplemented by hordes of impressed peasants, 'the old and the young', who were forced to march

A leather lamellar armour from Szechwan, still in use early in the 20th century. Its general appearance is typical of the early medieval period. (The Board of Trustees of the Royal Armouries, no. XXVIA-106)

ahead of the fighting troops and shield them from defenders' missiles. In this and other respects, Liao tactics foreshadowed those of the later Mongols. Both seem to have emphasized denser formations than the usual nomad horse-archer swarms.

Ordo cavalry was organized into regiments of 500 or 700 men, ten of which formed a division, with ten divisions making up an army. Attacks were carried out through a succession of controlled charges, each regiment advancing in turn before being replaced and withdrawn to rest. Banners and drums were symbols of command among the Khitans, and were no doubt used to control these manoeuvres. As soon as a unit succeeded in breaking the enemy line, the rest of the division advanced to support it.

This tactic was supposed to be repeated as often as necessary – sometimes for several days – until the enemy tired and could be broken by a concerted charge. Like many such theoretical systems, however, this would have depended on the enemy remaining passive and waiting to be attacked; it must have been very difficult to apply in practice. Certainly there were cases where Chinese opponents successfully took the initiative against the Khitans (see, for example, the battle of Ting-hsien, page 152). Chinese sources also describe them as being proficient at ambushes, and at skirmishing tactics involving swift advances and retreats. Another favourite ploy was to set fire to dry grass and let the wind blow the flames towards the enemy.

In 1125 the Jurchen, former vassals of the Liao, brought an 11-year rebellion to a successful conclusion and overthrew the dynasty. A Khitan remnant escaped to the west under an imperial prince, Yeh-lu Ta-shih. There they set up the Qara-Khitan regime, which defeated the Seljuk Turks and played an important role in the history of Central Asia for almost a century, until destroyed in its turn by the Mongols.

This state retained much of the Chinese culture which the Khitans had acquired, and was treated in later scholarly tradition as a bona fide Chinese dynasty – the Western Liao. However, it does not seem to have employed Chinese military technology or personnel, and it had little or no direct contact with China itself.

The Hsi-Hsia, 1038–1227

During the reign of Yuan-hao (1032–48), the Hsi-Hsia state is said to have deployed a total of 158,000 troops, of which 100,000 were stationed on the border with Sung China, and another 30,000 on the western frontier facing the Uighurs and Tibetans. There were also 8,000 Imperial Guards – including 3,000 heavily armoured cavalry – based in the capital, Chung-hsing. Little is known of Hsi-Hsia military equipment and organization, but their territory contained what in T'ang times had been the best horse-raising pastures in the empire, and they are known to have relied heavily on their cavalry; it was superior in both number and quality to that of the Sung.

Hsi-Hsia armies were at first simply a collection of tribal contingents, but a Chinese-style bureaucracy was eventually set up, and the country was divided into 12 military districts under two commanding generals. Tenth-century pictures from Tun-huang show dismounted warriors wearing long, Turkish-style coats of armour and wielding bows and lances, as well as infantry equipped with fire-lances and explosive bombs. A Kin source pays tribute to the Hsi-Hsia people as 'fiercely stubborn … and valiant in battle'. The country was also well provided with fortified towns, and these played a major role in their defensive strategy.

On the whole the Tanguts were successful in their series of wars with the Sung, but in 1209 the Mongols began their career of world conquest with an attack on Hsi-Hsia. A Tangut army commanded by Kao Liang-hui was defeated outside the town of Wu-la-hai. Another force of 70,000 men under Wei-ming Ling-kung was covering the fortress of K'ei-men, but was lured out of its defensive position and also beaten. Chinggis Khan then besieged Chung-hsing, which was saved when the defenders resorted to their usual tactic of breaking the dikes on the Yellow River. Hsi-Hsia was nevertheless forced to submit, and agreed to provide troops for future Mongol campaigns. This they did against the Jurchen in 1214, but their 80,000-strong army was defeated at Lin-t'ao.

When summoned again to join the Mongols in their western campaign against the Khwarizmshah, the Hsi-Hsia king refused. This foolish decision led to another Mongol invasion in 1227. The Tanguts were decisively defeated outside Chung-hsing – in a battle which, according to one source, took place on the frozen flood-plain of the Yellow River – and the Hsi-Hsia state was extinguished.

The Kin dynasty, 1125–1235

The Jurchen fought as mounted archers, and had a reputation for making good-quality armour and weapons. It appears that they were by no means as barbarous as their Chinese victims later claimed, having inherited many P'o-hai

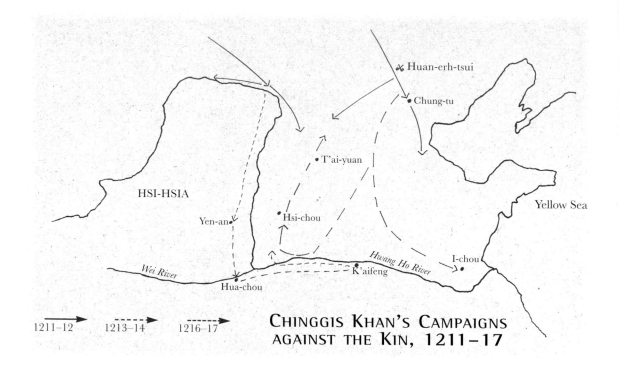

HSI-HSIA

Yellow Sea

Huan-erh-tsui

Chung-tu

T'ai-yuan

Yen-an

Hsi-chou

I-chou

Wei River

Hwang Ho River

K'aifeng

Hua-chou

1211–12   1213–14   1216–17   **CHINGGIS KHAN'S CAMPAIGNS AGAINST THE KIN, 1211–17**

institutions and having already begun to set up a state structure even before they broke from Liao control. Wan-yen Akuta, who led the successful revolt against the Liao, died in 1123 and was succeeded by his brother Ukimai, who took the Chinese-style title of Emperor T'ai-tsung of the Kin dynasty. During the next few years the Jurchen armies overran not only that part of northern China which had been occupied by the Khitan, but the whole of the Yellow River plain as far south as K'aifeng.

Unlike the Liao, the Kin abandoned early any attempt to control the Mongolian steppes directly, preferring instead to prevent the emergence of any threat from that direction by supporting selected client chiefs, and so inciting the nomads against one another. This policy tended to inspire resentment rather than loyalty, and finally backfired when Kin support for Chinggis Khan's rivals antagonized the Khan, who united the Mongols in 1206. In 1209 a series of Mongol attacks on the Kin Empire began. The state was already weakened, partly due to continual revolts by the Chinese peasantry, exacerbated by a change in the course of the notoriously unstable Yellow River in 1194, which brought catastrophic floods. At the same time the once formidable Jurchen cavalry had been neglected. The Kin were repeatedly outmanoeuvred and defeated in the field, and in 1215 their northern capital, Chung-tu, fell to the invaders. Incredibly, in 1217 Emperor Hsuan-tsung ordered an attack on the Sung, who had stopped the payment of the agreed tribute, and despite initial successes the Kin soon found themselves trapped between the Mongols in the north and the Chinese in the south. In 1235, with the fall of K'aifeng to the Mongols, the Kin Empire disappeared.

Military organization was derived from the traditional system of the tribal Jurchen, based on units called *Meng-an mou-k'o*, or 'units of a thousand and a hundred'. These were not just military formations, but social and economic units which also formed the basis of military-cum-agricultural colonies in the conquered territories. Two *p'u-nien* of 50 men each made up a *mou-k'o*, whose manpower and supplies were provided by a unit of 300 families. Ten *mou-k'o* formed a *meng-an*, or thousand. All these troops were originally mounted, and Jurchen armies of the period before their entry into China are said to have consisted entirely of cavalry. The most prestigious weapon was the bow, and Akuta himself impressed Liao ambassadors by hitting a target at the exceptional range of 320 paces. Both metal and quilted armour were known. In each *p'u-nien* 20 men were supposed to be armoured and equipped with lances or halberds, and formed the front two ranks of the standard five-deep battle formation – known as the *kuai-tzu ma*, or 'horse team'. The other three ranks consisted of lightly equipped archers. It has been suggested that this formation was designed to protect the archers from missiles while they softened up the enemy in preparation for a charge. One tradition – similar to that on page 91 regarding the Mu-jung Hsien-pi mounted archers – claims that the horses of the *kuai-tzu ma* were chained together. This unlikely tale probably reflects a habit of fighting in unusually close order, or perhaps the close cooperation between different wings of the army. The standard deployment in battle was in three bodies – a centre and two wings – and control was exercised by signalling with drums and banners.

After the conquest of the Liao Empire, Khitan, P'o-hai and Chinese troops were incorporated into the Jurchen forces, which came to rely heavily on Chinese infantry and artillery. For the campaign of 1161, Hai-ling Wang raised 120,000 Jurchen and 150,000 Chinese – the latter including 30,000 sailors. A regular Chinese infantry force, the 'Ever-Victorious Army' – which had originally been raised by the Liao – defected to the Kin from the Sung in the 1120s. Other native soldiers, the *chung-hsiao chun*, or 'loyal and filial', troops, were less well disciplined, but could nevertheless fight well. As often happened when invaders from the north established themselves in China, the cavalry eventually declined in effectiveness due to horse shortages, the difficulty of administering the traditional recruitment system under new social conditions, and the growing distaste of the aristocracy for military affairs as they began to adopt the values of the Chinese gentry. In the wars against the Mongols, therefore, the Kin relied heavily on subjects or allies like the Uighurs, Tanguts and Khitans to supply cavalry. These could be very effective, and the stubbornness of Kin resistance to

Representative of a long tradition is this leather-laced plate armour from Yunnan in south-western China. Nan-chao infantry of the 8th–13th centuries would have worn virtually identical equipment. (The Board of Trustees of the Royal Armouries, no. XXVIA.161)

the Mongols testifies to the quality of many of their troops even at this late stage: at the siege of Chung-tu, 5,000 Imperial Guards initially repulsed the Mongols, while at Ta-ch'ang-yuan in 1228, Wan-yen Ch'eng-ho-shan defeated 8,000 Mongols with just 400 cavalry and an unknown number of Chinese infantry.

Fortifications had been an important feature of Jurchen warfare since predynastic times. A favourite tactic was to block mountain passes with wooden or stone defences. After their arrival in China the Jurchen erected some impressive and technically advanced defences, including a system of long walls in Mongolia – well to the north of the present Great Wall – to control the nomad tribes. Surviving stretches show that these consisted of an outer and an inner wall, each fronted by a moat and provided with battlements, beacon towers and protruding semicircular shooting platforms known as *ma-nien* or 'horse-faces'.

Cities were similarly fortified, sometimes supplemented by ingenious devices such as fields of caltrops scattered outside the walls. Chinese gunpowder weapons were also in use as early as the 1120s, and initially made a great impression on the Mongols, who quickly adopted them in their turn.

Military science and technology

In parallel with the great changes occurring in social and economic affairs, the period between 590 and 1260 saw significant advances in the military art. Of especial interest to historians is the appearance of a genre of military manuals, of which the earliest surviving is the *T'ai Pai Yin Ching* of 759. Two others from the early 11th century are also in existence: the *Hu Ch'ien Ching* of 1004, and the best-known and most influential, the *Wu Ching Tsung Yao* dating from 1044. These works differed from earlier books on the art of war by including not only general tactical and strategic precepts, but detailed descriptions and illustrations of weaponry.

At the same time, interest persisted in the older tradition exemplified by works like the *Sun Tzu* and *Wu Chi*; influential commentators on *Sun Tzu*, for example, included Tu Mu (803–852), Mei Yao-ch'en (1002–60) and the late Sung writer Chang Yu, who also wrote a book entitled 'The Biographies of One Hundred Generals'. It was under the Sung, in fact, that the definitive list of military classics was established. Traditionally there are seven of these, attributed to periods ranging from the founding of the Chou before 1000 BC to the reign of T'ang T'ai-tsung. Most of the earlier ones, however, probably achieved roughly their present form in the Han era, and continued to undergo modification and editing until Sung scholars settled on the current versions.

It was in the field of military technology, however, that the most spectacular advances were seen. Stone-throwing artillery, based on a pivoted throwing arm powered by men pulling on ropes, had been in use as early as the Han, but it was under the Sung that it reached the peak of its development, and most of our information is derived from the manuals of that era. Three main types of machine were known. The lightest had its arm mounted on a single column support which could be fitted to a cart or wheeled base; it was therefore mobile enough to accompany the field armies, but could only shoot relatively small projectiles. The other types were fitted to triangular or semi-pyramidal four-legged bases, which were able to cope with greater stresses and so throw heavier missiles. These were often constructed on site for siege work. Although the even heavier Western type of counterweighted trebuchet was not known until the 1270s, these traditional Chinese types could be quite large, with missiles of up to 130lb (59kg) propelled by several hundred men pulling on the ropes. Effective ranges were of the order of 80 to 160 paces.

Sung artillery. A drawing in the *Wu Ching Tsung Yao* of 1044 shows this 'Sitting Tiger' stone-thrower. It is apparently so called because the triangular shape of the base reminded observers of an animal crouching ready to spring. It was powered by men pulling on ropes, and is said to be the most powerful, for its size, of all the Sung engines. By the mid-11th century a primitive bomb, which was made of paper with a gunpowder filling, was in widespread use. (Michael Perry © Osprey Publishing Ltd)

Sung manuals set out precise formulae for the construction of the different types of stone-thrower, with optimum throwing arm dimensions for each weight of projectile. Range and accuracy were less than for the counterweighted type of artillery, but rate of fire was considerably better, so that they were better suited to anti-personnel work – for example clearing defenders from the walls of a besieged town – than to actually battering down fortifications. A new, mobile type of artillery, with a range of 200 paces, was invented in 1176 by an officer who was being besieged by the Kin at Haichow, but it is not clear precisely how this differed from earlier models.

The defenders of towns sometimes used a rather sophisticated form of indirect fire against besiegers, with the machines themselves hidden within the walls and the fall of shot spotted by an observer in a high tower or other vantage point. Missiles were made from stone, terracotta, metal or even ice, but at some time during the early Northern Sung they began to exploit the explosive capabilities of a new discovery – gunpowder.

Apart from simple fire-arrows, which are attested as early as the 4th century BC, the first incendiary weapon used in China was naphtha or Greek Fire, which

The use by the Sung navy of Greek Fire, which is projected from the stern of a ship during a sea battle against the Kin c. 1160. (© Stephen Turnbull)

was introduced from the 'southern seas' – probably by the Arabs – several centuries after its first appearance in the West. 'Flying fire' was used at the siege of Yu-chang in 904, but exactly what this was is unclear; the first definite mention of a naphtha weapon is the 'fierce fire oil' the king of Wu-Yueh offered to the Khitans in 917. This burned on contact with water and was intended mainly for naval use, being squirted onto the water in front of enemy ships by a kind of flamethrower. Wu-Yueh employed it successfully in 919 in a naval battle at Lang-shan Chiang against the rival southern state of Huai-nan, and in 975 Chu Ling-pin, an admiral of the Southern T'ang, was defeated by the Sung on the Yangtze at Chin-ling when a sudden change of wind blew his own oil back onto his fleet. Projectors were also devised to shoot the blazing liquid at the besiegers of cities. The Khitans, however, did not adopt it. They saw no reason to change their successful cavalry tactics, and their Queen Shu-lu is said to have laughed at the idea of 'attacking a country with oil'.

The first surviving mention of gunpowder in the military manuals is in the *Wu Ching Tsung Yao* of 1044, which describes soft-cased bombs thrown by artillery, but a silk banner from Tun-huang, said to originate from the middle of the 10th century, shows that primitive gunpowder devices were already in use at this date. Among the weapons illustrated in this source are a hand-hurled bomb and a fire-lance – a short barrel on the end of a pole, from which flames emerge. This latter weapon was eventually to give rise to the handgun, but at this time it was no more than a close-range flame-projector,

probably with an effect more moral than physical. If the date for the Tun-huang banner is correct, it must have taken a long time to become popular, since fire-lances do not start to appear in manuals and accounts of battle until the early 13th century.

They became particularly associated with the Red Jacket troops of Li Ch'uan, a Shantung warlord who fought alongside both the Sung and the Mongols.

By the 11th century the main function of explosives was as a filling for paper- or bamboo-cased bombs thrown by artillery. The formulae then used for gunpowder were relatively low in saltpetre and only semi-explosive, so that the damage caused by these projectiles was probably due mainly to incendiary rather than blast effects. Eventually this was rectified by increasing the proportion of saltpetre to around 75 per cent, and the true fragmentation bomb, enclosed in an iron casing, appeared. This weapon was known as *chien-t'ien-lei*, or 'heaven-shaking thunder', and is first described in use by the Kin at the siege of the Sung city of Ch'i-chou in 1221, although it is not known whether it was a Kin or a Sung invention. The Kin Official History describes the effects of such a bomb at the siege of K'aifeng in 1232:

> … there was a great explosion … audible for more than a hundred *li* [about 30 miles or 48km] … When hit, even iron armour was pierced through … the attacking soldiers were all blown to bits, not even a trace being left behind.

Each bomb was said to affect 'more than half a *mou*' – an area of about 60 feet square (5.6 metres square). The devices could also be lowered from city walls into the besiegers' earthworks by means of iron chains.

Significant battles of Imperial China

Wei River, 203 BC

During the civil wars with Ch'u, which led to the foundation of the Han dynasty, Han Hsin faced Lung Chu of Ch'u and his Ch'i allies across the Wei River. During the night, Han Hsin ordered his men to fill more than 10,000 sandbags and block the river upstream. He led his army over to the west bank to attack Lung Chu, then pretended to flee. Lung, exclaiming, 'I always knew Han Hsin was a coward!', pursued him back over the Wei, whereupon the Han broke open the temporary dam. Most of the Ch'u army was not able to follow Lung across the rapidly rising river, so he was trapped on the far bank and killed. Lung's Ch'i

OPPOSITE Martial music had a prominent role in early Chinese warfare. This bronze drum from Szechwan is dated to the Western Han period. (British Museum OA 1936.11-18.84)

This cavalryman from the Northern Wei wears lamellar *liang-tang* ('double-faced armour') fastened over the shoulders and down the sides. What appears to be a complete one-piece suit may be intended to represent a combination of the customary front and rear torso-pieces with chaps for the legs. His foreign features suggest that he may be one of the 'iron-clad' Ehrchu who fought against the mutinous Six Garrisons. (British Museum OA 1973.7-26.181)

allies withdrew on seeing this, and the Ch'u fled. Han Hsin followed and captured most of them.

T'ien Shan, 99 BC

A campaign was planned against the Hsiung-nu in the T'ien Shan Mountains, west of Mongolia, utilizing 5,000 Chinese infantry led by Li Ling and a force of cavalry under Liu Po-te. Liu objected to serving under Li, and whether by accident or design the cavalry was sent to the wrong place. Li Ling advanced into the steppes regardless, apparently believing that the Hsiung-nu could be defeated by infantry alone. When he reached the mountains he was surrounded by 30,000 nomad cavalry. Li set up a camp between two mountains, protected by a wagon laager, then deployed his men with spears and shields in the front

Infantry of the Western Han. This spearman, swordsman and crossbowman are derived from the miniature 'terracotta army' from Yang-chia-wan near Sian, which comprises over 2,000 pottery figurines and is believed to date from the early 2nd century BC. (Michael Perry © Osprey Publishing Ltd)

rank and crossbowmen behind. The Hsiung-nu attacked, but the crossbows drove them off, leaving several thousand dead. Li retired towards the Chinese frontier, fighting rearguard actions on the way, but eventually ran short of ammunition. The barbarians ambushed him in a defile near the frontier, blocking the path and rolling rocks down the slopes. Some of the Chinese fled, but Li and the remaining 3,000 fought on, the crossbowmen using cart axles as makeshift spears. After dark Li ordered his men to disperse and break out, but only 400 escaped. Li Ling was captured by the Hsiung-nu.

Kang-chu, 36 BC

Chih Chih, one of several rival claimants for the title of Shan-yu of the Hsiung-nu, set himself up in Kang-chu in Sogdiana, where he antagonized the Han by raiding their allies, the Wu-sun. At the time, the protector general of the Western Regions, Kan Yen-shou, was ill, so his second-in-command, Ch'en T'ang – believing that the threat to the trade routes required immediate action – forged an imperial decree authorizing him to raise troops for a campaign. On his recovery Kan went along with this, and in 36 BC they led 40,000 men west in two separate columns, travelling north and south of the Takla Makan Desert. Chih Chih may have thought that supply problems would prevent the Chinese campaigning so far afield, but on arrival in Sogdiana, Kan and Ch'en took fresh provisions by capturing the livestock which the Sogdians had taken from the Wu Sun.

Chih Chih was occupying a town on the Tu-lai River; outside the earth wall, the stronghold was defended by a wooden palisade sheltering archers, while 100 Sogdian cavalry and 100 infantry were drawn up outside the defences. (Dubs' theory that the infantry were Roman legionaries captured by the Parthians at Carrhae need not be taken seriously.) The cavalry charged the Han army as it made camp nearby, but was beaten off by crossbowmen. The Chinese then advanced, with men carrying 'great shields' in front and spears and crossbows behind. Protected by a barrage of crossbow bolts which drove the defenders from the walls, they drained the moat, then stacked firewood against the palisade and burnt it. That night a Sogdian relief force of 10,000 cavalry appeared and made several charges against the Han camp, but was driven off. Chih Chih, shooting from a tower, was outshot by the crossbowmen. Many of the women of his harem were killed and Chih Chih was wounded. At dawn the Chinese broke into the town. The king's palace was set alight and stormed, and Chih Chih was stabbed to death and beheaded. Kan and Ch'en were pardoned for the crime of falsifying imperial documents, but the court was reluctant to reward them, fearing the consequences of encouraging other officials to undertake such adventures.

Ch'eng-tu, AD 36

After the overthrow of Wang Mang the empire remained in disorder, with several local warlords setting themselves up as independent kings. Kung-sun

Shu, king of Shu in modern Szechwan, blocked the Yangtze gorges with a floating bridge, fortified with towers and supported by defensive works on both banks of the river. A Han fleet using towered warships and rowed assault boats attacked and burnt the bridge and advanced upstream, supporting an overland attack on Ch'eng-tu, Kung-sun's capital. However, the terrain caused delays, and when the Han army arrived outside the city it had only one week's provisions left. It took up position in two widely separated camps while its commander made preparations for a withdrawal. Kung-sun led a sortie out of the city at this point and attacked one of the camps. Liu Shang, in command of the other camp, led an unexpected counter-attack in which Kung-sun was fatally wounded, demoralizing his army. Ch'eng-tu surrendered the next day.

Kuan-tu, AD 200

When Ts'ao Ts'ao faced his rival Yuan Shao in what was described at the time as the 'great crisis of the empire', he was at first driven back by the sheer weight of numbers, and he entrenched himself in a fortified camp at Kuan-tu in north-eastern China. Yuan Shao laid siege to the camp, shooting artillery from towers and an artificial mound. Ts'ao's own stone-throwers replied and gained the advantage, so Yuan tried tunnelling. This also failed because Ts'ao had dug a moat within the fortifications. Both sides were running short of supplies when a defector informed Ts'ao that a large supply train, escorted by 10,000 men, was attempting to rendezvous with Yuan's army. Ts'ao extricated 5,000 horse and foot from his camp by night and intercepted the column, bottling up the escorting troops within their own improvised defences. Yuan Shao meanwhile attacked Ts'ao's camp again, but was still unsuccessful. He also sent a force of cavalry to relieve the supply column, but before it arrived Ts'ao had attacked and captured it. Yuan's army was demoralized by this setback and several of his officers defected. Yuan himself escaped across the Yellow River, leaving behind his baggage and 70,000 casualties.

Hsien-mei, AD 221

Chang Chi, commanding a Wei army, was threatened by several thousand nomad cavalry. The Wei were tired, after several long marches, and their morale suffered when strong winds blew up and they feared that the enemy would take advantage of this to set fire to their camp. Chang, however, deployed 3,000 men in ambush positions under cover of darkness, then sent Ch'eng Kung-yin with 1,000 cavalry to provoke the enemy. The Wei horsemen made a feint attack and then fell back, luring their pursuers into a series of ambushes. The undisciplined

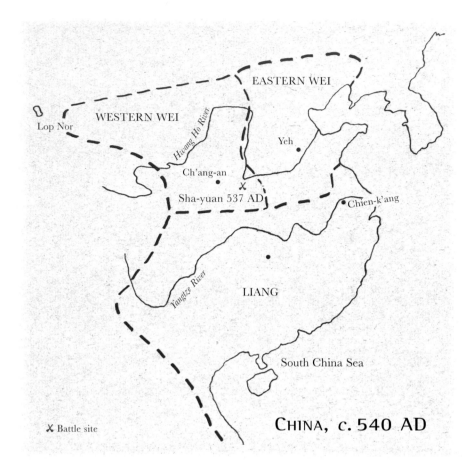

barbarians were hit from front and rear and were massacred. Tens of thousands were captured, along with huge numbers of sheep and cattle.

The siege of Ch'en-ts'ang, AD 229

Chu-ko Liang of Shu besieged the Wei city of Ch'en-ts'ang, held by Hao Chou. Hao rejected a summons to surrender, so the Shu army, which outnumbered the defenders by ten to one, launched an assault using scaling ladders, supported by artillery shooting from wooden towers. The defenders burned the ladders with incendiary missiles, and used millstones swung on ropes to demolish the towers. Chu-ko then filled in the moat and attacked again, but although the outer wall fell, Hao Chou had built another wall inside the original, and this continued to hold. The Shu tried tunnelling, but the Wei dug their own tunnels to intercept them. The city held out for more than 20 days, and by the time a Wei relief force arrived, Chu-ko, short of supplies, had already given up and left.

Fei River, AD 383

By 376 the Former Ch'in dynasty of the Ti warlord Fu Chien had established itself as the leading power in northern China. Fu planned to reunite the empire by conquering the Eastern Ts'in in the south, and raised an enormous army, said to have comprised 600,000 infantry and 360,000 cavalry, including Ti tribesmen, Hsien-pi and Hsiung-nu cavalry and conscripted Chinese infantry. When warned of the difficulties of the campaign and the poor state of training of his heterogenous army, Fu preferred to rely on weight of numbers, saying, 'My army is so huge that if all the men throw their whips into the Yangtze this will suffice to cover it.' However, as they approached the Yangtze valley in separated columns, the cavalry suffered in the unhealthy marshes, and it proved impossible for supply wagons to keep pace. Cavalry and infantry became hopelessly mixed up. The Ts'in forces under Hsieh Hsuan, though greatly outnumbered, ambushed the attackers at various points and concentrated swiftly against isolated units. Some of these were destroyed; others were bribed to retire. The coordination of the Ch'in columns soon broke down, and at the Fei River, Fu Chien ordered a tactical withdrawal. According to one account, the intention was to lure the Ts'in army across the river onto more open ground, but Ts'in agents raised the cry 'Ch'in is defeated!' and panic spread. Fu's army disintegrated in rout; only one Mu-jung Hsien-pi unit withdrew intact, accompanied by Fu and 1,000 cavalry. The Ts'in followed up, and over half the Ch'in force was slaughtered in the pursuit.

Military official, AD 580–620. Another example of the cloaked and helmeted warrior style, from the Northern Chou or Sui. (Victoria and Albert Museum)

Yeh, AD 528

After the Ehrchu, under their chieftain, Jung, had placed their own nominee on the throne of the Wei Empire, they faced an invasion by a huge army, said to have been a million strong, from the mutinous Six Garrisons. The mutineers advanced across the Yellow River plain north of the city of Yeh in a great crescent measuring several miles from tip to tip. Ehrchu Jung had only 7,000 cavalrymen, so he split them into small units to raise dust and make noise in order to conceal their lack of numbers. Then, concentrating them against part of the enemy line, he led a massed charge. The use of swords was forbidden, apparently in order to prevent men breaking ranks to take heads, and the troopers were issued with a weapon called *shen-pang*, to be held beside the horse. Unfortunately the nature of this weapon is not entirely clear; it has been suggested that it was an early example of the use of the couched lance, but the name translates as 'miraculous cudgel', so it may have been a type of mace. The

Ehrchu broke right through the mutineers and wheeled to come at them from the rear, routing them and capturing their commander.

Sha-yuan, AD 537

During the wars following the collapse of the Northern Wei, the successor state of Eastern Wei sent an advanced guard in three columns through the T'ong Pass to attack Western Wei. The Western army, under Yu-wen T'ai, concentrated against one column and defeated it; the others then retreated. Yu-wen followed up, only to run into the main Eastern army, which was alleged to number 200,000. The Westerners were pushed back through the pass, but as the Eastern army emerged from the mountains it was unexpectedly charged in the flank by 10,000 Western cavalry, and 6,000 Easterners were killed and 70,000 captured. This was the most celebrated victory in a series of attacks and counter-attacks through the Tong Pass which lasted until 542.

Huo-i, AD 617

During Li Yuan's march from T'ai-yuan to the Sui capital, the 30,000-strong T'ang army faced a Sui force under Sung Lao-sheng. Li's sons, Li Chien-ch'eng and Li Shih-min, each commanded a wing of the army, which included 500 warriors supplied by the Turkish Qaghan. Provoked by a detachment of T'ang cavalry, Sung Lao-sheng ordered a mass charge, which was at first successful; Li Chien-ch'eng was unhorsed, and the T'ang fell back in some disarray. However, Sung's advance exposed the flank and rear of his army to the elite 'iron-clad' T'ang cavalry, under the command of Li Shih-min, who was waiting in a concealed position. He led a counter-attack which broke through into the enemy's rear, while the T'ang main body rallied and attacked them frontally. Sung Lao-sheng was captured and his army crushed.

Mount Ta-fei, AD 670

A T'ang army, said to be 100,000 strong, was sent under Hsieh Jen-kuei to expel the Tibetans from the Tarim Basin. Hsieh left 20,000 men with his subordinate Kuo Tai-feng on Mount Ta-fei, instructing Kuo to build two palisades to protect the baggage train, while Hsieh himself pressed on to the Chi-shih River. There he surprised and defeated a force of Tibetans, apparently not realizing that this was not the enemy main body. Kuo had disobeyed the order to erect palisades, and when summoned to join Hsieh he brought the baggage with him. On the way he was attacked by 200,000 Tibetans under Mgar Khri-brin, who captured the Chinese supply train. Hsieh was forced to fall back to Mount Ta-fei, but was

Pottery figures from the T'ang dynasty. The military official on the right wearing fabric *liang-tang* armour and a hat with characteristic bird of prey motif, comes from the tomb of Liu T'ing-hsun, who died in AD 728. In the centre is an armoured 'lokapala' or tomb guardian figure. (British Museum OA 1936.10-12.220-9)

quickly overwhelmed by the pursuing Tibetans. Thus was the Tibetan occupation of the Tarim Basin secured.

Kao Yu, AD 685

The rebel leader Li Ching-yeh was defending the Hsia Ah Creek in Kiangsu against a T'ang army coming from the north under Li Hsiao-i. Five thousand imperial soldiers attempted to cross the creek in boats at night, but the defenders' best troops were waiting on the far bank and drove them off. Many were drowned. Wei Yuan-chung, a court official attached to the T'ang army to oversee the military commanders, then proposed a plan, which Li Hsiao-i adopted. As the wind was blowing from the north, the dry reeds along the creek were set on fire, and the government forces crossed while the enemy was blinded by the thick smoke. Li Ching-yeh had by this time withdrawn his elite fighters into reserve and replaced them with 'old and weary' men, who broke when the T'ang troops closed with them. The reserves were rushed to the front line, but arrived too late to stop the rout. More than 7,000 rebels were killed in the fighting, while others were driven into the creek and drowned.

The siege of Shih-pao, AD 745–749

The stronghold of Shih-pao, high in the Red Hills near the Koko Nor Lake, had been held by the Tibetans since 741, and was a serious obstacle to any T'ang invasion of the Tarim Basin. Emperor Hsuan-tsung therefore ordered that it be taken at all costs. In 745 Huang-fu Wei-ming attacked the fortress, but failed and was disgraced, as was his successor, Wang Chung-ssu. Chinese armies found the conditions at this high altitude very difficult – especially in winter, when they were virtually immobilized and were forced to watch helplessly while Tibetan cavalry rode in to reinforce the garrison and harvest the grain the besiegers had sown during the summer. T'ang losses were very heavy, and the Koko Nor region became notorious for the thousands of skeletons that lay unburied in the vicinity. Eventually command was given to a Turk in T'ang service, Qosu Khan, who in 749 launched an all-out attack with 63,000 men. After days of fighting no progress had been made, so Qosu threatened to execute his subordinate officers unless the city was taken. Desperate, they promised to do it within three days. Half the army is said to have been killed in the ensuing series of assaults, but Shih-pao finally fell within the time limit. Inside, the Chinese found a Tibetan general and a mere 400 soldiers.

T'ong Pass, AD 756

The rebel army of An Lu-shan, trying to reach Ch'ang-an, was halted at the T'ong Pass by Qosu Khan, the victor of Shih-pao, with 180,000 T'ang troops. Other T'ang armies were closing in on the rebels from several directions, but the emperor ordered Qosu to leave his impregnable position in the pass and attack at once. The experienced general at first refused, but the emperor – advised by Qosu's rival Yang Kuo-chung – insisted. The T'ang army advanced, but was ambushed by the rebel commander Ts'ui Ch'ien-yu in a narrow defile between the mountains and the Yellow River. With his army disintegrating Qosu fought on, trying to organize a last-ditch defence, but he was surrounded by the rebels and his own officers forced him to surrender. This unnecessary disaster allowed Ts'ui Ch'ien-yu to storm through the pass and take Ch'ang-an.

Ting-hsien, AD 945

A Khitan invasion of northern China was opposed by the Later Chin under Fu Yen-ch'ing, who pinned the enemy by advancing in the centre with his main body of infantry, while concentrating 10,000 Sha-t'o cavalry against one flank.

T'ang dynasty tomb model of a horse, unglazed, but with traces of pigment. (Topfoto)

The Khitan army was routed, and their emperor escaped in a cart pulled by camels. This proved not to be fast enough, and he transferred ignominiously to a riding camel. Many horses and weapons were captured by the Chin.

Pei-chou, AD 1048

The *Mi-le-chou* rebels under Wang Tse were besieged by Sung forces in the city of Pei-chou. Dissidents within the city allowed the imperial troops inside the walls, but the rebels drove them out again. Conventional siege operations also failed disastrously: Wang's men burnt the Sung siege engines, and when the besiegers threw up a huge rampart to overlook the defences, that too was set on fire. After a month the Sung commander was replaced by a court official, Wen Yen-po, who adopted different tactics. A tunnel was dug under the city wall, and one night 200 besiegers – gagged to prevent them making any unnecessary noise – entered Pei-chou secretly by this route, overcame the guards on the walls, and let down ropes for the rest of the army to climb up. A ferocious battle raged in the streets for the next 24 hours, until superior Sung numbers began to tell. Wang Tse then released oxen with blazing tow tied to their tails, which stampeded into the government soldiers and caused panic. The rebels followed up and began to gain ground, but Wen committed special penal units which met the animals with a hail of missiles and forced them back, disordering their own side. Seeing the failure of his last-ditch ploy, Wang fled.

Hsiang-yang, AD 1207

The frontier city of Hsiang-yang on the Han River was held for the Sung by Chao Shun. A force of Jurchen Kin cavalry blockaded it, so Chao sent out 1,000 men to drive them off, which they did successfully. However, the Kin soon returned, and on the 25th day of the siege a larger sortie was planned. Two Sung officers led more than 30 boats, carrying a total of 1,000 crossbowmen, 500 spearmen and 100 drummers across the river to the Jurchen camp under cover of darkness. The expedition was also equipped with fire arrows and explosive 'thunderclap bombs'. Reaching the river bank beneath the enemy camp undetected, the Sung attacked with repeated volleys of missiles, supported by artillery on the city walls. The Kin horses panicked, and their army was driven off in confusion. The Sung troops then withdrew, having suffered no casualties. Later a Chinese prisoner who had escaped from the Jurchen returned to Hsiang-yang with the information that the enemy had been surprised when asleep, and had lost 2,000–3,000 men and 800 horses.

Huan-erh-tsui, AD 1211

Chinggis Khan, invading the Kin Empire, was opposed by an army said to number up to 500,000 men, under Ke-shih-lieh Chih-chung. The Kin army consisted of Jurchen and Khitan cavalry as well as large numbers of Chinese infantry. Chih-chung rejected advice to strike quickly with his cavalry while the Mongols were grazing their horses after crossing the Gobi Desert, preferring instead to advance slowly so that his infantry could keep up. However, he declined to wait for a second Kin army to reinforce him.

The opposing armies met at Huan-erh-tsui, north of the passes leading to Chung-tu. Chih-chung deployed his cavalry in line in front of the infantry, but the Mongols attacked them with arrows, followed by a charge by their left wing. The Kin cavalry recoiled, colliding with their Chinese infantry and throwing both lines into confusion – 'men and horses trampling each other down in the rout and the dead being without number'. The whole army broke and was pursued through the passes, leaving the route to Chung-tu open.

PART III

The Yüan dynasty

In 1260, when Kubilai came to power, the Mongols had been fighting in China for over 40 years; Kubilai himself had commanded armies in the region since 1251, and the following year consolidated his reputation with a campaign that outflanked the Sung by capturing Ta-li, an independent kingdom in the remote and mountainous south-west. In 1257 he led one of a number of attacks that failed to break through the Sung defences, and in 1259 his brother Mongke, Great Khan of the Mongols, died on the western borders of China. Instead of attending the traditional council to choose a new khan, Kubilai, who relied heavily on Chinese troops and was increasingly influenced by their culture, had himself proclaimed ruler by his own army at Shang-tu. A rival claimant, Arik Boke, took Mongolia and launched an invasion of northern China, but was defeated by Kubilai at Simultu in 1261. For seven years Kubilai therefore ruled, from his base in China, an empire extending as far as Siberia, Poland and Syria. In 1268, however, another Mongol prince, Kaidu, led a revolt that caused the effective breakup of this vast realm, and although Kubilai remained nominally Great Khan his power in practice extended only over the conquered regions of China and part of Mongolia. In 1271 he proclaimed himself the first emperor of a new Chinese dynasty, the 'Yüan' or 'Origin'.

Meanwhile, war continued on two fronts. A series of raids and skirmishes with Kaidu's supporters made the Central Asian frontier a perpetual drain on manpower and resources, but the emperor's first priority remained the completion of his task in China. As early as 1260 he had offered the Sung autonomy if they would recognize him as 'Son of Heaven', and his policy of adopting Chinese culture and encouraging surrender with good treatment is often regarded as an enlightened change from the brutal tradition of his Mongol predecessors. Nevertheless, he could revert to old-fashioned severity if he considered it necessary: 20,000 rebels were executed in one incident in 1281, and according to Marco Polo the entire population of Chang-chow was put to death in retaliation for the murder of some soldiers. However, as the only power that seemed capable of bringing peace to the country, the Yüan continued to receive a steady flow of defectors from the Sung.

Kubilai unites China

The war resumed in earnest in 1265, when Kubilai's forces won a major battle at Tiao-yu Shan in Szechwan, capturing warships that became the nucleus of a Yüan river fleet. The twin cities of Hsiang-yang and Fanch'eng, which had denied access via the Han River to the lower Yangtze, fell in 1272, and four years later the Sung capital surrendered to the Mongol general Bayan. Sung die-hards fell back towards the east coast, keeping up the struggle from offshore islands;

PREVIOUS PAGE Two cavalrymen of the Yüan dynasty are attacked by Red Turbans c. 1350. (© Stephen Turnbull)

but a fleet under Fu Shou-keng defected to Kubilai, and in March 1279 the Sung navy was defeated at Yaishan. The young Sung emperor was drowned, and Kubilai found himself the first ruler of a united China since the T'ang.

Yet victory did not bring peace. Apart from the ongoing troubles in Central Asia, the Chinese found themselves embroiled in a series of attempts by Kubilai to extend his rule even further, involving expeditions to Japan (1274 and 1281), Champa and Annam in what is now Vietnam (1283 and 1287), Burma (1275) and Java (1293). None of these was very successful, and most incurred heavy losses from a combination of native resistance, disease and natural disasters. In addition the Yüan had to deal with internal revolts in China, which broke out in many places immediately after the fall of the Sung. Another threat was the revolt of the Mongol Nayan in 1287, requiring the deployment to Manchuria of Chinese as well as Mongol troops. In 1285 Tibet rebelled, not being pacified for five years; even then it remained a source of unrest, requiring constant punitive expeditions as late as 1354. Despite Kubilai's personal moderation his regime was an oppressive one, based on discrimination against the native Chinese; economic mismanagement was rife, combined with a lack of centralized control which enabled dissent to spread. The result was that unlike the Sung, who had kept their troops on the frontiers, the Yüan were forced to use theirs as an army of occupation, stationing units in every province.

After Kubilai's death the overseas ventures ceased, but the northern frontier remained troublesome, while the Chinese underground resistance flourished. In

Although illustrating an incident from the career of Mahmud of Ghazni, this picture from Rashid al-Din's world history, made in Ilkhanid Persia around 1310, shows warriors in contemporary Mongol armour. It is also one of the best medieval illustrations of the counterweight trebuchet or *Hsiang-yang p'ao* introduced into China by the Yüan and operated, as here, by Arab engineers. (Edinburgh University Library, OR Ms. 20)

1308 the government banned the Buddhist White Lotus Society, which subsequently became the most formidable of the secret anti-Mongol groups, and in 1315 the first of a series of major rebellions broke out. Plague (probably imported by Kubilai's armies from Burma), famine and natural disasters added to the regime's problems – census results show a steep decline in population under the Yüan, although it is not clear how much of this was due to tax evasion and the breakdown of authority. The bubonic plague epidemic between 1351 and 1354, however, may have halved the population in some areas; 50 per cent mortality is recorded among troops in the Huai valley. The Mongol elite, always a tiny minority in China, increasingly devoted their energies to feuding with each

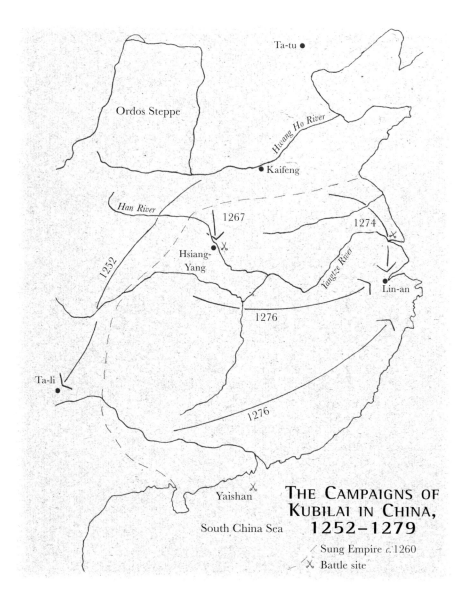

THE CAMPAIGNS OF
KUBILAI IN CHINA,
1252–1279

/ Sung Empire *c.* 1260

/✗ Battle site

other, while under a succession of weak emperors the government continued to pour China's wealth into the Central Asian garrisons and increasing numbers of unproductive Tibetan monks. In 1351 an army of peasants assembled for flood-control work broke out in what became known as the Red Turban revolt, a movement which was not to end until the Yüan were swept from power.

The Yüan army

The Mongol army that proclaimed Kubilai in 1260, and that provided the basis of his power throughout his reign, was in origin a *Tamma* or frontier army, created specifically for the task of conquering China by drafting a proportion of the strength of each Mongol tribe. As was their custom these Mongols fought as mounted archers, but lack of numbers and the unsuitability of this tactic for fighting in the broken terrain and walled cities of China had obliged them to make extensive use of native auxiliaries.

At first the khan's forces were a conglomeration of private armies led by Mongol princes and local warlords without proper central administration; his efforts to introduce a Chinese-style bureaucracy were at first unpopular with

Detail from a Ming dynasty painting showing a Mongol horse-archer in summer dress. (Victoria and Albert Museum, no E33-1964)

161

both peoples, but after the rebellion in 1262 of Li T'an, a Shantung warlord, the Chinese commanders were brought under Kubilai's direct control and their troops incorporated into a new formal organization. The *Yüan Shih*, the official history of the dynasty, describes the army as made up of four elements: the *Meng-ku Chun* or Mongol army was composed of Mongol cavalry units under the emperor's control, in contrast to the *T'an-ma-ch'ih Chun* or *Tamma* army, formed from the followings of semi-independent Mongol lords. The five clans known as the *t'ou-hsia*, for example, seem to have fought for the Yüan as allies under their own leaders. Mongol units were theoretically organized according to their traditional decimal system into *toumans* of 10,000 and *minghans* of 1,000, commanded by officers with the Chinese titles of *Wan-hu* and *Ch'ien-hu* respectively; but in practice Yüan *toumans* varied in strength between 3,000 and 7,000, being divided into *minghans* of correspondingly small size. A *minghan* was further divided into ten companies, each led by a *Po-hu*. The term *i*, or wing, was used under the Yüan and early Ming for a military unit of any size.

All Mongol males between the ages of 15 and 70 were liable to serve, forming a hereditary military caste; but this system, which had worked well on the steppes, was a failure in China. As nomads they had been able to make the transition between peace and war without much difficulty, but to those in China, forced by lack of pasture to become farmers, the call-up caused great hardship. They no longer kept large horse herds and often had to buy animals or arrange to have them requisitioned by the state; China was mostly unsuitable for horse-breeding, and imports from Mongolia and Korea were never sufficient. Therefore by the early 14th century many Mongols could not afford even to travel to join the army, and their military potential was seriously weakened.

The third element of the army was the *Han Chun*, comprising the troops from northern China, including not only ethnic Chinese but Khitans, Jurchens, Koreans and Tibetans. Conscription had been introduced in the conquered areas as early as 1235, based on hereditary military families who had to find replacements when soldiers died, but extra mass levies could be raised in emergencies. The troops were organized according to the Mongol system, which in fact had much in common with that of the Jurchens, already in use under the Kin dynasty. Many had originally been cavalry, but by the 1260s it was becoming policy to retain them mainly as infantry, leaving the Mongols to provide the mounted element of the army, and Chinese cavalry units were sometimes ordered to hand over their horses to Mongols.

The captured Sung forces were formed into the fourth element, the *Hsin-fu Chun* or 'Newly-Adhered Army'. This was almost exclusively infantry and artillery and was regarded as the least reliable part of the armed forces, being placed wherever possible under Mongolian or northern Chinese officers. *Hsin-fu* soldiers were also incorporated into the standard organization but it is likely that

Thought to have been manufactured in northern China in the late 13th century, this silver-decorated helmet was probably worn by a Yüan officer. A fabric neckguard, possibly reinforced with internal iron plates, was originally attached. (By permission of the Board of Trustees of the Royal Armouries, XXVIA.192)

many units in the early period retained the Sung system. A late Sung commentator on the *Sun Tzu* describes a rather idealized table of organization according to which an 'army' of 3,200 men is made up of two sub-units, each progressively divided into two, down to a 'platoon' of five sections of ten men each. A section consists of two squads of five, each made up of a 'pair' and a 'trio'. This suggests that a squad may have contained men with different weapons, perhaps three spearmen and two archers, but another Sung source condemns the practice of mixing close-combat and missile weapons. Chinese infantry fought with either spears and halberds or bows and crossbows, the bow probably being the most popular weapon. It is significant that when, in 1289, Kubilai wished to make the people of Chiang-nan incapable of further rebellion, he prohibited the possession of bows. Civilians had always been discouraged from using crossbows, and although widely used by regular troops they would have been much less common among peasant rebels.

The Yüan army contained other units, often temporary, which did not fit into this system – e.g. the *T'ung-shih Chun*, Mongol mercenaries captured fighting for the Sung and incorporated into Kubilai's forces in 1279; and the *Kan-t'ao-lu* or 'looters', independent bands of Chinese that had accompanied the conquerors in search of profit. Notoriously inefficient, these latter discredited the Yüan when defeated, and if victorious ruined conquered provinces by plundering and enslaving the people; in 1274 Kubilai disbanded them and drafted their troops into regular units. Specialist units included the *P'ao Chun* or 'Artillery Army', and

Cavalry of the Yüan period, c. 1260. This encounter between a Chinese and a Mongol cavalryman illustrates examples of the respective armour styles of the two peoples. Either, however, could be found fighting for or against the Yüan or even the Ming. (David Sque © Osprey Publishing Ltd)

OPPOSITE This early-15th-century presentation sword is a rare surviving example of the Ming armourers' art. The hilt is gilded, and the scabbard of wood covered in green leather and lined with red silk. (The Board of Trustees of the Royal Armouries no. XXVIS. 295)

Nu Chun or 'Crossbow Army'. The aboriginal peoples of southern China and Ta-li also provided contingents, most of which were used in their home provinces for fear that they might desert if moved far away. The so-called Miao Army, however, raised from other related peoples as well as from the Miao tribe, was used in the Yangtze valley in the 1350s, where it garrisoned the cities of Hangchow and Soochow. Other tribes, particularly the She, were unreliable and often rebelled. Marco Polo describes some of these tribal troops as riding with long stirrups, unlike the Mongols, wearing armour of buffalo hide and fighting with spears, shields and crossbows shooting poisoned bolts. A dozen elephants, or possibly more, were acquired as tribute from Burma, but the only mention of an elephant in battle in a Yüan army is as a mount for Kubilai himself.

The Imperial Guard

Separate from the rest of the army was the *Su-wei* or Imperial Guard based in the capital, which was not simply a palace bodyguard but the emperor's private army. Guardsmen, either conscripted or drafted from other units, were regarded as of higher quality than the provincial troops, so that they grew steadily in numbers as the regime came to rely more heavily on them. In 1260 Kubilai's guard numbered 6,500 but by 1352 there were more than 100,000, although by then their quality and training had declined and they were beginning to be replaced by Chinese mercenaries. The force was divided into *wei* or guard units of varying strength, of which 34 were established between 1271 and 1337. Most *wei* were recruited from a single ethnic group, sometimes Mongols, Manchurians or Koreans, but more often Chinese or *Se-mu*. The latter term covered troops from the central and western parts of the Mongol Empire, including Kipchaq Turks from the Caspian region, Alans from the Caucasus and even a unit of *Wo-lo-ssu* or Russians, formed by the Emperor Toq Temur in 1330. The Chinese *wei* fought as infantry and the others mostly as cavalry; the *Yüan Shih* describes all the guards as 'carrying quivers and bowcases', but this may be an archaic formula for soldiers generally rather than an accurate description. The old Mongol *Keshig*, the bodyguard of the early khans, survived in Yüan China as a mainly bureaucratic and educational institution, although its members could fight in emergencies.

Yüan generals were conscious of the suitability of the different contingents of the army for different tactical roles, and regularly selected them according to the task in hand. A commander ordered to lead a force in mountainous territory, for example, would request the addition of infantry from the *Han Chun* to supplement his Mongol horsemen. The *Hsin-fu* troops were more experienced in naval operations and so were deployed in coastal areas and on overseas expeditions (although the first invasion of Japan in 1274, undertaken before the fall of the Sung, used mostly Mongols, northern Chinese and Koreans). Most importantly, the Mongols had to rely on Chinese or Muslim engineers for their siege artillery. Muslims from the west were skilled in this work, but the Yüan seldom trusted them with military command, partly because most were prisoners of war. The 'Newly-Adhered' troops had the advantage of being familiar with gunpowder, already in use in explosive bombs; an accidental explosion in the arsenal at Wei-yang in 1280 was attributed to the employment of inexperienced northerners instead of ex-Sung men. Garrisons were provided mainly by Mongols in the north and Chinese in the Yangtze delta, while the rest of the south was less firmly held, depending on local

165

The processional ways leading to the tombs of Chinese emperors were often guarded by large carved figures. This statue from the massive tomb complex of the Yung Lo Emperor and his successors outside Peking, represents a military official in the elaborate armour typical of the Ming period. (© Stephen Turnbull)

levies. On occasion, however, commanders in the south would request Mongol reinforcements if trouble was expected, in the same way as men from the *Han Chun* would be sent to the coast to stiffen the *Hsin-fu* units. Garrisons along the frontier with Central Asia and Tibet were mainly Mongolian, supported by non-combatant Chinese agricultural colonists; military-agricultural colonies were set up in many areas, the intention being that the soldiers would save the state the cost of feeding them. Although this did not work well in practice, Kubilai's successful strategy against Kaidu involved denying him the use of advanced grazing grounds in the Ordos loop of the Hwang Ho by encouraging irrigation and agriculture there.

Wide discrepancies between theoretical and actual strengths of units make it difficult to estimate the total size of the Yüan armed forces, and in fact this information was kept strictly secret at the time, but there can be little doubt that they were very large by contemporary standards. In Hangchow alone, admittedly the largest city of the empire and in a region that was particularly tightly controlled, there were 30,000 men stationed, and the total of garrisoned towns and cities ran into hundreds. Expeditionary forces were often between 10,000 and 30,000 strong, but in some cases much larger armies were amassed. Ninety *toumans* were deployed in China in 1259, and this figure does not include the Chinese troops who probably outnumbered the Mongols. Some 50,000 levies were raised for the siege of Hsiang-yang in 1268, and in 1283, 83,600 *Hsin-fu* soldiers were in service. The 360,000 quoted by Marco Polo for the campaign of 1287 could thus be of the correct order of magnitude, but we must bear in mind the logistical problems of moving and supporting such a host in the arid frontier regions. A Ming expedition of 1422, for instance, numbering 235,000 men, required 117,000 wagons and 340,000 pack donkeys, a collection of animals which would have rapidly exhausted the available grazing.

The Civil Wars, 1351–68

In 1351 prophecies of the return of a descendant of the Sung emperors spread by the White Lotus Society encouraged the growth of the anti-Yüan Red Turban movement out of the cooperation of several insurgent peasant armies. In the following year the rebels defeated the Miao army at I-feng Bridge, but were unable to dislodge it from Hangchow, and so turned their attention to the north. They made several incursions into the Hwang Ho plain between 1352 and 1359, at one point taking K'aifeng and proclaiming a restored Sung dynasty. Much of the early success of the rebels was due to the Yüan's failure to maintain city walls, or even to repair the breaches made in their own conquest 80 years earlier – a reflection of their contempt for fortification and mistrust of the urban

The Red Turban revolt, c. 1350. The Red Turbans would have differed at first from the mass of peasantry only by their adoption of red headgear. The rebel here is unarmed and relies on martial arts techniques disseminated by the secret societies. Some authorities believe that the high kicks for which northern Chinese unarmed combat styles are famous were originally developed as a counter to Mongol cavalry who rode with very short stirrups and were easily unseated by a hard blow. (David Sque © Osprey Publishing Ltd)

populace. The government, weakened by internal dissension, was more than once on the verge of crushing the rebels but abandoned the campaign without achieving final victory. Mongol warlords set up their own virtually independent states; and although the Red Turbans were eventually suppressed in 1363, they had distracted the Yüan long enough to ensure that it would never regain its grip on the south. In the Yangtze valley, as central authority collapsed, rebel armies and the forces of local officials set up a number of independent states. Most important of these were a revived Sung Empire at Hanyang in the south-west, Chou in the far south, Wu on the coast south of the lower Yangtze and Han on the middle reaches of that river. Sandwiched between the latter two were the lands of Kuo Tzu-hsing, one of the original Red Turban leaders.

Kuo died in 1355 and was succeeded by Chu Yuan-chang, who had once been a beggar but had risen quickly through the ranks of Kuo's army. Early in the following year Chu defeated a Yüan river fleet at Ts'ai-shih and took the city of Chin-ling, which he fortified as a base. He then fought several battles with the Miao army but failed to take Hangchow, which fell to his more powerful neighbour, Chang Shih-cheng of Wu. By 1360 the Yüan had been driven out of the lower Yangtze valley and Chu found himself surrounded by his fellow warlords, who were mostly content to hold the territories they had taken. This

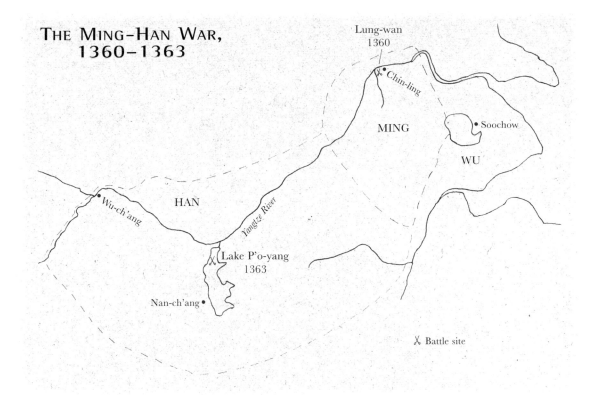

enabled Chu to build up his forces in peace, and to pursue a policy of appealing to the common people by storing grain for famine relief and forbidding his troops to plunder. Soon he felt strong enough to take on his rivals.

It is surprising to find that the armies of these rebel states had quickly attained a high level of sophistication. Although short of cavalry they were far from mere peasant mobs, and deployed massive fleets of ships and hundreds of artillery pieces, including cannon. Much of this material was taken over from Yüan units, but even so it suggests that the country had not been as ruined economically as is often thought. The reasons for the success of Chu's forces, however, lie not in superior technology but in superior leadership, and in particular the strict discipline of the army.

The Ming–Han War

In 1360 the more populous kingdom of Han under Ch'en Yu-liang, which dominated the Yangtze with a fleet of several hundred ships, woke up to the threat posed by Chu and moved to eliminate him. The ensuing conflict is usually known as the Ming–Han War, although strictly speaking it is anachronistic to refer to Chu's state as the Ming, a title it did not take until later.

This Ming tomb figurine wears an elaborate suit of armour very similar to those of the larger statues at the imperial tombs. (British Museum, G Eumorfopoulos collection, OA + 530)

The Han attempted to take Chin-ling by an amphibious assault but were defeated at Lung-wan; in the following year, using ships captured in the battle, the Ming won another victory on the Yangtze. Early in 1363 Ch'en raised an army, allegedly of 600,000 men, and sent it down the river in a new fleet of enormous warships (described by their awestruck enemies as 'like mountains') to besiege Nan-ch'ang on Lake P'o-yang. A Ming army of 100,000 sailed to raise the siege, defeating the Han in a decisive battle on the lake by the use of fireships and superior mobility. Naval warfare is unfortunately outside the scope of this book, but it is interesting to note that the fleets deployed very much as if for a land battle, with the largest ships in the centre and the lighter and faster vessels on the wings; and that the Han tried to close with and board the smaller Ming craft, relying on hand-to-hand fighting and close-range missiles. At the end of the battle Ch'en was killed by an arrow, and the following year his son surrendered to Chu.

Chang Shih-cheng of Wu, who had foolishly refused an alliance with Han, was the next victim. In 1365 his army was broken by a Ming cavalry charge at the relief of Hsin-ch'eng, and in October 1367 his capital, Soochow, fell after a ten-month siege; 250,000 Wu troops were drafted into the Ming army. A month later Chu ordered the simultaneous conquest of the rest of China. A fleet sailed down the coast and up the Si River, receiving the surrender of the states of Sung and Chou, while the general Hsu Ta led 250,000 men in a two-pronged attack on K'aifeng. By now the Yüan were in complete disarray, and in September 1368, almost unopposed, Hsu entered Ta-tu, now renamed Pei-ping ('The North is Pacified'). The Emperor Toghon Temur fled back to Mongolia, and Chu Yuan-chang was proclaimed the first emperor of the 'Ming', or 'Brilliant', dynasty. It is symptomatic of the shift of wealth and power from north to south during the medieval period that, for the first time in Chinese history, a power based in the Yangtze valley had been able to unify the country, reversing the north's political dominance.

The Ming dynasty

The capture of Ta-tu did not bring the war to an end, as while the Yüan emperor and many of his Mongol followers had escaped, remaining a threat to China's northern provinces, the new regime was determined to take over the whole of the Yüan Empire including the Central Asian provinces. Shensi and Kansu in the north-west were secured after a victory over a Mongol army at Ting-hsi in 1370, and in the following year the Shu state in Szechwan was conquered; but in 1372 an army under Hsu Ta was decisively beaten in Mongolia near Karakorum. This ended the Ming dream of ruling a steppe empire; but security on the northern frontier continued to be maintained by an aggressive policy, with fortified garrisons pushed well forward beyond the boundary of settled agriculture. The strategic key to the security of northern China against nomad invasion was the Ordos steppe, and, just as Kubilai had done, the new emperor denied it to his enemies by encouraging irrigation projects to make it suitable for settlement by Chinese. In 1387 the expeditions into Mongolia resumed, culminating in a battle at Lake Buyur in which the Ming general Lan Yu trapped a nomad army against the shore of the lake and annihilated it, but in 1398 the death of the emperor brought the northern war once again to a temporary halt.

The Hung Wu Emperor's strong centralized rule had been in many ways a blessing for China, despite the paranoia that marred his later years; but he had made the mistake of granting huge semi-independent fiefs to his relatives, the Imperial Princes, and permitting them to raise private armies. The result was

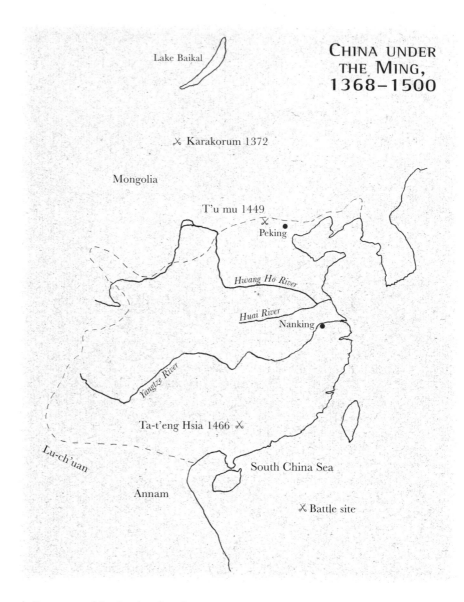

CHINA UNDER
THE MING,
1368–1500

Lake Baikal

Karakorum 1372

Mongolia

T'u mu 1449

Peking

Hwang Ho River

Huai River

Nanking

Yangtze River

Ta-t'eng Hsia 1466

Lu-ch'uan

South China Sea

Annam

Battle site

civil war on his death; the throne passed to his grandson, the cultured and unwarlike Chien-wen Emperor, who was soon challenged by his uncle, the prince of Yen. At this time the Ming capital was still at Chin-ling, now Nanking, while the prince's power base was in the north around Pei-ping, so most of the fighting was concentrated on the plain between the Hwang Ho and Yangtze, and in particular the vital Grand Canal by which grain was transported to the north.

The rebel army began with about 100,000 men, a third of the strength of the imperial forces, but the northerners were stronger in cavalry and more accustomed to the harsh winters of this theatre than those from the south. On the other hand the emperor seems at first to have had a monopoly of gunpowder

Ming troops, c. 1400.
Shown here, left to right,
are a halberdier, standard
bearer and handgunner.
(David Sque © Osprey
Publishing Ltd)

weapons. In May 1400 the prince won a victory at Pao-ting, but for nearly two years the struggle swayed back and forth along the canal. Then in January 1402 the prince, employing large numbers of Mongol horsemen, advanced on Nanking. Although beaten several times in the field he repeatedly outmanoeuvred his opponents, helped by the emperor's mistrust of his best general, Hsu Hui-tsu. In June the rebels reached the Yangtze and crossed with the aid of a defecting imperial fleet; a month later the gates of Nanking were opened by sympathizers and the city was taken after fierce street-fighting, in

Detail of the sword hilt and scabbard fittings of one of the statues from Peking. (© Stephen Turnbull)

which the emperor was killed. The prince, ascending the throne as the Yung Lo Emperor, quickly restored the aggressive policies of the Hung Wu reign, beginning with a brutal purge of his opponents in which thousands died.

One of the first acts of the new ruler was to move the capital to Pei-ping, once again renamed Peking ('Northern Capital'). This placed the emperor nearer the vital northern frontier, but involved the empire in enormous disruption and expense, the necessary fortification work dragging on into the 1440s. He rewarded his supporters by creating a new military aristocracy, but did not allow them to raise their own armies or to forge close links with individual units by remaining too long in one place. The fiefs of the imperial princes were abolished.

At first the aim was to secure peace in the north by diplomacy, settling loyal Mongol tribes within the empire to form a buffer zone, and the garrisons on the steppe were pulled back to more defensible positions. At the same time a policy of expansion was adopted in the south; Annam was invaded in 1406 and turned into a province, but the natives carried on a guerrilla war which drained Chinese resources and led to several defeats before the province was abandoned in 1427. Between 1405 and 1433 the eunuch Cheng Ho was sent on seven long-distance sea voyages with fleets said to have carried as many as 70,000 men. The aim was diplomatic rather than military, but Ming forces did intervene in succession disputes in Java, Sumatra and Ceylon. States on the Malay Peninsula and in Indonesia accepted nominal Chinese overlordship, and on his longest voyage Cheng Ho crossed the Indian Ocean to the coasts of Arabia and Africa.

The north was not at peace for long, however, as a new tribal grouping, the Oirat Mongols, began to launch raids from beyond the settled buffer zone. The emperor personally led five expeditions into Mongolia between 1410 and 1424 with the intention of breaking up the Mongol confederation and punishing the raiders; all won battles, but none was decisive due to the difficulty of pursuing the mobile horsemen. On the last campaign the Yung Lo Emperor died, bringing to a close this new phase of offensive warfare.

Ming decline

After the Yung Lo reign, although the empire remained a formidable military power, the numbers and efficiency of Ming armies began to decline. The story of this decline is often repeated in discussions of the Ming, but for our period at least it should not be over-emphasized: Chinese forces were on balance successful against their enemies until a defensive mentality really took hold from the 1540s onwards. The main problems were cultural and economic.

Chinese society had drifted away from warlike pursuits under the Sung, and the military ethos of the early Ming emperors was not shared by most of their educated subjects. Troops had therefore to be raised by forming families into an hereditary military caste with an obligation to serve; unlike the feudal obligation of the European nobility this carried little social status, often involved great hardship, and was evaded where possible. Chinese generals had long been accustomed to use their men as labourers when not on campaign, which was detrimental to morale. This situation was made worse by the environment in which many units were deployed, for while the Yüan had been prepared to tax China to support the garrisons on the steppe, the Ming emperors were

Restored in the same style as the 15th-century original, the impressive architecture of the Forbidden City in Peking illustrates the style of early Ming buildings. (© Stephen Turnbull)

determined to make them pay for themselves as agricultural colonies. This, through a combination of the harsh climate and the inexperience of the men, never worked properly, and eventually incentives had to be introduced to persuade merchants to send grain to the frontier. Isolated and often starving, the men deserted in growing numbers, while their officers kept false records in order to embezzle the rations. By the late 15th century units were regularly found to be at half strength or less, and mercenaries had to be hired to supplement the regulars. No Chinese dynasty could ever afford enough mercenaries to guard its enormous borders, and a series of financial crises further weakened the army. In the 1440s natural disasters added to the burden, in particular the disastrous flooding of the Hwang Ho in 1448; and major rebellions began to break out in the south. From then on the main military preoccupation of the dynasty, apart from the ever-threatening Mongols, was the maintenance of order in China itself.

In the same period, however, trouble on the south-western border, in Yunnan, led to a series of campaigns in which local Chinese forces took the offensive once more. The Shan people of Lu-ch'uan raided Yunnan and in 1440 defeated a punitive expedition. The local governor, Wang Chen, formed an alliance with the rival Burmese states of Ava and Hsien-wi and thrust repeatedly into the tropical forests as far as the west bank of the River Irrawaddy. This was successful in protecting Yunnan, but was to have an unfortunate result in another theatre.

In July 1449 the Oirats under Esen Khan launched a major offensive in the north and Wang Chen, now at the court in Peking, persuaded the Cheng-t'ung Emperor to lead a counter-attack, with Wang as military commander. Wang's

Another view of the Forbidden City. The construction of this palace and the surrounding fortifications strained the resources even of the Ming Empire. (© Stephen Turnbull)

Ming elite troops, c. 1500. Shown here are a cavalry trooper, a rocketeer and drummers. (David Sque © Osprey Publishing Ltd)

inexperience in steppe warfare led to a disastrous defeat at T'u-mu which plunged the country into temporary chaos. Worst of all, control of the Ordos region was permanently lost to the nomads.

A major reorganization in 1464 restored some of the efficiency of the army, but the days of large-scale offensive action were over. Henceforth the government was to fluctuate between a policy of punishing the Mongols with small, fast-moving cavalry columns, as advocated by the scholar-turned-general Wang Yueh, and an entirely defensive one involving the building of walls to pen them up in the Ordos loop. Proposals for another offensive to occupy the Ordos were still sometimes considered and once, in 1472, actually set in motion, but each time financial worries and the caution of the generals caused them to be abandoned. The Oirat confederation broke up soon after their victory in 1449, but by prohibiting trade with Mongolia the Chinese missed an opportunity to make a lasting peace. By now the tribes had become dependent on Chinese goods and livestock, and were forced to continue raiding in order to obtain them.

In 1473 work began on a system of walls in Shensi Province requiring months of labour by 40,000 troops; between then and 1485 nearly 600 miles of rammed earth walls were built, overlooked by watchtowers and anchored on fortified towns, and in 1482 they passed their first important test when a Mongol army became bogged down among the defences and was forced to abandon an attack into China. It is worth mentioning at this point that there had been no Great Wall along the frontier under the Yüan and early Ming. The original Ch'in wall had long since fallen into ruins and although subsequent dynasties, notably the Han and the Kin, had built walls, they had been far to the north of the Ming frontier and in any case had been so completely neglected that few traces had survived. Initially the Ming system covered only the Ordos region in the north-west, the eastern sections dating from the 1540s and later.

Of the internal revolts that plagued the Ming in the 15th century the worst was the Ching-hsiang Rebellion of 1465 to 1476, based on the area west of the Han River around the old fortress of Hsiang-yang. In Sung times this had been a very rich and populous district, but it was depopulated during the Mongol conquest, and in Ming times formed a sort of internal 'frontier region' where central control was weak and bandits flourished. The first serious outbreak was crushed in 1466; but four years later a charismatic leader known as the *T'ai-p'ing Wang* or 'Prince of Great Peace' again raised a rebel army, which took six years and 250,000 men to suppress. Other sources of trouble were the tribes of the south, especially the Miao, Yao and Lolo, who resented the appropriation of their lands by Chinese settlers.

For the majority of subjects of the Ming, however, the 15th century was a period of peace, accelerating the decline of the army. The new policy of aggression in Mongolia died with Wang Yueh in 1499; until the previous year, at the age of 71, he had still been in the habit of leading his cavalry raids in person. In 1504, when the Hung-chih Emperor announced his intention of leading another expedition northwards, his ministers united in dissuading him, admitting that the army was far inferior to that of the Yung Lo period. Within a few years the arrival of the Portuguese off the southern coast was to mark the end of China's long period of independent military development.

The Ming army

Until the end of the Ming–Han War in 1363 Chu's army consisted of various separate contingents, many taken over intact from the Yüan or rival warlords, under their own leaders. Units of the Miao army were incorporated in this way after 1360. In 1364, however, a major reorganization broke up the existing units and redistributed them into *wei*, or brigades, of 5,000 each, divided into five battalions, *chien-hu so*, each of ten *po-hu so*. Independent battalions, *shou-yu*, each 1,000 strong, also existed. The influence of the Yüan system is obvious. After 1368 this was regularized into the *wei-so* system, under which units corresponded to military districts where they were stationed, and combined with the *t'un-t'ien* or military colonies. Up to four-fifths of the soldiers grew food to support the remainder, who were responsible for guard duties. At first this worked acceptably, as the wars had left large regions of underpopulated land which could be settled; but as population pressure grew and military necessity forced the troops to concentrate in arid regions it broke down, with the results discussed above. There were about 500 *wei* throughout the empire, each nominally 5,600 strong, giving a total of between two and three million hereditary troops, but they gradually fell below their theoretical numbers until by the late 15th century most were below half strength. Additional to these were the guard units stationed around the capital, and the generally better-equipped garrisons of the fortified cities on the northern frontier.

Statue of a Ming official from the processional way at Peking. This form of headgear was worn by courtiers in civilian dress. (© Stephen Turnbull)

Guard units fell into three groups. The *Ch'in chun wei*, like the *Yüan Keshig*, was a bureaucratic organization comprising the emperor's personal bodyguard and the secret police. The *Hu-wei* or 'Princely Guards' came under the control of the imperial princes and were disbanded by the Yung Lo Emperor early in the 15th century. This left the *Ching-wei*, eventually consisting of 72 units making up the *Ching Chun* or Imperial Army. This provided the core of all major expeditions until 1449, when it was lost at T'u-mu. It was later re-formed, but no longer as an elite force – in fact it was employed so rarely that it became ineffective. By 1504 the guards had declined so far that a minister argued against sending them to reinforce the border garrisons on the grounds that they would run away and demoralize those whom they had been sent to help. As early as 1434 volunteers had been hired to supplement the hereditary troops, and after 1449 these mercenaries came to bear the brunt of the wars against the Mongols and internal rebels. Many were in fact Mongols themselves, greatly valued for their traditional cavalry skills. The native Chinese mercenaries, however, were usually recruited from criminals and vagabonds and were noted for their resistance to discipline. Conscripted militia were also used in the crisis of 1449 when the Oirats threatened Peking, and called up on occasion thereafter, although the practice was not placed on a legal basis until 1494.

In the Hung Wu period there was little difficulty in finding large numbers of experienced soldiers in a country militarized by the long series of wars, but savage discipline was needed to ensure that hereditary officers trained their sons to succeed them: at least one man had his nose cut off when his son was discovered playing the flute instead of working at his military exercises. This system was regularized in the Yung Lo reign by the establishment in Peking of three *ying* or training camps, to which troops were sent in rotation. The *Wu-chun ying* drilled recruits and specialized in infantry manoeuvres; the *San-ch'ien ying* employed Mongol instructors to teach cavalry warfare, scouting and signalling; and the *Shen-chi ying* trained men in the use of firearms. (Surprisingly, in the country which had invented gunpowder, many Annamese gunnery instructors were imported.) There was also a horse training camp where army mounts were broken in by Mongols. Several times this system fell into decline and was revived, notably in 1464 when 12 units were set up under a veteran general to train infantry, cavalry and artillery together in combined-arms tactics.

Despite the sophistication of the training programme, however, it failed to produce enough high-ranking officers of ability and experience. Military examinations were set up in parallel with the civil service ones, but the low status of the army did not attract the required calibre of applicants. Inevitably the descendants of hereditary commanders were of much more mixed ability than the original appointees had been, and officers of lower rank were selected mainly for their physical strength and skill at archery, so lacked potential for promotion. After the Yung Lo period the emperors tended to live very sheltered lives at court, and so were not able or inclined to supervise the army personally; military affairs were left to the bureaucrats of the Board of War, who regarded the generals as their social inferiors and often suspected

Chinese or Tibetan helmet, early 15th century. Helmets constructed of overlapping iron plates were a common alternative to the one-piece bowl, but this example is unique in the number of plates used; eight or fewer would be more usual. (The Board of Trustees of the Royal Armouries no. XXVIA. 150)

the able ones of disloyalty. The last emperor to take the field himself was Hsuan-te, who in 1428 personally killed several Mongols. Other sources of generals were court eunuchs and the scholar gentry, who could on rare occasions produce a commander of the calibre of Wang Yueh.

Many non-Chinese troops were still used by the Ming. Mongols, either those remaining in China after the fall of the Yüan or from allied tribes along the frontier, were employed in most Ming armies. The success of the prince of Yen in 1402 was largely attributable to his 100,000 Mongol cavalry, while smaller numbers could be found serving even in the far south. Armies in Central Asia, like those sent to Hami in 1473 and 1495, could consist almost entirely of Mongols. Like the Yüan the Ming used contingents from the southern tribes in regions close to their homelands, when possible setting one tribe against another. In the Burmese campaigns the states of Ava and Hsien-wi provided allies, probably including elephants (which were certainly used by Ava in an earlier invasion of China), but again these were only used in close proximity to their areas of origin. It was considered undesirable to deploy northerners in the south and vice versa, but in the case of Chinese troops it was not always possible to avoid this.

By the mid-14th century firearms were in use in considerable numbers – they were instrumental in the defeat of the state of Shu in 1371, and in 1388 an army including 2,000 handgunners was sent to crush an Ava invasion. At about this time the first field pieces on wheeled carriages also appeared. In 1412 the emperor ordered five cannon to be set up on mountain passes near Peking, many other strategic sites being so protected by the 1440s; in one year, 1465, 300 large bronze cannon were manufactured. But these figures can give a misleading impression, as production was restricted for security reasons to the capital, and elsewhere firearm-equipped troops were a very small minority, most infantry still relying on bows, crossbows, swords and the huge variety of pole weapons illustrated in the manuals. The cavalry, whether Mongol or Chinese, were mostly mounted archers.

Military technology

It was inevitable that a society as advanced as China should have looked to technology for the solution to its military problems, and as early as the Han dynasty we find victories over the barbarians attributed to possession of inventions like the crossbow. This weapon had been considerably improved by Sung times, notably by the addition of sights for aiming and stirrups to aid in drawing. The repeating crossbow, probably first used by the Sung, could discharge bolts at a rate of almost one a second at the cost of reduced accuracy

Rocket launcher, c. 1450. One of the most ingenious uses ever devised for the wheelbarrow – itself a Chinese invention – was as a mobile rocket launcher. This illustration is based on a reconstructed scale model in the National Historical Museum in Peking, and on the *Wu Pei Chih*. Six box launchers were carried, four on the top row and two below; hundreds of rockets could thus be fired in a few seconds. (David Sque © Osprey Publishing Ltd)

and penetration; it was useful in sieges, but in this period was not as popular as the single-shot type. Large artillery crossbows spanned by winches were in use: but the more common 'light artillery pieces' seem to have been single-armed stone-throwers operated by men pulling on ropes. These were used not only in sieges but also in naval warfare, the defence of camps and even in the field, especially for covering river crossings. The rope-operated system, however, was inferior to the true counterweighted trebuchet, introduced by the Yüan, which eventually replaced it.

The aspect of military technology most often associated with China in this period is of course the use of gunpowder. The Mongols were terrified by gunpowder weapons, such as flamethrowers and explosive bombs, when they first encountered them in China. By Kubilai's time, however, they had adopted them from the Kin and were using them against the Sung. Bombs with metal casings, which burst to scatter lethal splinters, were now common, a famous illustration of one appearing on the Japanese Mongol Invasion Scroll of 1293. These were mass-produced in tens of thousands and were made in a variety of sizes, ranging from enormous bombs, which had to be hauled by draught

元至正辛卯铳

制造于元至正十一年（1351年），为世界上
现存最古老的手铳。

The oldest accurately dated handgun in the world. It is from 1351. The end of the barrel on the right is a socket into which was fitted a wooden handle. (© Stephen Turnbull)

animals, to grenades, which could be thrown by hand. The Ming sometimes strapped them to oxen, which were driven into an enemy camp. The same technology also gave rise to defensive mines, made from lengths of bamboo filled with powder, which by the late 14th century could be buried under gates and at frontier passes and exploded by a tripwire attached to a flint-and-steel detonator.

More significant for the future were two types of artillery developed under the Yüan – the true gun and the rocket. Although the latter was invented about the 11th century there seems to be no firm evidence for its use in war by the Sung, who used the term later used for rockets to denote fire-arrows. Battle accounts start to mention rockets in the 1340s, and multiple launchers may have first appeared in the civil war of 1399–1402. Explosive warheads were not used, the missiles being no more than small rocket-propelled arrows, but a wheeled launcher could fire several hundred at once. They were placed in holes in wooden frames, drilled at an angle to increase dispersion; inaccuracy was considered an advantage, as while their approach could be seen from a distance their eventual point of impact was unpredictable, and this had a demoralizing effect on enemy units over a wide front.

Often carried on wheelbarrows, the launchers were mobile enough to be used widely in battles as well as sieges. Smaller versions could be carried by individual men, massed into a bodyguard or dispersed for surprise among conventionally armed troops. But they had to be fired within range of enemy archery, which is no doubt why drawings generally show their users as heavily armoured. Extreme range for the larger launchers, however, may have been well in excess of 500 paces. The *Huo Lung Ching* describes a number of ambitious attempts to improve rocket technology, including multi-stage rockets, a device shaped like a bird and carrying a bomb for use against ships and encampments, and one which ignited a second rocket as it burned out, and flew back to the launcher after dropping a bomb. It is hard to believe that these were ever successfully used in battle, and in fact the use of rockets declined in the 16th century when modern guns became available, testifying to their lack of killing power. Long before this the explosive bombs thrown by trebuchets had apparently fallen into disuse.

Development of the true gun

The true gun had its roots in a 10th-century invention, the *huo-ch'iang* or 'fire-lance'. Originally no more than a firework tied to a spear, by 1260 it was evolving into a variety of types, still usually incorporating some sort of blade but shooting out smoke, small projectiles or even poison along with the flames. These weapons were particularly associated with peasant rebels but were also adopted by regular Sung troops, who took them into Yüan service. They had a range of only a few feet and so were basically close-combat weapons, but were cheap to make and remained popular until well after the Ming period, sometimes being combined in mobile racks for the defence of cities. Fire-lances were in use for centuries before the two advances were made that would lead to their evolution into effective firearms – the development of a formula for gunpowder that gave the necessary explosive force, and the use of projectiles fitting the bore of the weapon that could be propelled with sufficient force to kill.

Because this was an evolutionary process it is difficult to fix an exact date for the invention of the true gun, but Needham (see Bibliography) has identified a bronze handgun from Manchuria as dating from Kubilai's expedition of 1287–88, and believes that their first appearance may have been around 1250. The earliest definitely dated cannon, an example in the National Historical Museum in Peking, is ascribed to the year 1332. These dates are not much earlier than the first firearms in Europe and the Middle East, but the fact that both the weapons and the formulae for gunpowder which appeared in Europe in the first decades of the 14th century are identical to Chinese types, and show no prior history of experimentation and development in the West, strongly suggests that they were transmitted from Yüan China.

The early Ming saw the appearance of new types of firearm, perhaps developed secretly under the Yüan in preparation for revolt. The *Ming Shih* claims that guns were first acquired by the dynasty from Annam in 1410, but other evidence disproves this. In fact the *Huo Lung Ching* states that they were an important factor in the Ming victory over its rivals. The later Yüan, however, also possessed both handguns and heavier pieces, as did the rival warlord Chang Shih-cheng; the commander in 1356 of the first Ming unit of handgunners was a defector from the Yüan army, where he had learned his skills.

Surviving 14th-century guns are usually of bronze, although cast iron was also used; they generally have bulbous, thickened breeches and flared muzzles like contemporary European weapons, and were designed to fire arrows, metal or stone balls, or case shot consisting of up to a hundred small pellets in a bag. By the 15th century thick metal bands were being cast on barrels to strengthen them, again paralleling developments in Europe. Despite the enthusiasm of the manuals and other contemporary writings, however, there is reason to believe that Chinese firearms were fairly unsatisfactory, and accidents with gunpowder were very common. A 15th-century writer, Ch'iu Chun, remarks on the guns' very low rate of fire, enabling an enemy to overrun them before they could reload. Handgunners were therefore deployed in groups of five: one or two to shoot, and the rest to help with loading. Hardwood guns firing arrows were brought back from Annam in 1410 and regarded as superior to Chinese weapons, as were European types when introduced in the 16th century – in fact the latter replaced traditional guns and rockets within a surprisingly short time.

After about 1400 Chinese military technology began to stagnate – a consequence of the low social status of soldiers, the lack of sophisticated enemies to stimulate development, and the suspicion with which emperors in the Hung Wu tradition regarded innovations, especially those which might weaken the power of the state. Although in Europe gunpowder strengthened royal control by enabling governments to destroy the castles of the nobility, in China it tended instead to aid the defence; the enormous thickness of rammed earth fortifications resisted cannon fire in a way which the vertical stone walls of contemporary Europe could not.

There was a great deal of continuity throughout the period in armour construction; illustrations from the 1620s show armour and helmets identical to those in paintings of the Sung era and even before. Lamellar already had a long history in China when the Mongols introduced their own versions, and although surviving sets are much later there is no reason to doubt that it remained popular under the Ming. Chinese versions, however, were generally inferior to armours made in Central Asia or Tibet, and in 1374 the Hung Wu Emperor had to introduce regulations to improve their manufacture, insisting for example that they were laced with leather thongs rather than cord. Such armour was often protected with a coat of red or black lacquer. A more distinctively Chinese type of protection was brigandine, of riveted plates covered with fabric. Mail was used only by the western guard units of the Yüan. To judge from illustrations the majority of infantrymen did not wear armour, although it may sometimes have

A sentry stands guard beside the slope leading up to the Great Wall where it enters the sea at the 'Dragon's Head' – its eastern extremity. (© Stephen Turnbull)

been hidden under robes. Horsemen were generally better protected and horse armour was known, but probably used only by a minority of cavalry.

Strategy and tactics

The ancient Chinese tradition of the art of war, dating back to the Chou dynasty, was still very much alive; one of the classical commentators on the *Sun Tzu*, Liu Chi, was an advisor to Chu Yuan-chang. The surviving manuals represent only a fraction of the body of writing on military affairs available to the commanders of the period: a Sung bibliography lists 347 such works, of which only two are now extant.

Strategy was often fairly ambitious, involving for example the converging attacks by widely separated forces which were sent against Lin-an in 1276 and K'aifeng in 1368; equally impressive are the distances covered by expeditions across difficult terrain, whether the mountains of Szechwan in the Ta-li campaign of 1251, the Burmese jungle or the Gobi Desert in Mongolia. Supply was no doubt made easier by Chinese road-building skills and by the excellent road network that existed within the empire. Large numbers of bridges also facilitated river crossings. In 1484 an attempt was made to improve the mobility of the infantry on the northern frontier by carrying them in carts, but this was not successful.

Battlefield tactics emphasized surprise, either through deceptions such as the use of smoke or dummies on horseback, or by manoeuvring independent divisions against the enemy's flank or rear; Ming armies usually consisted of three or five such divisions, controlled by a system of signal flags. When fighting Mongols the main problem was to prevent them using their superior mobility to avoid battle or to escape from pursuit if defeated. This was overcome by swift surprise raids on their encampments, or by trying to force them to give battle with their backs to an obstacle, as happened at Lake Buyur in 1388.

At the level of individual unit tactics, however, little subtlety was in evidence. Infantry attacks took the form of wild charges, the men making faces and screaming to frighten the enemy and accompanied by as much noise as possible from drums, gongs and trumpets. The natural indiscipline of the troops was made worse by the practice of rewarding them for taking heads, making it difficult to rally them after a victory. It seems that when necessary missile troops took cover behind those armed with spears and halberds, but the *Wu Ching Tsung Yao* recommends that crossbowmen are deployed separately, and claims that they could defeat a cavalry charge by firepower alone – although in fact resisting cavalry was never a strong suit of Chinese infantry. Crossbowmen used a circulating formation to compensate for their low rate of fire, with men advancing to shoot and retiring to reload. In terms of equipment and tactics it was probably often difficult to tell Chinese cavalry from Mongols, so closely were nomad methods copied; most cavalry thus fought as mounted archers, especially in the north, although this need not imply exclusively skirmishing tactics.

Most Mongol battles were won by hand-to-hand fighting after an initial softening up with arrows, and Ming cavalry are recorded as making impetuous charges, as at Hsin-ch'eng in 1365. Against Nayan in 1287 Kubilai strengthened his cavalry with units of Chinese infantry carried behind their saddles, who dismounted to attack the horses of the enemy.

An army forced onto the defensive generally made use of field fortifications, as at Ting-hsi in 1370 when part of the Ming line was protected by a stream and the rest by palisades. The techniques available for fortifying camps were very sophisticated and often involved the use of artillery. Siege warfare was also highly developed, although defensive techniques were neglected under the Yüan. City walls were of rammed earth, sometimes faced with stone, and overlooked by high towers. Large central towers were also built inside the walls of major towns. These walls, especially when protected with layers of rope matting or clay, could absorb the impact of missiles and so were seldom breached, although rebels took Nan-ch'ang in 1362 by destroying a gate with cannon fire. Blockade, assault and mining were more usually successful techniques. Gunpowder weapons were popular for the defence of towns, in which role they were more effective than in the field; in beating off an assault on Tung-ch'ang by the prince of Yen in 1400, for example, they are said to have caused tens of thousands of casualties, including a number of generals.

Significant battles of Medieval China

Hsiang-yang and Fanch'eng, 1268–72

These two cities, situated on either side of the Han River, were garrisoned by the Sung to prevent the Mongols advancing downriver to the Yangtze. Initially the Yüan forces, including thousands of Chinese levies, attempted to blockade the cities by patrolling the river and building siege works; but although the Sung failed in several break-out attempts the blockade was not close enough to prevent supplies getting through. Two Sung officers, Chang Shun and Chang Kuei, led a flotilla of boats to break in and re-provision Hsiang-yang, an operation which was successful despite the deaths of both leaders.

The Sung commander, Lu Wen-huan, showed no sign of giving up after four years of siege. Kubilai therefore employed two Muslim engineers, sent from Persia by his nephew Abakha, who built large counterweight stone-throwing engines of a type not previously seen in China. With these they bombarded Fanch'eng with rocks and explosive bombs, leading to a successful assault. Turned against Hsiang-yang, one of the engines wrecked the central tower of the city and the garrison surrendered. Marco Polo in his account attempts to take the credit for the construction of these devices, but Chinese sources make it clear that the engineers were Iraqis. The Arab type of counterweighted trebuchet was henceforth known in China as the *Hui-hui p'ao* or 'Muslim engine', or as the *Hsiang-yang p'ao*.

Lung-wan, 1360

Ch'en Yu-liang of Han attempted to sail his fleet up the San-ch'a River, a tributary of the Yangtze, and take Chin-ling from Ming troops by surprise. Finding his way blocked by a stone bridge and the river banks covered with sharpened stakes to deter a landing, he returned to the mouth of the river and built a fortified camp. Chu Yuan-chang of the Ming had anticipated this, and devised a plan to lure him out. Chu himself took up a position in front of Ch'en's camp with a third of his army, deploying a flanking force under Ch'ang Yu-ch'un behind a range of hills; he then led an attack on the fortifications. As expected, the Han, seeing an inferior force attacking them, sallied out to eliminate it, whereupon Chu hoisted a yellow flag. At this signal Ch'ang charged into the flank of the enemy and routed them: 20,000 Han were killed and 7,000 captured. Meanwhile the tide had gone out and stranded the Han fleet in the mud; hundreds of ships, soon to form the core of a Ming fleet, were taken.

Ch'u-t'ang Gorge, 1371

The state of Shu in the western province of Szechwan built a defensive position across one of the great Yangtze gorges to stop the advance of a Ming river fleet

The defence of Peking by the Ming against the Mongols in 1449. (© Stephen Turnbull)

under Liao Yung-chung. Iron chain booms were stretched across the river to obstruct
the ships, while between the cliffs on both banks were three suspension bridges sited
to command the booms with fire. On the bridges and on both banks the Shu
deployed artillery, probably stone-throwing trebuchets but possibly including
cannon. A Ming attempt to break through was repulsed; so Liao landed a
detachment of infantry, who wore green clothing and cloaks made of leaves for
camouflage as the banks were thickly wooded. These men worked their way round
the Shu position and attacked it from behind, while cannon on the Ming ships fired
at the bridges – a tactic that suggests a high-trajectory weapon like a mortar. The
bridges were destroyed, and Liao's ships, their bows armoured with iron, broke
through the chains and forced the position.

T'u-mu, 1449

The Cheng-t'ung Emperor led an expedition against the Oirat Mongols, giving military command to Wang Chen. The army, which included the whole of the *Ching-wei*, was said to number 500,000, and the Mongols characteristically fell back before it into the steppe. The march was slowed by heavy rain, and when the army reached Yang-ho only to find the corpses of a Ming force massacred by the enemy, Wang decided to retire, claiming a victory. The Mongols closed in behind them, wiped out a rearguard and ambushed a cavalry force sent to rescue it. At T'u-mu, eight miles short of the walled town of Huai Lai, Wang ordered a halt, refusing to press on, although the site was waterless, for fear of having to abandon the baggage train. The next day the camp was surrounded by 20,000 Mongols, who promised to spare the lives of the troops if they threw down their arms. Made desperate by thirst, many did so, and the army disintegrated as they ran in disorder towards a nearby river. The Mongols slaughtered them and captured the emperor.

Ta-t'eng hsia, 1466

The rebellious Yao and Chuang tribes of Kwangsi in south-western China assembled in the Ta-t'eng hsia Gorge on the Ch'ien River, a steep ravine flanked by jungle-clad mountains. A Ming force under Han Yung, consisting of 160,000 local levies and 30,000 regular soldiers including 1,000 Mongols, was sent to blockade the mouth of the gorge, but ordered not to risk an attack. Han ignored both his orders and local advice and entered the ravine, where the Yao resisted from behind a series of wooden stockades. At first unsuccessful, Han resorted to setting fire to the stockades with incendiary missiles and then storming them. The Yao fled and were massacred, while many of the Chuang, who were deadly archers renowned for their use of poisoned arrows, surrendered and were recruited into the government forces. They were then used to occupy the gorge, denying it to the rebels.

Hung-yen-ch'ih, 1473

Wang Yueh, a scholar by training, devised a policy of striking back at the Mongols by adopting their own tactics. He led 4,600 horse-archers, equipped like nomads, into the steppes north of Ning-hsia. At Hung-yen-ch'ih he surprised the camp of Bag Arslan's Mongols while the warriors were away raiding, overwhelmed the few guards and captured many horses and other livestock. Bag Arslan learned of this and rode back in haste, but fell into an ambush laid by Wang. The tribesmen were decisively defeated and retreated to the north-west.

PART IV

The late Ming, 1517–98

Although the Ming dynasty had expelled the Mongols from China in 1368, in the 16th century the main external threat still came from Mongol descendants on the northern frontier, who were intermittently united into confederations under leaders claiming descent from Chinggis Khan. The Cheng-te Emperor of the Ming, who reigned from 1506 to 1521, has been judged harshly by traditional historians, in part because he showed an unseemly interest in military affairs and was not content to remain a figurehead. He achieved some success in battle against the Mongols, but under his successor, Chia-ching (1522–67), the gains were quickly thrown away. The new ruler presided over endless factional disputes at court, which prevented the development of a consistent military policy, but at the same time he was fanatically anti-Mongol and blocked all attempts at reaching an accommodation with them, punishing officials who dared to undertake negotiations.

Typical of Chia-ching's style was an edict that ordered that the character 'i', referring to the northern 'barbarians', should always be written as small as possible. Not surprisingly, such measures failed to deter them. In the 1540s the Oirat leader Altan Khan reunited the eastern Mongols and began to lay the foundations of an organized state, building cities, promoting agriculture, and attracting Chinese renegades to serve him. He repeatedly asked permission to trade with China, but this was refused. The Ming instead toyed with plans for an attack on him – an enterprise eventually abandoned because of the government's growing financial difficulties. In any case, in 1548 Altan struck first, capturing and demolishing the frontier walls in the Hsuan-fu area. Two years later his troopers rode round the eastern flank of the unfinished Great Wall and laid siege to Peking. Although Altan eventually withdrew, this humiliation highlighted the powerlessness of the Ming field armies, and gave extra impetus to the policy of building walls to keep the nomads at bay. Two decades of destructive raiding followed, until in 1571, after the death of Chia-ching, Altan was finally allowed to trade peacefully. For the next 20 years the Mongol frontier was relatively quiet.

The same indecisiveness characterized the Chia-ching reign on other fronts. In 1513 Hami – an outpost on the Silk Route which had been controlled by the Ming since the 14th century – was occupied by the sultan of Turfan, one of a number of independent Muslim rulers who had succeeded the Timurid and Chagatai Mongols in the Tarim Basin. The Chinese retaliated by hiring several armies of Mongol mercenaries to recapture Hami, but without success. In 1528 the city was finally written off, but the revelation of Ming weakness provoked raids from Turfan into north-western China, as well as revolts by Muslims within the empire. In 1537 a major expedition was planned against Vietnam, which had

PREVIOUS PAGE The tower on the Great Wall at Huangyaguan. (© Stephen Turnbull)

stopped paying tribute, but after three years of dithering the emperor dropped the idea. Subsequently the Burmese and Vietnamese, also sensing weakness, began to raid the southern provinces of Yunnan and Kwangsi.

Another serious problem arose in the 1540s, when the pirates who had long plagued the south-east coast began to organize themselves into an effective military force. The main cause of this situation was the short-sightedness of the Chinese government, which from 1525 had attempted to isolate the population from foreign influences by a series of edicts restricting trade and seafaring. Local merchants seized offshore islands to use as bases for illegal trading with the Japanese and Portuguese, and soon graduated to full-scale piracy, raising large armies and even attacking cities on the coast. The pirates were initially supported by merchant families from Kyushu and Honshu, and reinforced by contingents of the Japanese pirates who had been operating for two centuries around the coasts of south-east Asia. The latter were always a minority, however; despite the name the Ming gave to the insurgents – *wo-k'ou* or 'Japanese pirates' – more than two-thirds of their manpower was Chinese. In 1547 Chu Wan was sent to suppress the insurgency, but the merchants had friends in the provincial government who engineered Chu Wan's dismissal.

Despite its mythological subject matter, this 16th-century painting, 'The Conversion of Hariti', contains many interesting details of late Ming military equipment. (British Museum 1926.4-10.02)

OPPOSITE General Ch'i
Chi-kuang, the great
reformer of the Ming
army who died in 1587,
as depicted on his statue
in front of the Great Wall,
for which he had an
important responsibility.
(© Stephen Turnbull)

Yet more stringent restrictions on shipping prevented even fishermen from making a living and drove them to join the rebellion, so that by 1554 the *wo-k'ou* were stronger than ever, defeating several Ming armies on land, and threatening major coastal cities like Nanking and Hangchow.

It was a combination of measures that finally brought the situation under control: two able generals, Hu Tsung-hsien and Ch'i Chi-kuang, intensified the military pressure, enabling the capture of the leading pirate, Wang Chih, in 1557. Then, in 1567, the ban on overseas trade was lifted. Profiting from the newly discovered route across the Pacific to the Spanish possessions in America, the region began to prosper and discontent receded.

The Wan-li Emperor, who came to the throne in 1573, was not without ability, but was a prisoner of a system that by now kept emperors virtually imprisoned within the palace, isolated from the world outside. His reign was noted for the 'Three Great Campaigns', often quoted at the time as proof that the Ming armies were still formidable. Two of these campaigns, however, were relatively insignificant. The Po-chou War was sparked off in 1587 by a warlord in Szechwan, Yang Ying-lung, who drew his support mainly from the native Miao tribes. Yang remained independent for several years while the government was occupied elsewhere, but in 1600 an army – also mainly of local tribesmen and led by Li Hua-lung – defeated him in a hundred-day campaign. The Ordos Campaign of 1592 was even more localized. The garrison of the city of Ninghsia revolted and allied itself with a Mongol chieftain, but the uprising collapsed in October of that year when government troops diverted water from a nearby lake to undermine the walls of the town.

The main focus of attention in the Wan-li reign was the third of these 'Great Campaigns', in Korea. In 1592 the Japanese, under Hideyoshi Toyotomi, invaded the peninsula – apparently with the ultimate objective of conquering China. At first they made rapid progress, taking the cities of Seoul and P'yong-yang before halting to regroup. In January 1593 a Ming army, under Li Ju-sung, crossed the Yalu River into Korea and beat the Japanese outside P'yong-yang. Hideyoshi's men were suffering supply difficulties – exacerbated by Korean naval activity and by Chinese agents, who had burned a large food depot behind the lines – and withdrew to a bridgehead in the far south, near Pusan. An uneasy truce followed, until in October 1596 a Chinese embassy visited Japan with the aim of making peace.

The outcome illustrates one of the defects of Chinese foreign policy: the Chinese were unable to come to terms with the idea that 'barbarian' rulers might expect to be treated as equals. Hideyoshi had anticipated a partition of Korea, and perhaps the hand of a Ming princess in marriage, but all the Chinese were prepared to offer him was recognition as king of Japan (of which he was already the de facto ruler), provided that he accepted the status of vassal and agreed

never again to invade the mainland. Incensed by what he saw as an insult, Hideyoshi advanced on Seoul again the following year, but was blocked by a force of 50,000 Chinese. The Korean admiral Yi Sun-sin, helped by a Ming fleet under the artillery expert Ch'en Lin, had command of the sea, preventing supplies and reinforcements from reaching the Japanese, and again forcing them to fall back as winter approached. During 1598 Chinese attacks at Ulsan, Sunchon and Sochon were all beaten off with very heavy losses, but they succeeded in keeping the Japanese penned up in their bridgehead. When news of Hideyoshi's death arrived at the end of the year, both sides were exhausted and happy to make peace. The Japanese evacuated Korea, giving the Ming a strategic victory.

Late Ming armies

The story of the corruption and inefficiency undermining the hereditary *wei-so* military system of the early Ming has been outlined previously. By the 16th century the old guards and battalions were becoming a liability rather than an asset: they were chronically under strength, since officers continued to keep men

Ming mounted archer, 16th century. (Topfoto)

on the rolls after they died or deserted in order to claim extra pay, and were lacking in training and discipline. Ch'en Chien, writing of the Chia-ching reign, describes the *wei-so* army in the following terms:

> [the army is] the source of many troubles. They start riots and try to revolt whenever the authorities are slow in paying them … whenever there is a rumour of war there is actually fear that the army may be injured. Accordingly, village guards and mercenaries are employed to deal with the bandits. In a word, civilians are used to protect the soldiers.

By the middle of the 16th century the core of the Ming forces consisted of mercenaries hired from the general population – a system similar to that employed by the Sung dynasty. Like those of the Sung, however, these men tended to be of low social status, the days when a military career was considered respectable in China having long passed. They were recruited mainly from vagabonds and amnestied bandits, were poorly and erratically paid, and were often robbed by their officers. Being of many different origins, the mercenaries formed a heterogeneous army with units that varied widely in size and fighting qualities. Men from Hsiang-fu in Honan, for example, were easy to control but cowardly. On the other hand the Mao-hu-lu ping, who were ex-miners, were considered brave but undisciplined. The men of Szechwan were inveterate looters, and easily distracted from a pursuit by discarded enemy baggage. In general, peasants were thought to make better soldiers than the streetwise urban misfits who sometimes volunteered; the latter were inclined to give too high a priority to self-preservation.

Against internal rebels it was thought advisable to employ men from distant provinces: soldiers from Liao-tung were especially effective against the Shensi rebels in the 1630s, as they could not understand their dialect and so could not be bribed or subverted. (Troops recruited from Shensi itself proved to be useless, as they often came from the same villages as the rebels and tended to fraternize with them instead of fighting.)

Foreign troops were also recruited. Mongols were employed in contingents varying in size from whole tribes, hired for expeditions into Central Asia, to small bands of prisoners of war, who were transported to remote parts of the empire as garrison troops, and were distinguishable from the Chinese only by their red caps.

Pubei, the leader of the Ordos revolt of 1592, was a Mongol whose family had served in the Ming army for generations. Several of the Jurchen tribes of Manchuria were vassals of the Ming and also provided soldiers, fighting – like the Mongols – as cavalry. Small groups of Japanese were hired in the late 16th century, and an allied Korean contingent fought alongside the Ming in the 1618–19 campaign against the Manchus.

Traditionally the troops were encouraged to fight by a system of rewards for enemy heads taken, but by the 17th century this practice was being widely abused. Prisoners of war and innocent civilians were often slaughtered to provide evidence of fictitious victories, and there was even a well-established procedure for steaming Chinese heads to remove the traces of their headgear and so enable them to be passed off as Manchus. This helped to keep the government in ignorance of the true military situation by inflating the reported numbers of enemy dead. In 1640 the Ch'ung-chen Emperor tried to abolish the system, but by then the dynasty was crumbling, and it was too late to restore discipline.

Like the *wei-so* troops, many mercenary units quickly became liabilities. In 1620 Shen Kuo-yuan submitted a report on the Peking garrison quite as damning as Ch'en Chien's verdict on their predecessors:

> It would be impossible to depend on them for the defence of the capital if war should break out. It is said that the authorities dare not reform them lest the attempt at reform should lead to a riot. They dare not train them since this might cause the same disaster.

This Chinese two-handed sword dates from the 19th century, but blades of identical shape were already in use in the 16th. (Topfoto/HIP/The Royal Armouries)

European observers tended to be equally scathing about the quality of Ming armies. Matteo Ricci, for example, writing at the end of the 16th century, considered that their strength lay in their numbers rather than their skill. Many reform movements were started – notably that of Chang Chu-cheng in the Wan-li period – but little progress was made against the weight of vested interests involved. Corruption had become institutionalized: in one area, for example, the officers had established fixed tariffs for such privileges as exemption

Ming standard bearer and swordsman, 16th century. The standard bearer is based on a painted scroll in the National Palace Museum in Taipei, depicting an imperial procession, probably of the Chia-ching Emperor (1522–67). Several units wear this combination of blue coat and red hat. The armour, constructed of iron plates fastened to the back of a fabric garment, is well known from the early Ch'ing period and later, but no Ming examples have survived. The swordsman is based on a c. 1590 Ming scroll now in San Francisco which shows figures of this type in several scenes from the Korean campaign of 1592–98. Most of the infantry in this source carry spears, but two-handed swords were popular among officers and their bodyguards. (Christa Hook © Osprey Publishing Ltd)

Late Ming dynasty helmet from the 16th century. At the base of the skull is a gilt band retaining fragments of a blue silk covering or neckguard. (Topfoto/HIP/The Royal Armouries)

from drill, or permission to 'borrow' army horses for private use. On one typical occasion in the 1560s, only 30,000 soldiers could be found in the Hsuan-fu district to repel a Mongol invasion, although the local commander had been drawing salaries for 120,000.

In the field, the diversity of units made central control difficult. To some extent sheer numbers compensated for this. The armed forces of the early Ming were said to number around three million men, although because of the chronic maladministration it is impossible to establish what the real strength was. The Spaniard Martin de Rada gives a list of garrisons for the late 16th century totalling 4,178,500 foot and 780,000 horse. This no doubt represents a paper strength never achieved in practice, but the steadily increasing population of the empire – from perhaps 65 million in 1400 to 150 million in 1600 – did ensure that by the standards of the time late Ming armies could be very large.

In strategic terms they were also fairly mobile, assisted by the advanced infrastructure of roads and bridges, which had grown up as a result of the economic boom of the 11th–13th centuries. In the Ninghsia campaign of 1592, for example, a train of 400 artillery pieces covered 300 miles over difficult terrain in about a month. The campaign of 1619 against the Manchus, involving a converging attack by four separate columns totalling 200,000 men, shows that the sort of ambitious operations characteristic of the early years of the dynasty could still be undertaken.

On the battlefield itself, rather than trying to manoeuvre these huge and sketchily trained masses, generals tended to put themselves at the head of specially picked units of not much more than battalion size and use these to spearhead attacks. Liu T'ing, for example, led a bodyguard of 736 men in 1619, fighting personally in the front rank with a two-handed sword. Many such elite troops were ferocious fighters who took vows to die with their commanders rather than flee, and their desperate charges greatly impressed their allies in Korea. However, with most of the able officers fighting as ordinary soldiers, the problems of control became even worse; the tactical manoeuvre warfare practised by earlier Ming armies had become largely replaced by a reliance on massed frontal attacks.

European observers commented on the amount of training and drilling that occurred even in peacetime, but the emphasis tended to be on individual weapon skills rather than manoeuvring in formed bodies. According to de Rada, Chinese archers were 'very skilful', but of their infantry generally he comments, '... their manoeuvres were not done in ordered array ... but in crowds and all huddled very close together'.

There were, however, exceptions to the general decline in military science. Outstanding among Ming commanders was Ch'i Chi-kuang, who took command of an army in Chekiang in 1555, tasked with defeating the *wo-k'ou* pirates. Finding that the latter had established a moral superiority over the government troops, Ch'i imposed a strict system of discipline. On occasion he personally executed officers who retreated without orders. The men were also motivated through speeches and religious imagery, and they received intensive training in small-unit tactics and individual combat techniques. At a higher level, Ch'i's operations were carefully planned, often with the aid of clay models of the terrain.

Ch'i's most famous innovation was the 12-man 'mandarin duck' squad, in which each soldier had a precisely defined role. Four of them carried long spears, with which they could outreach the Japanese swords on which the pirates' best troops relied; the spearmen were protected in close combat by two swordsmen –

Ming figurine, depicting
an official wearing
a ceremonial version
of traditional armour.
(Topfoto/British Museum)

one on the right with a large shield and one on the left with a small round shield and some javelins – and two men carrying bamboo saplings, with the branches still attached. These could be used to entangle the enemy and keep him at a distance. A rearguard of two men with three-pronged fire-lances, an officer, and a porter, completed the squad. This arrangement seems rather inefficient, with only one man in three actually equipped for offensive action, but in the context of Ch'i's isolated command, with plenty of peasant manpower available but no capacity for manufacturing sophisticated weapons, it was no doubt a logical approach.

Ch'i Chi-kuang's army, c. 1560. Derived from drawings in Ch'i Chi-kuang's own manuals, these figures represent peasant soldiers of the army with which Ch'i defeated the *wo-k'ou* pirates in southern China. They are dressed in what is essentially the day-to-day dress of working-class Chinese. The weapon of the figure on the left is simply a bamboo tree, complete with branches, which was used to pin an enemy while the accompanying spearmen despatched him. (Christa Hook © Osprey Publishing Ltd)

A distinctive feature of the *wo-k'ou* themselves was the Japanese swordplay employed by some of their infantry – both Japanese and Chinese who had learned their methods. They raised and lowered their swords in unison, signalled by officers with folding fans, and wielded them so swiftly that an enemy 'could see only the flash of the weapon, not the man'.

At first the pirates were better disciplined than the government troops and frequently outmanoeuvred them, but when possible they preferred to stand on the defensive. Ch'i Chi-kuang noted the pirates' surprise tactics:

the pirates always manage to sit on the heights waiting for us. Usually they hold on until evening, when our soldiers become tired. Then they dash out … They adorn their helmets with coloured strings and animal horns of metallic colours and ghostly shapes to frighten our soldiers.

Ch'i gradually gained the upper hand over the pirates, and in 1568 he was transferred to the northern front at Chichou to fight the Mongols. Here too he introduced innovative organizations and tactics suited to the local conditions. These were essentially defensive – as befitted a mainly infantry force facing cavalry on the open steppe – and were based on a section of 20 men deployed around a two-wheeled mule-drawn war wagon. Each wagon carried two light artillery pieces manned by a team of ten, who also manhandled the vehicle in battle. The remaining ten men carried various close-combat weapons, although four of them also had muskets. Ch'i was opposed to excessive reliance on firearms, because those he had encountered in the south were badly made and prone to misfire or even explode.

Ming artillery

The question of firearms was one frequently debated in the Late Ming period, but it was generally agreed that wherever possible their numbers should be increased. In 1530 a proposal was submitted for replacing garrison troops with small cannon, each manned by three men, thus releasing nine-tenths of the manpower for agriculture. Several thousand of these weapons were manufactured over the next few years, but production was never sufficient to achieve the ideal. Around this time, the traditional Chinese artillery began to be replaced by Western types. Advanced matchlock weapons seem to have been introduced into north-western China from the Ottoman Empire, via Turfan, during the Hami campaign of 1513–24, and into the rest of the country in the 1540s by Japanese pirates, who had only recently copied them from the Portuguese. The weapons were known to the Chinese as 'bird's beak muskets', presumably because of the 'pecking' action of the cock which held the match.

Fo-lang-chi p'ao, or 'Frankish cannon', were probably first encountered on board two captured Portuguese ships in 1523, and were being manufactured in China by 1529. Originally they were iron breech-loaders of the type mounted on Portuguese warships, but it seems that later the same term was used for larger bronze or iron muzzle-loaders, as well as for light, portable wooden copies. The quality of Chinese gun founding seems to have varied greatly from one area to another: de Rada describes their artillery as small and 'most inferior', but in 1585 Juan de Mendoça described cannon 'of huge greatness, and better made than ours'. Methods of employing artillery could also be very sophisticated: a

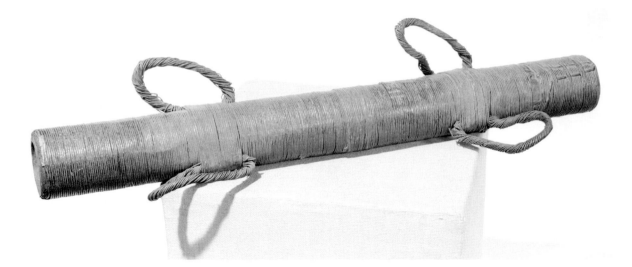

17th-century bronze 'silk gun', which would originally have been bound with raffia and covered with silk. (Board of Trustees of the Royal Armouries)

local history of Soochow describes gunners spotting by telescope in the wars of the Ch'ung-chen reign (1628–43) against Li Tzu-ch'eng's rebels. This predates the widespread use of the technique in Europe.

By the end of the 16th century European heavy artillery was considered so superior to indigenous types that the latter had almost disappeared except for the defence of city walls, where their mobility and rate of fire were less important than in the open field. During the T'ien-ch'i reign (1621–27) sacrifices were offered to the great *fo-lang-chi* cannon as though they were gods. Europeans themselves were generally recognized as the experts in the use of artillery, and the Ming frequently sought European help in the wars against the Manchus. When, in 1621, three Portuguese guns manned by African slaves arrived on the Manchu front, they were credited with beating off the enemy virtually unassisted.

It was mainly because of their ability to cast cannon that a succession of Jesuit missionaries was permitted to reside in Peking. The first of these was Matteo Ricci, who arrived in 1602 and was soon coerced into producing guns for the Ming, as was his successor, Adam Schall, in 1642.

Conservatism and xenophobia led some to oppose the adoption of new foreign weapons. As late as 1642 Liu Tsung-chou was advising the emperor against relying on firearms, on the grounds that the T'ang and Sung dynasties had managed without them. In fact soldiers from many areas remained unfamiliar with guns, and the lack of experience of Chinese artisans led Hsu Kuang-ch'i to argue in 1630 that the manufacture of powder and shot should be left entirely to Europeans. At the same time, Hsu had to fend off a suggestion from the emperor that they could make better use of the expensive imported cannon by increasing the recommended charge of powder. The Chinese were notoriously casual with gunpowder, and accidents were common: hundreds were killed in one explosion in 1605 after a group of soldiers, finding that their powder supply had been stored for so long that it had congealed into a solid block, attacked it with axes.

Even in Late Ming times the majority of soldiers were equipped with more traditional weapons. Cavalry were mainly mounted archers – a technique adopted from the Mongols. They had declined in importance since the Early Ming because of a shortage of horses – a problem common to all dynasties without easy access to the northern grasslands. Infantry used bows, crossbows, long swords and polearms, of which many different types are illustrated in books such as the *Wu Pei Chih*. The majority of infantry wore no armour, but lamellar and probably brigandine armour, made of leather or iron plates, was in use, especially for cavalrymen and officers.

Battlements and musket holes on the Great Wall at Jinshanling. (© Stephen Turnbull)

THE MING GREAT WALL SYSTEM, c. 1640 (A simplified diagram)

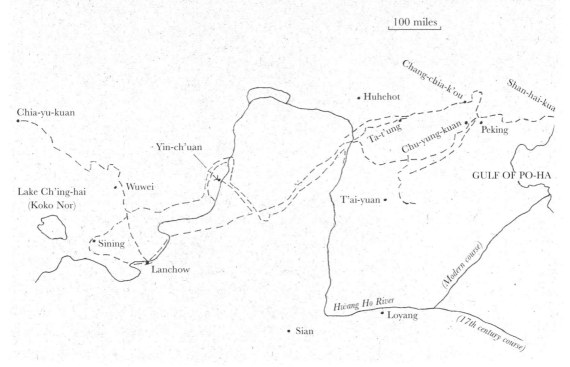

The Great Wall
==============

Of all the military accomplishments of the Chinese, the best known in the outside world has been the 'Great Wall'. Many of the claims made about it are misleading, however. Although the first continuous frontier wall was constructed under the Ch'in dynasty in about 215 BC, the usual assumption that it has enjoyed an uninterrupted existence since that time is incorrect. As mentioned previously, the succeeding Han dynasty (202 BC–AD 220) also maintained a 'Great Wall', which extended as far west as modern Kansu Province, but much of this was newly built; it is not clear how much of the Ch'in construction survived even then. In later years the whole system fell into disuse, and although some regimes did build new lines in various places, others maintained no such walls. The present construction dates from the 16th and 17th centuries, and along most of its course it runs well to the south of the line of the Ch'in original.

The Ming, ever conscious of the danger from the northern steppes, began erecting fortifications as soon as they took over the frontier zone in the 1370s, and systematic wall building began in the Ordos region in the 1480s, under the minister of war Yu Tzu-chun. By 1540 Yu's rammed earth walls were already

Cannon on the Great
Wall at Shan-hai-kuan.
(© Stephen Turnbull)

being eroded away. The growing threat from Altan Khan's new Mongol state was then countered by the construction of a series of defence lines in stone and brick, built mainly by the local garrison troops. This was not undertaken as a single project, but as a series of responses to Mongol attacks, beginning in the west and moving eastwards as successive raids were blocked and diverted in that direction. In some places the Mongols demolished the walls, and they had to be repeatedly rebuilt.

The wall's actual line probably owes much to the vicissitudes of politics at the Ming court, where proponents of aggressive 'forward' policies and defensive wall-building ones were constantly competing for power.

Some sectors in the west were never finished in stone, and remain to this day as low banks of earth; others, such as those protecting the cities of Ta-t'ung and Peking, were much more solidly constructed. At Badaling, north of the capital, the wall averages about 24 feet (approx. 7.4m) in height, 20 feet (approx. 6.1m) wide at the base and 16 feet (approx. 4.9m) wide on top – broad enough for five horsemen to ride abreast. It is faced with stone, with battlements at the top, and loopholes in places to enable the defenders to shoot from inside. Projecting buttresses every 150 yards (approx. 140m) permitted enfilading fire, and stone towers were added every 300 yards or so (approx. 280m), with firing ports for artillery and crossbows.

The three most important forts on the wall were Chia-yu-kuan, the 'Heroic Pass in the Sky' in the Chilian Mountains at the western end, built in 1372, but only linked to the line along the Yellow River in the 1570s; Chu-yung-kuan, near Peking, which had also been a major fortress since the beginning of the Ming period, but whose present walls date from about 1580; and Shan-hai-kuan in the east, on the Gulf of P'o-hai. Impetus was given to the construction of this eastern sector by the rise of the Manchus in the last decades of the 16th century, but the work was still not complete when Wu San-kuei, the commander at Shan-hai-kuan, let the Manchu armies through in 1644. The Manchus thus came into possession of the territory on both sides of the wall.

At the end of the 16th century the length of the wall was divided into nine *chen*, or military zones, each commanded by a general and subdivided into *lu*, or garrisons, of varying strength. Many sectors were manned only by patrols and sentries, but in the most important areas the wall itself became the core of an elaborate system of defence. Outlying forts, or *pao*, were built on either side in order to break up and channel an attack, or to provide a base for counter-attacks.

Immediately in front of the wall was a strip of raked sand to show the tracks of enemy raiding parties. Sentries could give warning of attacks by means of a prescribed system of bonfires and gunshots. For example, if the enemy was less than 100 strong, one gun was to be fired and one fire lit; for over 10,000 invaders, five shots and five bonfires were used. Coloured smoke or mounted messengers could be used to convey additional information.

Well behind the wall, the main garrisons were kept in reserve in walled camps, or *ch'eng*. They deployed heavy crossbows and guns located permanently in the towers. The value of firearms for defence against nomad cavalry was recognized early on, and from 1412 cannon were deployed in the northern frontier fortifications. They were supplied to the garrisons in considerable numbers: in Shensi between 1536 and 1538, for instance, 9,300 iron and brass guns were issued.

The European impact

While the attention of the Ming government remained concentrated upon the northern frontier, an entirely new threat was growing in the south. The Portuguese had discovered the sea route round the Cape of Good Hope to India in 1498, and soon began working their way further eastwards in search of the 'Spice Islands'. In 1511 they captured Malacca, a city-state on the Malay Peninsula that paid tribute to the Ming, and in 1517 the first Portuguese fleet reached China itself. It departed peacefully after selling its cargo of pepper, but

three years later another party, under Simao Andrade, undermined prospects for further friendly relations by attacking Chinese ships near Canton, and building a fort without permission on an offshore island. A short but indecisive naval war followed, after which the Portuguese were allowed to trade at Chang-chuen-shan and Ningpo, until they wasted this gain by once more indulging in piracy. During the 1540s they often collaborated with the *wo-k'ou* in smuggling their goods into the empire via the south-east coast. In 1557 they established a base on the peninsula of Macao, which was informally tolerated by the Ming government. It eventually became the main port for trade between China and Europe.

The next Europeans to establish relations with China were the Spanish, who began acquiring bases in the Philippines in the 1560s. After 1567, when the Ming ban on overseas voyages was lifted, a lucrative trade with Spanish America grew up. As we have seen, 16th-century European observers generally had a low opinion of Chinese military prowess, and it was perhaps natural that the Spanish, fresh from the conquest of vast empires in America, should entertain similar ambitions in Asia. Several proposals for the conquest of China were made – notably that of Andres de Mirandola, who outlined his plans in a letter to Philip II in 1569 – but the invasion never took place. In fact in 1574 the tables were turned when the Cantonese pirate Lin Feng nearly captured Manila – then protected only by a small wooden fort – in a surprise attack. He used ships so well provided with cannon that they were at first mistaken for Portuguese. The Spanish later cooperated with the Ming naval commander of Fukien Province in an attempt to catch Lin. It was suggested that they might receive a base at Amoy on the Chinese coast in return for their help, but as Lin managed to avoid capture, this concession was never granted.

In 1622 a Dutch fleet occupied the Pescadores Islands off the south coast and used them as a base for preying on Chinese shipping. The Ming repeated their earlier mistake by prohibiting trade, in an attempt to deprive the Dutch of victims and potential collaborators; however, this only succeeded in forcing many local people to resort to piracy and smuggling. In 1624 an improvised Ming fleet drove out the Dutch, who moved to Taiwan. The Chinese pirates, however, continued to flourish under the leadership of Cheng Chih-lung, who built up a strong power base in the southern coastal regions.

Overall, the Europeans made an unfavourable impression on the Chinese, who with some justification regarded them as little more than pirates. European behaviour reinforced the tendency of the Ming towards isolationism – a policy also favoured by the Manchus.

The fall of the Ming

In the 16th century the descendants of the Jurchen tribes, who in the 12th century had conquered northern China and established the Kin dynasty, were still living in Manchuria. They were nominally vassals of the Ming, who knew them as the 'Chien-chou Commandery'. As late as the 1590s they fought alongside the Chinese in Korea. From 1583, however, a leader named Nurhachi began the process of moulding the tribes into a centralized state. In 1601 he set up the famous 'Banner' system, which, like the *meng-an mou-k'o* of the medieval Jurchen, organized the whole population into military units and their supporting households. Then, in 1616, Nurhachi took this process to its logical conclusion and proclaimed himself, in Chinese style, Emperor T'ien Ming of the Later Kin dynasty. (The term 'Manchu', by which his people became known, is commonly applied to the period of Nurhachi's rule, although it was not in fact adopted until 1635. For convenience, despite the anachronism, we will follow this usage here.)

By 1618 all but two of the Manchu tribes acknowledged Nurhachi's authority. The exceptions, the Yehe and the Haihsi, were still under Ming protection – a fact that inevitably set Nurhachi on a collision course with China.

OPPOSITE The siege of Kweilin, 1647. Kweilin was held for the Ming by a detachment of Portuguese allies. A mobile pavise is being pushed into action by the invading Manchus, manned by either archers or handgunners. The primitive-looking multi-barrelled handguns are very similar to Ming types, and were no doubt captured or copied from the Chinese. They were thought to be more reliable in the fierce winds of the north than more modern weapons. The Portuguese colonial troops were formidable fighters, and highly valued by the Ming for their expertise with firearms. Their African slaves were surprisingly loyal, and were often considered to be their best troops. Even in the 17th century many of them were still armed with halberds, or with sword and buckler. (Christa Hook © Osprey Publishing Ltd)

The Manchus began by attacking the town of Fu-shun, which quickly surrendered, and destroying a Ming army sent to relieve it.

The Chinese response was to raise a force of 200,000 troops, including Yehe and Korean allies, under the command of the eminent general Yang Hao. In April 1619 they crossed the frontier, advancing in four widely separated columns on the Manchu capital at Hetu-ala.

Nurhachi was outnumbered by perhaps three to one, but he was operating on interior lines and his troops – mainly Manchu and Mongol cavalry – were more mobile. He concentrated against each Ming column in turn, and in a single week won three decisive victories – at Sarhu, Siyanggiayan and Niu-mao-chai. The fourth Chinese column hastily withdrew. The territory east of the Liao River quickly fell into Manchu hands. The able Ming strategist Hsiung T'ing-pi managed to restore order and hold the line of the Great Wall, but one of his subordinates took the offensive against Nurhachi again in 1621, and was defeated. Huang was unfairly blamed for this disaster and eventually executed.

The Manchus were unable to follow up their successes immediately. In 1626 they suffered a major defeat outside the town of Ning-yuan – mainly due to Ming superiority in firearms. Nurhachi received a wound in this engagement

OPPOSITE Chang Hsien-chung, the 'Yellow Tiger', who terrorized Szechwan. (© Stephen Turnbull)

The Great Wall snakes down the side of the 'yellow cliff' from which the Pass of Huangyaguan takes its name. (© Stephen Turnbull)

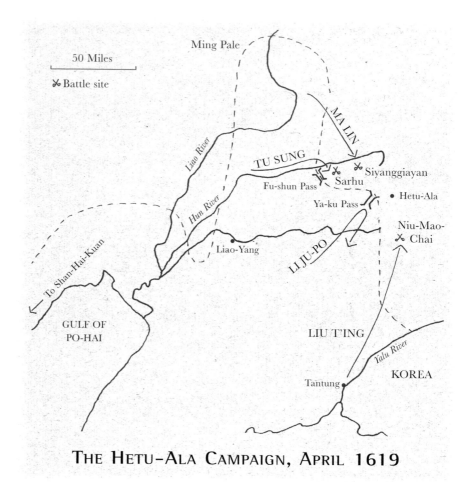

THE HETU–ALA CAMPAIGN, APRIL 1619

which may have been the cause of his death soon afterwards. They also experienced difficulty in absorbing the Chinese population of their new territories. Attempts to conciliate them in order to make use of their manpower were often frustrated by traditionalist generals, who still thought in terms of plunder rather than permanent conquest. The people of Yung-p'ing and Ch'ien-an, for example, were massacred when these towns fell in 1629, in defiance of official policy.

The capture of Yung-p'ing did bring with it an unexpected breakthrough, however. Manchu armies had until then been at a disadvantage in positional warfare, because they had no artillery train to match that of the Ming. Within the city the victors found European-trained gunsmiths, who were removed to Manchuria. By 1631 the Manchus were casting their own cannon.

By this time, however, another danger had arisen to distract the Ming. Peasant rebellions had been frequent throughout the 16th century, and now unrest was growing as a result of unfair taxation, official corruption and poverty

cxaccrbated by population growth and natural disasters. This was a pattern the Chinese had learned to associate with the withdrawal of the 'mandate of heaven' from a doomed dynasty. By the mid-1620s, government control had already been lost in several areas.

In 1627 the province of Shensi in the north-west erupted into open revolt. The people there were noted both for their poverty and for their skill at arms; many of them were excellent horsemen. Reinforced by thousands of defecting soldiers, they at first avoided pitched battles with government troops, but despite numerous setbacks, they gradually expanded. By the mid-1630s they had overrun most of central China, as far east as the lower Yangtze valley.

Eventually the various rebel bands coalesced into armies, led by loosely allied warlords. One of these was Chang Hsien-chung – known as the 'Yellow Tiger' – who left a reputation as the worst mass murderer in Chinese history. In 1642 Chang was in Anhui on the lower Yangtze, but under pressure from the Ming armies he moved upriver to Cheng-tu in Szechwan, where he began a reign of terror. The inhabitants of captured cities were routinely massacred, as were the owners of any land or property that Chang coveted. He killed officials and scholars wherever he found them, and responded to any disobedience by slaughtering whole units of his own men. Although the toll of victims attributed to this lunatic must be exaggerated – contemporaries quoted numbers as high as 600 million, far greater than the entire population of China at that time – he seems to have virtually eliminated the upper classes of Szechwan society. Chang remained at large until 1647, when his own followers handed him over to the Manchus.

More rational – and hence more dangerous – was Li Tzu-ch'eng, whose policy was to present himself as a protector of the common people. Supporters flocked to him as Ming authority collapsed, and in 1643 he proclaimed himself the first emperor of the Shun dynasty. In May 1644 he entered Peking, whereupon the Ming emperor, Ch'ung-chen, committed suicide.

However, the establishment of the new dynasty was thwarted by the commander of the north-eastern frontier, Wu San-kuei, who made an alliance with the Manchus. With their help he defeated Li outside the fortress of Shan-hai-kuan on the Great Wall. The Manchus, led by Prince Dorgon, lost no time in seizing their opportunity. They occupied Peking and set up their own imperial court, ruling as the Ch'ing dynasty. Li Tzu-ch'eng fell back to the north-west, where he fortified the T'ong Pass against his pursuers. Early in 1645 the Manchu Prince Dodo forced the pass and drove him further westwards. Li died soon afterwards, and his followers dispersed.

The Ming policy of centralization meant that the loss of the capital was a fatal blow. There was nowhere else in the empire that could provide a strong enough power base to permit reoccupation. Nevertheless, the Ming Empire did not collapse immediately. A successor to the late emperor was selected and installed at Nanking, where the regime became known as the Southern Ming. Its fatal weakness, however, soon became apparent: the court was distracted by disputes between rival princes, and its armies were depleted by a spate of defections to the Manchus. The remaining troops, still numbering several hundred thousand, could not be paid or supplied from the reduced territories under Ming control, so had to be allowed to plunder, thus alienating the populace.

To many Chinese of the official class, the Manchus now seemed to be the only power capable of restoring order. There was much popular opposition to the conquerors – in particular to a decree that forced the Chinese to shave their heads and wear the pigtail, in Manchu style – but the Ming leaders proved unable or unwilling to mobilize it. In 1645 Chin Sheng tried to organize a local militia in Chiang-nan, a task that would have involved the total militarization of the villagers – even the women were to be taught to fight.

Li Tzu-ch'eng, the founder of the short-lived Shun dynasty in 1643. (© Stephen Turnbull)

But the revolutionary implications of this were unacceptable to his colleagues, whose experiences had made them wary of arming the people. Their attitude was typified by Yang T''ing-shu, who was invited to join a pro-Ming guerrilla band in the Soochow region. He accepted their protestations of loyalty, but asked, 'From where will you get your supplies?' The guerrillas replied, 'From the people.' 'If that is the case', said Yang, 'then you are bandits. What has that to do with loyalty?'

A Ming counter-attack early in 1645 collapsed, and Prince Dodo swept into the Yangtze valley, where the local commanders surrendered. Early in June the Manchus crossed the Yangtze at Chen-chiang; Nanking fell soon afterwards. The

Ming loyalists fell back towards the south-east coast, where in a series of campaigns between 1646 and 1650 their strongholds were gradually reduced by the Manchus and their growing band of Chinese allies. The Ming appealed in desperation to the Portuguese and Japanese for aid. The latter stood aloof, but in 1647 the Portuguese provided 300 arquebusiers from Macao, who were involved in an epic but doomed defence of the city of Kweilin under the command of a Christian Chinese general, Ch'u Shih-ssu. In 1659 the last Ming emperor, Yung-li, was forced to flee to Burma. Two years later the Chinese general Wu San-kuei, fighting for the Ch'ing, followed him and forced the Burmese to hand him over for execution.

The Shun army

When he founded his short-lived Shun dynasty in 1643, Li Tzu-ch'eng had about 60,000 men under his command. They were organized into five divisions, split in turn into a varied numbers of units; each unit had 50 cavalry, 150 infantry and 30–40 servants. The largest division had 100 such units, while a further 130 or so were divided among the other four divisions. Perhaps inspired by his surname, which was the same as that of the founder of the T'ang dynasty, Li tried to gain an aura of legitimacy by adopting T'ang titles for his officials.

Earlier in his career, Li had lost his army after a defeat by the Ming at Tzu-t'ung in 1638; then he had had to ask for help from the Muslim rebels of Ma Shou-ying, who were also based in the north-west. Ma had given him some men, who formed the core of his new army. Muslims were therefore a significant element in the Shun forces, and there were even rumours that Li himself had adopted Islam. The main Muslim rebel forces continued to cooperate with Li, and in fact outlasted him. They fought on against the Manchus until 1650, when they were crushed by an army under Meng Ch'iao-fang.

Although the Shensi rebels had originally been poorly equipped, by the 1640s they had handguns and artillery in large quantities. These had not only been captured from the government; some had been manufactured in their own foundries. (One Ming official lamented, 'What we possess [in firearms] cannot be compared with theirs.') Li's victory over Tso Liang-yu in 1642 was attributed to this superiority of artillery. The Shun were also strong in cavalry, and some sources suggest that many of the infantry were mounted when on the march. The *K'ou-shih pien-nien* describes the spectacle of the rebel armies crossing rivers on their horses, of which there were so many that they seemed to block the flow of the water. Li is said to have needed boats only when crossing the Yellow River. By the time of their entry into Peking, in 1644, the Shun troops were uniformed, in green coats and white caps.

Discipline was good at first, although it deteriorated after the fall of the capital. Li had little interest in employing the talents of existing officials, whom he regarded as corrupt. But the vast fortunes Li had counted on seizing from them turned out to have been a myth. The resultant financial crisis made it difficult to pay or even feed the troops, and they began to rob the people. When Wu San-kuei's approach was reported, many men were reluctant to fight, having supposed that the war was over. In the crucial battle at Shan-hai-kuan the Shun army collapsed, and the disillusioned citizens of Peking welcomed the Manchus as liberators.

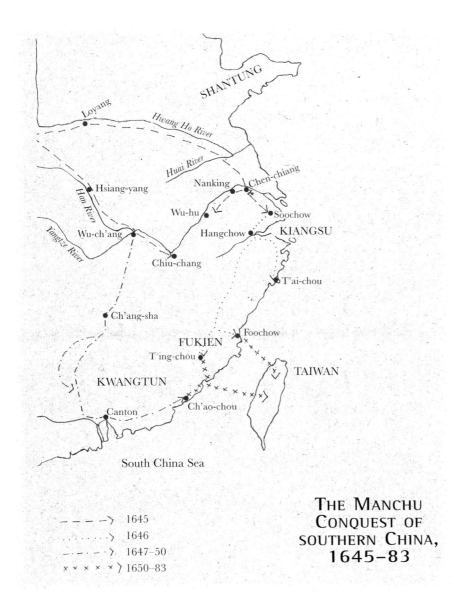

THE MANCHU
CONQUEST OF
SOUTHERN CHINA,
1645–83

- - - -> 1645
........> 1646
-.-.-.> 1647–50
× × × ×> 1650–83

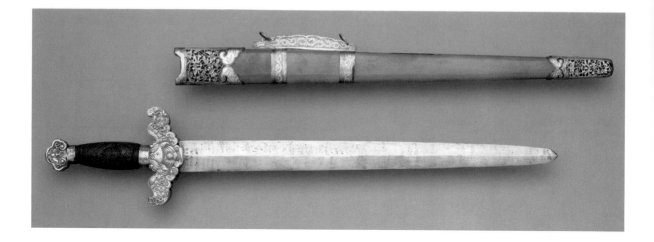

The Ch'ing dynasty, 1644–1842

It was to be some time yet, however, before the Manchus were able to enjoy their conquests in peace. The son of the pirate Cheng Chih-lung, Cheng Ch'eng-kung (better known in the West as Coxinga), remained at large along the south-east coast, building up a formidable force of Ming loyalists. In 1655 he advanced northwards with 250,000 men and 2,300 ships, with the avowed aim of restoring the Ming. The Ch'ing sent a fleet of their own, but their inexperience in naval matters led to its loss in a storm. In 1659 the overconfident Cheng besieged Nanking with the aim of luring his enemies into a decisive battle on land. The Manchus obliged, routing Cheng, who was forced to retreat with his fleet to the island of Taiwan.

There he found the Dutch in possession, but drove them out of their main stronghold, Fort Zeelandia, after a nine-month siege. Shortly afterwards Cheng died, but his successors held Taiwan for another 20 years. The island was poor, however, and a Ch'ing blockade imposed further hardship. The Cheng regime was never able to raise enough men or ships for an invasion of the mainland, and by 1664 the whole of the mainland coast was firmly in Manchu hands.

In 1673 a major revolt, known as the 'Rebellion of the Three Feudatories', broke out against the Ch'ing in southern China. This crisis was provoked by the young and inexperienced K'ang-hsi Emperor, who had attempted to reduce the privileges that had been granted to some of the leading Chinese generals in return for their support. The most powerful of these generals was Wu San-kuei. He retained command of the army with which he had invaded Burma, and ruled almost independently over much of the west and south-west, making enormous profits from his control of mines and trade routes. Joined by several other commanders, Wu proclaimed his own 'Chou' dynasty, and for a time threatened to overrun the whole country. But other Chinese generals remained loyal to the Ch'ing, and in 1676 Wu was weakened by the defection of two principal allies, Wang Fu-ch'en and Keng Ching-chung. Wu died in 1678, and the Ch'ing armies gradually closed in on K'un-ming, the remote city in Yunnan where he had established his capital. His successor, Wu Shih-fan, committed suicide in 1681, bringing the rebellion to an end.

Despite his previous record and his own dynastic ambitions, Wu presented himself as a Ming loyalist, and his men cut off their Manchu pigtails and wore their hair in the traditional Chinese style, under white caps. They also carried white flags, as a sign of mourning for the Ming. Wu's army was noteworthy for maintaining a corps of 45 elephants. It is not clear when this was first established, but the animals were presumably acquired through his contacts with Burma.

After the defeat of the Three Feudatories, most of the Chinese heartland enjoyed a period of peace under a series of able and long-lived emperors: K'ang-hsi (1661–1722), Yung-cheng (1723–36) and Ch'ien-lung (1736–96). Civil order was imposed somewhat heavy-handedly, but official corruption was brought under control, and the tax

burden on the peasantry was relatively light. For most of the 18th century China enjoyed unprecedented prosperity. Beginning in the K'ang-hsi reign, the empire was able to undertake a series of successful military campaigns, which expanded its boundaries to their greatest ever extent.

One of the first external threats came from the Russians, who were moving south and eastwards from their settlements in Siberia. In 1652 they invaded the Amur valley in Manchuria and massacred the tribes there, who were vassals of the Ch'ing. At first they were driven off by a Manchu expedition, but they

OPPOSITE 18th-century
cavalry. Shown here are
a Manchu horse-archer
and a Muslim musketeer.
In the background,
camel-mounted artillery
can be seen. (Christa
Hook © Osprey
Publishing Ltd)

returned two years later and attempted to take their boats up the Sungari River, a tributary of the Amur, which led into the Manchu heartland. In the spring of 1658 they were decisively defeated by a Ch'ing fleet of river boats armed with cannon. In 1685 fighting broke out again over the Russian fort at Albazin on the Amur. The issue was eventually settled in 1689 by a conference between the Russian ambassador and the Manchu prince Songgotu, who was backed up by an army of 15,000 men with 50 cannon. The Russians, who had no more than 2,000 troops in the area, were suitably impressed and agreed to make peace. This agreement, the Treaty of Nerchinsk, was the first between China and a European power, and was a clear victory for the former. Ch'ing rule over northern Manchuria was acknowledged, and it remained unchallenged until the 1850s.

The eastern Mongols or Khalka had been allied to the Manchus since before the Manchu conquest of China, but in the west a group of independent tribes known as the Oirats had occupied the Tarim Basin and Tibet and established an aggressive rival empire. In 1686 their leader, Galdan Khan, attacked the Khalka, provoking war with the Ch'ing. In 1696 K'ang-hsi himself led an expedition into Mongolia. Galdan attempted to avoid battle, but was trapped between converging columns and defeated at Jao Modo, near present-day Ulan Bator. The khan escaped, but was hunted down the following year.

This victory gave the Ch'ing control of most of what is now Mongolia, but further west one of the Oirat clans, the Jungars, was gradually rebuilding its strength. In 1755 war broke out again, and two years later a Manchu army under Chao Hui invaded the Ili valley. The Jungars were virtually wiped out, and the Muslims of the Tarim Basin, who had supported the Jungars, were also defeated, in 1759. The Ch'ing frontier was pushed forward as far as Lake Balkhash and the Pamir Mountains, where Chinese armies had not penetrated since the days of the T'ang.

Part of the reason for the Manchu success was their own affinity with the Central Asian nomads: their cavalry fought in the same style, as highly mobile mounted archers, and the Ch'ing armies could outmanoeuvre the Mongols on the steppe – something traditional Chinese forces had seldom managed to do. Furthermore, the nomads, who had for centuries relied on the vast spaces of the steppe for protection, could no longer retreat beyond the reach of armies based in China, for the Russians were advancing from the opposite direction, into what is now Kazakhstan.

Other influences were also at work to weaken the Mongols: those under Ch'ing rule had been impoverished by the government's policy of restricting them to specific grazing grounds, which in time of drought were unable to support their horse herds; tribes beyond the frontier suffered from chronic political disunity and a devastating series of epidemics, probably transmitted by farmers and traders moving into their lands as the settled population increased;

and the spread of Buddhism may also have encouraged some Mongols to abandon their traditional warlike pursuits. A combination of factors, therefore, lay behind the sudden evaporation of the Mongol menace which had dominated Chinese military policy for so long.

Success on other fronts led to the Ch'ien-lung reign being remembered for its 'Ten Great Victories', although they were not all of equal significance. Tibet had been reduced to vassalage in 1720, and nominal Ch'ing authority was maintained thereafter by sporadic expeditions. In 1790 Gurkhas from Nepal invaded Tibet and looted the rich monastery of Tashilhunpo. The Dalai Lama asked Ch'ien-lung for help, and an army of 80,000 men was despatched under the Manchu general Fu K'ang. Fu quickly drove out the invaders, pursued them over the Himalayan passes and defeated them at Nawakot, not far from Katmandu. The Gurkhas agreed to pay tribute to Peking, which they continued to do until 1908. In view of the well-known prowess of the Gurkhas in their later encounters with the British, this campaign provides an interesting insight into the performance of Chinese armies in the late 18th century. It is clear that they were still in the front rank of Asian powers, in terms not just of numerical strength, but also of strategic mobility and effectiveness on the battlefield.

Not all of Ch'ien-lung's campaigns were so successful, however. Between 1767 and 1771 four armies sent against Burma met with disaster, although eventually the Burmese king agreed to pay a nominal tribute. In 1786 an expedition was sent by land and sea to Vietnam in support of the last king of the Later Le dynasty (another vassal, who had been deposed by rebels). In 1789 the Ch'ing suffered a defeat and had to abandon the campaign, but the king of the new Nguyen dynasty also paid tribute. In practice, however, this amounted to no more than an agreement to restore trading relations.

In the south-western provinces of Yunnan, Kweichow and Szechwan, maladministration and an influx of Chinese colonists caused recurring trouble among tribes such as the Miao. The revolt in Chin-ch'uan in Szechwan lasted intermittently for 30 years after 1746, and the campaign which finally suppressed it, in 1771–76, is said to have cost twice as much as the wars against the Jungars. The tribes of Taiwan and the Muslims of the north-west also revolted in the 1780s, necessitating yet more expensive military operations.

The growth of the population of the empire under the Ch'ing was spectacular: from 140 million in 1740 to 360 million in 1812. Reasons often given for this include the decline of epidemic diseases and the importation of new food crops, but it is likely that a major cause was the long period of internal peace imposed by the Manchus. However, this vast increase in population brought its own problems. Natural disasters leading to popular unrest have been a recurring theme throughout Chinese history, but by the end of the 18th century the explanations being given were beginning to have a very modern ring.

Population pressure was forcing farmers to cultivate marginal land and cut down the trees on the hillsides. This led to soil erosion and silting of the rivers, with consequent disastrous floods.

Furthermore, as the ageing Ch'ien-lung Emperor lost his grip on the government, corruption reappeared. Soon the Chinese peasantry began to show signs of unrest. The revolts led by the White Lotus secret society after 1795 were especially serious: in 1813 a related group, the Eight Trigrams Rebels, entered Peking and nearly stormed the imperial palace. Early in the 19th century the Muslims of the Tarim Basin resumed their struggle for independence under a leader called Jahangir, who between 1817 and 1827 repeatedly challenged Ch'ing authority with the support of his co-religionists from Kokand, beyond the frontier. Economic recession made the situation worse. By the 1840s the Ch'ing dynasty was widely regarded as being in decline.

The issue of trade eventually brought about the fatal clash between China and Europe. The Ch'ing inherited the approach to foreign policy that had infuriated Hideyoshi, and persisted in the diplomatic fiction that regarded all embassies from other powers as proof that their rulers acknowledged the overlordship of the Son of Heaven. These 'tribute missions', however, were expensive for their hosts to receive with proper ceremony, and were generally unwelcome. In 1757 overseas trade was restricted to the city of Canton.

A Chinese military post, 1796. (Topfoto/Fotomas)

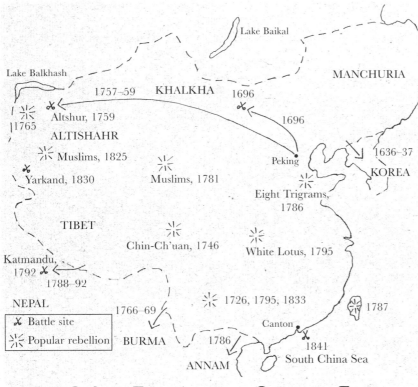

THE CH'ING EMPIRE AT ITS GREATEST EXTENT

Lake Baikal

MANCHURIA

Lake Balkhash

1757–59   KHALKHA   1696

Altshur, 1759   1696

1765

ALTISHAHR

Muslims, 1825   Peking   1636–37

KOREA

Yarkand, 1830   Muslims, 1781

Eight Trigrams, 1786

TIBET   Chin-Ch'uan, 1746   White Lotus, 1795

Katmandu, 1792   1726, 1795, 1833   1787

1788–92

NEPAL   Canton

✗ Battle site   1766–69   1841

Popular rebellion   BURMA   1786   South China Sea

ANNAM

OPPOSITE 17th- and 18th-century Tibetan infantryman and cavalryman. Tibet was nominally a Ch'ing vassal from 1720, and Tibetan troops fought alongside the Manchus in the Gurkha War of 1792. The Monlam festival – commemorating the inauguration of the fifth Dalai Lama, in 1642 – was celebrated until the 1950s with the aid of performers dressed in authentic armour and equipment of the period. These figures are based mainly on photographs taken by European visitors, with other details from Tibetan and Central Asian armours in the Royal Armouries. A Chinese account in the *Wei Tsang T'u Chih* of 1792 confirms that this type of equipment was still in use at that time. (Christa Hook © Osprey Publishing Ltd)

Ch'ien-lung's response to Lord Macartney's embassy from Britain has become famous: the British were informed that it was impossible for an ambassador to be allowed to reside in Peking, and that a trade agreement was unnecessary, as China had no need of foreign goods.

Ultimately, however, the growing military and commercial power of Europe could not be kept out. The British insistence on being able to sell the opium they produced in India, in spite of the social evils brought about by its consumption, gave rise to an episode that left a long legacy of bitterness in China. Opium had been banned by the Ch'ing in 1731, but since the 1770s smuggling had flourished. After 1816 the British East India Company began to flood the Chinese market with the drug, hoping to reverse the balance of trade, which until then had been in China's favour.

The effects of this policy – on law and order, on the currency, which risked collapse as silver poured out of the country, and on the individuals, including many soldiers, who became addicted to the drug – have sometimes been exaggerated, but they were enough to provoke the Ch'ing government to take action. In 1839 Lin Tse-hui ('Commissioner Lin') was sent to Canton, the main centre for opium imports, to stop the smuggling. He confiscated opium and expelled British merchants, who appealed to their own government for support.

In 1841 full-scale war broke out. The British advanced by land and sea from Canton to Nanking, smashing every attempt by Ch'ing forces to oppose them. In the following year the Chinese government was forced to sign the Treaty of Nanking, consenting to the opium trade and granting Britain a base at Hong Kong, as well as the right to trade at several other ports.

The series of 'unequal treaties' with the European powers that followed was doubly humiliating because such a relationship with outsiders was so completely unprecedented. For 3,000 years China had seen itself as the centre of the political universe, granting the privilege to trade or live in the 'Middle Kingdom' only to those who showed suitable reverence for China's institutions. Even when the military balance of power had temporarily swung in favour of the 'barbarians', invaders had generally been quick to acknowledge the superiority of Chinese culture. The Manchus, for example, had soon begun to outdo the Chinese themselves in their eagerness to maintain the dignity of the empire. Now that the myth of military superiority had been shattered, the prestige of the Ch'ing dynasty had suffered a serious blow. The 'Opium Wars' were thus one of the main causes of the great rebellions which convulsed the empire in the mid-19th century.

Ch'ing armies

The core of the Manchu military system at the time of the conquest consisted of the *pa-ch'i*, or 'Eight Banners'. When the system was set up in 1601, there were

A 19th-century sword, with scabbard. The angled hilt, covered with ray skin, is characteristic of Ch'ing period weapons. (Topfoto/HIP/The Royal Armouries)

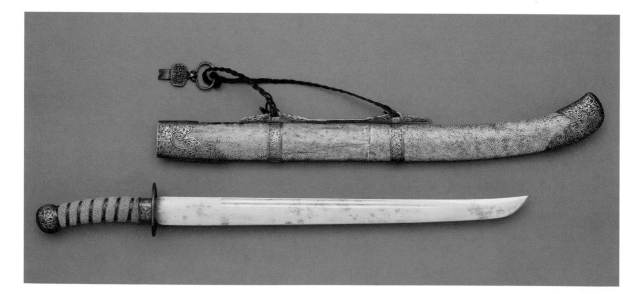

four Banners – the Yellow, White, Red and Blue – distinguished by flags of the respective colours. In 1616 four more Manchu Banners were created, using flags of the same four colours but with contrasting borders. In addition, an army carried a black silk flag, which was used as a rallying point and seems to have been regarded as sacred; Nurhachi is described as offering sacrifices to it. Each Banner was divided into five *jalans*, or regiments, each of five *nirus*, or 'arrows'. A *niru* had a nominal strength of 300 men.

An invaluable source for the appearance and equipment of Manchus of the conquest period is the *Tai-tzu shih-lu*, an illustrated biography of Nurhachi published in 1635. This shows armoured cavalry with bows, swords and lances, and also infantry equipped with spears, swords, bows and handguns. It has been suggested that the standard deployment was to shelter the cavalry behind three lines of infantry – spearmen, swordsmen, then archers. It is not certain how many of the infantry were Manchus rather than Chinese allies; nor how rigid the difference was at this time between members of the original Jurchen tribes and assimilated Chinese. It is often assumed that all the former were cavalry. However, before the conquest of China the Manchu state had not been wealthy and had suffered from recurring famines, so it is unlikely that the expense of mounting all the soldiers could have been met. The infantry in the *Tai-tzu shih-lu* are dressed very similarly to the Manchu cavalry and – apart from the guns that some footsoldiers carry – use the same weapons. Later, in the Ch'ing period, a logical division of labour was maintained where possible, with the Chinese providing the infantry and artillery, and the Manchus the cavalry.

From 1618 the Manchus also relied heavily on subject Mongol cavalry, although they regarded the Mongols as undisciplined, and a bad influence on Manchu warriors. In 1634 the Mongols were organized into their own Banners, which by 1644 also numbered eight. They were commanded by a hereditary Mongol aristocracy, the *jasaks*, or 'Banner princes'. The Banners were divided into *jalans* like those of the Manchus, each of which comprised six *sumuns*. Other Mongol groups, like the Khalka who assisted against Galdan in the 1690s, were allies rather than subjects, and remained in their own tribal units. The Mongols continued to fight in their traditional manner as mounted archers as late as the 1860s, although matchlock muskets were also in use by the mid-18th century.

In the 1620s the conquest of Liaotung brought large numbers of Chinese under Manchu rule. At first the conquerors levied one man in 20 to serve in the Manchu Banners, but this was raised to one in ten when the first Chinese Banner was formed, in 1630. Numbers increased rapidly, until in 1642 there were eight Chinese Banners, in which one in three of the male population was liable for service. Throughout the dynasty, however, Chinese and Mongols were also to be found in the Manchu Banners, although in diminishing numbers. Later the

Chinese Banners declined in importance, possibly as a result of the mistrust engendered by the Three Feudatories Rebellion.

By the 18th century the majority of native Chinese troops were to be found in the *lu-ying*, or Green Standard army. This had originally been a garrison force. It consisted of more than a thousand *ying*, or battalions, of widely varying strength scattered throughout the provinces, leaving the Manchus concentrated around Peking, on the northern frontier and in the more important towns.

The Chinese were not regarded by the Manchus as very good soldiers, and their loyalty was often suspect. At Yung-p'ing in 1630 they fought with signs reading 'New Soldier' pinned to their backs so that the Manchus could keep an eye on them. They were often accused of standing back and allowing the Manchus to do all the fighting, and of hiring incapable substitutes to serve in their place – a practice which had spread to the Manchus themselves as early as the 1630s.

Even in the 19th century foreign visitors observed that the Manchu troops were much better than the Chinese, and that it was to the advantage of the regime to keep it that way. However, Chinese numbers, along with their expertise with ships and artillery, meant that it was impossible to do without them. Chinese officers had held high positions in Ch'ing armies as early as the 1620s, when hereditary ranks were given to the most loyal. Li Yung-fang, who surrendered the town of Fu-shun in 1618, was the first defector of rank, and was eventually given command of a Banner. His sons all became officers in the Chinese Blue Banner.

Wu San-kuei and the other 'Feudatories', along with lesser collaborators, were of vital importance to the Manchu conquest of China after 1644, and were rewarded with generous grants of land and political privileges, which at first amounted to virtual independence. Even after Wu's revolt, in 1673, Chinese generals such as Chao Liang-tung remained loyal to the Ch'ing and led armies against the rebels. During the Ch'ien-lung reign Manchus and Mongols began to replace natives in the high command, but this process was never completed, and indeed was reversed after the middle of the 19th century.

Another *jian* or ceremonial sword, from the Ch'ien-lung reign (1736–96). (Board of Trustees of the Royal Armouries, No. XXVI-90s)

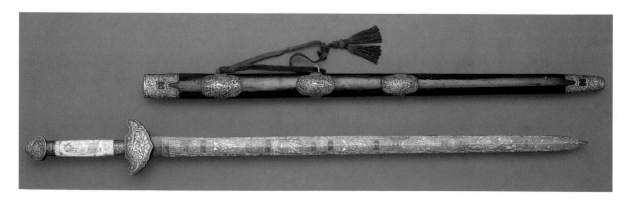

The Ch'ing rulers generally showed great respect for Chinese culture and literature, but there is little evidence that this extended to the traditional military classics. In fact the K'ang-hsi Emperor is reported to have dismissed them as 'full of nonsense about water and fire, lucky omens and advice on the weather, all at random and contradicting each other'. He advised his officers to ignore them and rely instead on strength of will and careful planning.

By the 1620s infantry handguns and even artillery were beginning to appear in Manchu armies, but the cavalry remained reluctant to give up their bows. Pictures of the Altshur campaign of 1759 show them still fighting as horse-archers against mounted Muslim musketeers, and even 30 years later the government was worried that the Bannermen might neglect their archery skills because of the new popularity of firearms. This was not necessarily an illogical preference, since matchlock firearms were awkward to handle and reload on horseback, and a well-trained archer could shoot much more quickly.

Nineteenth-century outsiders usually described Ch'ing troops as cautious to the point of timidity, but although sanctioned by some elements of Chinese tradition, this was largely a response to the Europeans' superiority in firearms. British observers during the Opium Wars remarked that the enormous casualties suffered initially by the Chinese were the result of their attempts to come to close quarters with steady infantry armed with the new percussion muskets. Excessive caution was certainly not in evidence among the Manchus in their heyday. K'ang-hsi, for example, described how he had pursued Galdan Khan into the steppes in the 1696 campaign – leaving behind first the Chinese infantry, then the artillery, and pressing on with the cavalry alone. He took the enemy completely by surprise, and was rewarded with all the signs of precipitate flight: abandoned armour; bowls of unfinished food; and women, children and the sick left behind.

Mobility was also required of the artillery. In the 1675 campaign against Wu San-kuei, the existing iron guns were found to be too heavy to take the field. Following the Ming example, the Jesuit Verbiest was ordered to supervise the casting of lighter bronze pieces, which proved very successful. From then on guns of this type, whether imported or cast

233

locally, were the mainstay of the Ch'ing artillery. Indigenous development had not entirely ceased, however, and Chinese inventors continued to approach the authorities with ambitious ideas, such as the 28-round repeating gun which Tai Tzu presented to K'ang-hsi in the 1670s. Like similar efforts in Europe, it was probably too complicated for existing construction techniques, and never saw action.

By the early 19th century, the Ch'ing army was beginning to show signs of deterioration. The long period of internal peace was partly responsible for this, for most units had no recent experience of action, and their training diverged more and more from the needs of actual combat. By the 1820s it seems to have finally been recognized that the gun was replacing the bow as the weapon of choice. One reason for this is likely to have been that it required much less training to use. According to a Chinese officer who attended Lord Macartney's party in 1793, matchlocks were preferred to flintlocks, since the latter, though quicker to reload, were more liable to misfire. In fact there were not even enough of the older weapons to equip the majority of the troops. Typically, J. F. Davis reported of the soldiers at Tientsin in 1841, 'Some few had matchlocks, but the greatest number nothing but swords, with bows and arrows.'

Davis also noted the skirmishing drill the musketeers practised: they 'shot in rapid succession, and kept up a sort of running fire round a man who stood with a flag in the centre, and served as a pivot to the rest'. In general the individualistic, almost gymnastic, style of military exercise which 16th-century observers had noted still prevailed, the lack of disciplined opposition during the long Manchu peace having provided no incentive for the rediscovery of the value of solid infantry formations. Huc's scathing description of a review in the 1840s is well known:

> It is impossible to imagine anything more whimsical and comic than the evolutions of the Chinese soldiers; they advance, draw back, leap, pirouette, cut capers, crouch behind their shields, as if to watch the enemy, then jump up again, distribute blows right and left, and then run away with all their might, crying, 'Victory! Victory!'

In defensive techniques too appearance was often valued above effectiveness. Lord Macartney observed that the firing ports in many city walls were not provided with guns, but with doors on which were painted 'the representations of cannon, which at a distance look somewhat like the sham ports of our men of war'. In 1841 Davis noted watchtowers made of mats, painted to resemble brick or stone. He ridiculed this as 'playing at soldiers', though he would not have known of the long and honourable Chinese tradition of using dummy fortifications to deceive an opponent. More serious symptoms of decline included the poor state of repair of many personal weapons, the shortage of horses among the Bannermen, which forced many who were nominally cavalry to fight on foot, and the growing addiction to opium among the soldiery.

At the same time, the relative military effectiveness of the tribal and Chinese peasant populations – the very people least likely to be loyal to the dynasty – was increasing. Chinese civilians were initially forbidden to possess firearms, but during the 18th century they became very common among smugglers and bandits – to the extent that in 1760 the prohibition had to be lifted in order to allow the law-abiding to protect themselves. By the 1830s some bandits even had their own artillery pieces, and feuding clans in Fukien Province built fortified 'gun towers' all over the countryside. The Miao of the southern mountains were well equipped with guns and crossbows, which K'ang-hsi had permitted them to keep despite their support for Wu San-kuei; K'ang-hsi recognized the practical impossibility of disarming them. The government was never able to subdue them, and was reduced to building forts at the bottom of the mountain passes in a largely unsuccessful attempt to stop them raiding into the plains. As late as the 1830s, Ch'ing troops seeking to advance into Miao territory suffered several severe defeats. Twenty years later many of the tribesmen were to throw in their lot with the Taipings.

Significant battles of late Imperial China

Ying-chou, 1517

In October 1517 a large Mongol force bypassed the border fortress of Ta-t'ung and advanced into China. On 18 October they were stopped at Ying-chou, 40 miles south of Ta-t'ung, by a Ming army. The first day's fighting was inconclusive, but the following day the Cheng-te Emperor himself arrived with reinforcements and took control of operations. He played an active role in the fighting and killed at least one Mongol; he also only narrowly avoided capture. The battle lasted for two more days, but at dusk on 20 October the Mongols withdrew towards the north. The Ming pursuit was swift, but was halted by a sudden dust storm.

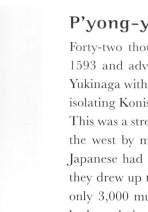

P'yong-yang, 1593

Forty-two thousand Ming troops under Li Ju-sung entered Korea in January 1593 and advanced on the city of P'yong-yang. Opposing them was Konishi Yukinaga with 18,700 Japanese. The Japanese garrisons of two nearby forts fled, isolating Konishi, who nevertheless deployed for battle on a hill north of the city. This was a strong position, which could not be outflanked, as it was protected on the west by mountains and on the south and east by the Tadong River. The Japanese had fortified their front with earthworks and palisades, behind which they drew up their arquebusiers. The Chinese possessed some artillery, but with only 3,000 musketeers were at a disadvantage in hand firearms. Li, therefore, had no choice but to order a frontal attack; this began on 10 February. Korean observers were shocked to see the unarmoured Chinese infantry repeatedly charging the Japanese line and being shot down in their hundreds. After two days of fighting, however, the Japanese were driven from their positions and retired inside P'yong-yang, leaving behind 2,000 dead. Li Ju-sung stopped to rest his exhausted troops, and Konishi took the opportunity to evacuate the city and flee southwards. Belatedly, Li followed him with 1,000 cavalry, but encountered a larger Japanese force near Seoul and had to abandon the pursuit.

Sarhu, 1619

Four separate Ming columns set out in April 1619 with the aim of converging on the Manchu capital at Hetu-ala. The first to encounter the enemy were the 25,000 troops of Tu Sung – a notoriously rash commander known to his enemies as 'Tu the Madman'. Tu forded the Hun River with his infantry and cavalry, in his haste leaving behind a unit of wagons equipped with artillery, which were unable to cross. He broke through some Manchu barricades on the far shore and took a few prisoners, then rushed forward at the head of his men, straight into an ambush by 30,000 Mongols. Cutting his way out, Tu attempted to seize the commanding high ground on a nearby mountain. This was a logical move, but Nurhachi had foreseen it and deployed his Manchus there in another ambush. Tu was killed, along with all his divisional commanders and most of his men.

Chen-chiang, 1645

The strategically important city of Chen-chiang, on the south bank of the Yangtze, was held against the Manchus by a large Ming garrison. This was commanded by Cheng Hung-k'uei and Cheng Ts'ai, the brothers of the pirate warlord Cheng Chih-lung, and included many men armed with muskets. The night of 1 June 1645 was foggy and visibility was poor, so the Manchus, under

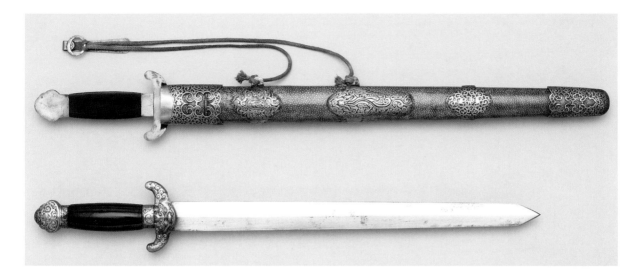

Prince Dodo, attempted a diversion. They floated unmanned rafts across the river, carrying burning torches. The nervous Ming troops opened fire on these, wasting most of their ammunition, while the real Manchu army crossed undetected further upriver. At dawn the defenders discovered the enemy advancing on them along the southern shore, and panicked. The Cheng brothers abandoned their men, escaping to Foochow by ship. Chen-chiang fell almost without a fight, leaving the new Ming capital at Nanking exposed.

The two sieges of Albazin, 1685–86

By 1685 the Russians had been evicted from the whole of the lower Amur valley in northern Manchuria, except for the fort of Albazin, which was held by about 500 Cossacks. The wooden fortifications consisted of a high stockade with corner towers on which artillery could be mounted, surrounded by a moat. Outside the moat was a palisade, and beyond that iron stakes hidden in pits. In June 1685 a Ch'ing army of 10,000 men arrived under the local Manchu governor, Sabsu. They built siege works and put gunboats on the Amur River to isolate the fort, then set fire to the outer palisade. The Russian commander, Tolbuzin, surrendered and was allowed to retire to Nerchinsk. The Manchus burned the fort and left, but neglected to destroy or harvest the crops that the Russians had sown in the vicinity. Soon afterwards Tolbuzin reoccupied the site with 826 men, 12 cannon and a Prussian engineer, who supervised the rebuilding. Albazin was now well stocked with food and gunpowder. In July 1686 Sabsu returned with 7,000 men and 40 cannon. He placed his heavy guns on a hill a third of a mile away and the lighter pieces about 500 paces from the palisade. Then, under cover of a bombardment, the Manchus shot fire arrows

ABOVE Early-19th-century pair of swords and scabbard. The scabbard is covered in ray skin. The swords would have been used one in each hand, but resembled a single weapon when sheathed. (Topfoto/HIP/The Royal Armouries)

LEFT 19th-century Indo-Chinese spearhead. This curved style, reminiscent of the Japanese *naginata*, was also widely used by Chinese troops. (Board of Trustees of the Royal Armouries, No. XXVI-198)

Chinese iron chain whip, 19th century. Such exotic weapons were associated with martial artists and members of secret societies rather than regular troops. (Board of Trustees of the Royal Armouries, No. XXVI-50c)

and attacked from the cover of wheeled shields. However, several attempts to scale the walls with ladders were repulsed by the Russian guns. Tolbuzin was killed leading a sortie, but the fort held out until November, when negotiations began between the two governments. By this time only 66 defenders remained alive. The Russians realized that Albazin could not be held, and in the subsequent peace treaty they agreed to abandon it.

Maymyo, 1767

Ming Jui, a son-in-law of the Ch'ien-lung Emperor, advanced on the Burmese capital at Ava with 50,000 men in two columns. The first proceeded through Bhamo and the second, under Ming himself, further south, via Hsien-wi. The first column was held up outside a fortified position at Kaungton, and contrary to Ming's orders, its commander retreated. The Burmese king, Hsinbyushin, then despatched two divisions to deal with Ming Jui. One, consisting of 10,000 infantry and 2,000 cavalry, advanced directly to meet the Chinese, while a larger force, under the overall commander Maha Thiha Thura, moved by a circuitous route over the hills to the south to get behind them. Ming quickly repulsed the frontal attack and resumed his advance, but the Burmese remained in contact and continued to harass him. The Manchu cavalry were prevented from foraging or protecting their lines of communication, and supplies began to run short. Two days later, 50 miles north-east of Ava, Maha Thiha Thura appeared in the rear of the invaders. In three days of fighting, the Chinese were encircled by the two Burmese divisions. Ming concentrated his entire army against the smaller enemy force in an attempt to break out, but the Burmese held on until their other division came up and attacked the Ch'ing from behind. By the battle's end 2,500 Chinese were taken as slaves, and the rest were massacred. Ming Jui committed suicide.

Yarkand, 1830

Ten thousand Kokandi cavalry crossed the Ala T'au Mountains into the Tarim Basin and seized the Chinese frontier city of Kashgar. The nearby garrison at Yarkand held out, despite numbering only 500 Bannermen and 4,500 poorly trained local militia. The Ch'ing commander, Pi-ch'ang, deployed 400 of his regulars outside the east gate of the city and left 1,000 militiamen to guard the Muslim town and the Manchu cantonment. He prepared fields of fire for his few artillery pieces by demolishing outlying market stalls and buildings. The Kokandis tried to rush the gate, but lost some 300 men to cannon fire in their first charge. They then regrouped and attacked again. When this charge was also broken they withdrew, taking with them a large haul of slaves and loot from the surrounding countryside.

Conclusion

The relationship between the Chinese and the outside world changed radically after the 1840s. The European powers exploited their new technical advantages to impose a series of humiliating treaties on the Ch'ing Empire, whose people found themselves in an unfamiliar position of inferiority. It took another century before their unity and self-confidence were fully restored, and during that time Westerners formed a negative view of Chinese military abilities, which still colours many accounts today. Reasons commonly suggested for their supposed unwarlike character include the pacifist influence of the Confucian-educated scholars, the defensive mentality typified by the Great Wall, and a supposed reluctance on the part of the imperial bureaucracy to adopt new ideas and inventions.

In fact, as this narrative has shown, the whole stereotype is a myth, which flourished only because the long history of Chinese warfare was so poorly understood. The scholar class did not achieve real power until halfway through the imperial era, and the Great Wall was maintained by only a handful of the regimes that flourished since its foundation by the Ch'in, most of which preferred to pursue an offensive strategy against the tribes of the northern steppes. The isolationist rule of the Ming did gradually begin to stifle innovation, but until then China had been at the cutting edge of military technology. Ironically, the economically advanced Sung dynasty was primarily responsible for developing the very gunpowder weapons that eventually enabled the West to subjugate its successors.

As for their individual fighting prowess, regardless of the particular dynasty for which they have fought, Chinese soldiers have never lost their reputation for courage and endurance. Far from being defensive-minded, their most characteristic tactic has always been a ferocious headlong charge, which their commanders have sometimes struggled to control and direct. As well as developing battlefield leadership to a fine art, Chinese generals were notably successful at raising large numbers of troops and supplying them on distant campaigns. Their contribution to the theory of generalship has been belatedly recognized today, when the writings of men like Sun Tzu on the 'Art of War' have become classics as much admired in the West as in their homeland.

Historians have often speculated about what might have happened if the armies of East and West had ever been pitted against each other. How would Alexander the Great have fared against the Ch'in, or Pan Chao against the Roman Empire? We will never know; it was its isolation from the rest of the great powers of Eurasia that gave Chinese warfare its distinctive character. It is sobering to realize that, even at the limit of his advance on the Oxus River, Alexander was less than halfway from Macedonia to the northern China plain. But it would be hard to deny that in men like Sun Pin, Han Hsin, Ts'ao Ts'ao and Li Shih-min, China possessed leaders who equalled any of the great captains of the West, and whose stories deserve to be remembered.

PREVIOUS SPREAD The Ch'ien-lung Emperor and bodyguards. These figures are based on a painting by the Italian Jesuit Castiglione, showing the emperor at an archery contest. As late as the end of the 18th century Manchu emperors continued to practise the archery skills of their ancestors; however, after K'ang-hsi (1661–1722) they no longer took the field in person. The system of coloured buttons worn on the cap to denote rank was an innovation of the Ch'ien-lung period. Until then, different coloured robes had been worn, with badges depicting animals for military and birds for civil officials – a continuation of the Ming tradition. (Christa Hook © Osprey Publishing Ltd)

OPPOSITE The 'First Pass Under Heaven', the most important gateway on the Ming Great Wall, now fully restored. The Manchu invaders marched through this very gate. (© Stephen Turnbull)

241

Bibliography

Primary sources in translation:

Chan-Kuo Ts'e, trans. J. I. Crump (Clarendon Press, 1970)

Loewe, M., *Records of Han Administration* (2 volumes) (Cambridge University Press, 1967)

Lord Macartney (J. Cranmer-Byng, ed.), *An Embassy to China*

Na Chih-liang, *The Emperor's Procession – Two Scrolls of the Ming Dynasty* (National Palace Museum, 1970)

Pan Ku, trans. H. Dubs, *The History of the Former Han Dynasty* (Kegan Paul, Trench, Trubner & Co., 1944)

Polo, Marco, *The Travels*, trans. R. Latham (Penguin Classics edition, 1958)

Records of the Grand Historian of China (extracts from Ssu-ma Ch'ien's *Shih Chih*), trans. B. Watson (Columbia University Press, 1969)

des Rotours, R., *Traite des Fonctionnaires et Traite de l'Armee, Traduit de la Nouvelle Histoire des T'ang* (Leiden, 1948)

Ssu-ma Kuang, trans. A. Fang, *The Chronicle of the Three Kingdoms* (Harvard University Press, 1952)

Sun Tzu – The Art of War, trans. S. B. Griffith (Oxford University Press, 1963), includes Wu Ch'i's *Art of War* in an appendix.

Tso Chuan in Vol. 5 of *The Chinese Classics*, trans. J. Legge (Oxford University Press, 1872)

Secondary sources:

Ancient Chinese Armour (Shanghai Chinese Classics Publishing House, 1996)

Beckwith, C., *The Tibetan Empire in Central Asia* (Princeton University Press, 1987)

Blunden, C. and Elvin, M., *Cultural Atlas of China* (Phaidon, 1983)

The Cambridge History of China, Vol. I: The Ch'in and Han Empires (Cambridge University Press, 1986)

The Cambridge History of China, Vol. 3: Sui and T'ang China, 589–906 (Cambridge University Press, 1979)

The Cambridge History of China, Vol. 6: Alien Regimes and Border States, 907–1368 (Cambridge University Press, 1994)

The Cambridge History of China, Vol. 7, Part 1 'The Ming Dynasty, 1368–1644' (Cambridge University Press, 1988)

Chan, A., *The Glory and Fall of the Ming Dynasty* (University of Oklahoma Press, 1982)

Cottrell, A., *The First Emperor of China* (Macmillan, 1981)

Cottrell, A., *The First Emperor's Warriors* (Emperor's Warriors Exhibition Ltd., 1987)

de Crespigny, R., *The Last of the Han* (Canberra, 1969)

Desmond Martin, H., *The Rise of Chingis Khan and his Conquest of North China* (Johns Hopkins Press, 1950)

Dien, A., *The Stirrup and its Effect on Chinese Military History*, Ars Orientalis XVI (University of Michigan, 1986)

Dien, A., *A Study of Early Chinese Armour*, Artibus Asiae XLIII 1/2 (1981/2)

Gernet, J., *Ancient China from the Beginnings to the Empire* (Faber and Faber, 1968)

Hsiao, C. C., *The Military Establishment of the Yüan Dynasty* (Harvard University Press, 1978)

Huang, R., *1587, A Year of No Significance – The Ming Dynasty in Decline* (Yale University Press, 1981)

Hulsewe, A., *China in Central Asia, The Early Stage, 125 BC – AD 23* (E. J. Brill, 1979)

Hummel, A., *Eminent Chinese of the Ch'ing Period* (Washington, 1943)

Institute of the History of Natural Sciences, Beijing, *Ancient China's Technology and Science* (Foreign Languages Press, 1983)

Jenner, W., *Memories of Lo-yang* (Oxford University Press, 1981)

Kierman, F. and Fairbank, J., *Chinese Ways in Warfare* (Harvard University Press, 1974)

Loewe, M., *Military Operations in the Han Period*, China Society Occasional Papers No. 12 (The China Society, 1961)

Needham, J., *Science and Civilisation in China Vol. 5, Part 7: The Gunpowder Epic* (Cambridge University Press, 1989)

Nicolle, D., *The Mongol Warlords* (Firebird Books, 1990)

Peers, Chris, *Warlords of China, 700 BC to AD 1662* (Arms and Armour Press, 1998)

Pulleyblank, E., *The Background of the Rebellion of An Lu-shan* (Oxford University Press, 1955)

Ranitsch, K-H., *The Army of Tang China* (Montvert Publications, 1995)

Rawson, J., *Ancient China, Art and Archaeology* (British Museum Publications, 1980)

Rossabi, M., *Khubilai Khan* (London, 1988)

Russell Robinson, H., *Oriental Armour* (Herbert Jenkins, 1967)

Skoljar, S., *L'Artillerie de let a l'Epoque Sung, in Etudes Song Series 1, Vol. 2* (Sorbonne, 1971)

Smith, B. and Weng, W., *China: A History in Art* (Studio Vista, 1973)

Spence, J., *Emperor of China – Self Portrait of K'ang-hsi* (Jonathan Cape, 1974)

Spence, J., *From Ming to Ch'ing* (Yale University Press, 1979)

Tao, Jing-shen, *The Jurchen in Twelfth-Century China: A Study of Sinicization* (University of Washington, 1976)

Waldron, A., *The Great Wall of China* (Cambridge University Press, 1990)

Walker, R. L., *The Multi-State System of Ancient China* (Shoestring Press, 1953)

Watson, W. *China, 'Ancient Peoples and Places' Series* (Thames and Hudson, 1961)

Index